The Governance Report 2014
Hertie School of Governance

OXFORD

The Governance Report 2014

OXFORD
UNIVERSITY PRESS

Great Clarendon Street, Oxford, OX2 6DP,
United Kingdom

Oxford University Press is a department of the University of Oxford.
It furthers the University's objective of excellence in research, scholarship,
and education by publishing worldwide. Oxford is a registered trade mark of
Oxford University Press in the UK and in certain other countries

© Hertie School of Governance 2014

The moral rights of the authors have been asserted

First Edition published in 2014

All rights reserved. No part of this publication may be reproduced, stored
in a retrieval system, or transmitted, in any form or by any means, without
the prior permission in writing of Oxford University Press, or as expressly
permitted by law, by licence or under terms agreed with the appropriate
reprographics rights organization. Enquiries concerning reproduction outside
the scope of the above should be sent to the Rights Department, Oxford
University Press, at the address above

You must not circulate this work in any other form and you must impose
this same condition on any acquirer

British Library Cataloguing in Publication Data
Data available

Library of Congress Cataloging in Publication Data
Data available

ISBN 978–0–19–870661–8

Managing Editor: Regina List
Book design: Plural | Severin Wucher
Cover illustration: Emilia Birlo
Information graphics: Kilian Krug
Typeset in Publico and TheSans

Links to third party websites are provided by Oxford in good faith and
for information only. Oxford disclaims any responsibility for the materials
contained in any third party website referenced in this work.

Table of Contents

Preface   7
Acknowledgements   13

I. Setting the Scene: Challenges to the State,   15
Governance Readiness, and Administrative Capacities
Martin Lodge *and* Kai Wegrich

II. Administrative Capacities   27
Martin Lodge *and* Kai Wegrich

III. Governance Challenges and Administrative Capacities   49
Martin Lodge *and* Kai Wegrich

IV. Governance Innovations   77
Ramsey Wise, Kai Wegrich, *and* Martin Lodge

V. Governance Indicators   111
Piero Stanig

VI. Enhancing Administrative Capacities for   151
Better Governance: Seven Recommendations
Martin Lodge *and* Kai Wegrich

References   171
About the Contributors   183

Preface

The Governance Report 2014 is the second in this annual series about the changing conditions of governance, the challenges and opportunities involved, and the implications and recommendations that present themselves to analysts and policy-makers.

Why the Governance Report?

In a world that seems to be changing fast and that seems to gain in complexity, how can we make sense of governance, i.e. how and how well those who are entrusted to do so manage public problems? What are the main issues and components of, and for, good governance? What governance innovations are taking place, what options emerge, how can we measure governance capacity and performance, and what policy recommendations come to mind?

Many initiatives have emerged over the past decades to attempt to grasp these phenomena. The various handbooks on governance might cover concepts and theories; others focus on innovations and improvements; indicators research seeks to elucidate one or another aspect of governance. None of these covers conceptual issues, examines current governance challenges and solutions, assesses innovations, and develops indicators and other data that illustrate and inform all under one umbrella–in a systematic way and over time–and focused on a central issue or topic. This is where the Governance Report comes in.

What the Governance Report Is

The Governance Report is an inter-disciplinary effort to examine the state-of-the-art of governance at the local, national, and transnational levels, and by looking at governments, public administration, business corporations, and civil society. In doing so, it enlists experts from the Hertie School of Governance but also from other institutions. Special attention is paid to institutional designs and approaches, changes, and innovations that state and non-state actors have adopted in response to the shifts that have been occurring. This applies to the profound geopolitical changes that are likely to gain momentum and become more entrenched in the future, as it does to the world's financial architecture and smaller, often more incremental developments at local levels, be it the spread of new approaches to public administration, the role of information and communication technology, or the capacities of civil society to support municipal governance.

The results are available in an annual series that includes this compact report, an edited companion volume, both published by Oxford University Press, and a dedicated website at www.governancereport.org. Together, these various outputs and outlets are designed to provide both policy-makers and analysts ideas, knowledge, and tools to consider and implement policies and programmes that lead to better solutions to public problems.

Each Report focuses attention on institutional changes and innovations that have been proposed or that state and non-state actors have actually adopted. We use critical policy fields and issues as a lens to see how different actor groups have adjusted and could adjust to new types of challenges. We look at constraints as well as opportunities that present themselves.

Critical Policy Fields and Issues

Launched in February 2013, the first edition examines the challenges of financial and fiscal governance, proposes a new paradigm–'responsible sovereignty'–for tackling global issues, highlights selected governance innovations, and introduces a new generation of governance indicators.

The governance performance model, based on Juan Linz and Alfred Stepan's approach to democratic regime performance, highlights the interplay of legitimacy (do the problem-solvers enjoy the trust of other stakehold-

Governance Performance Model

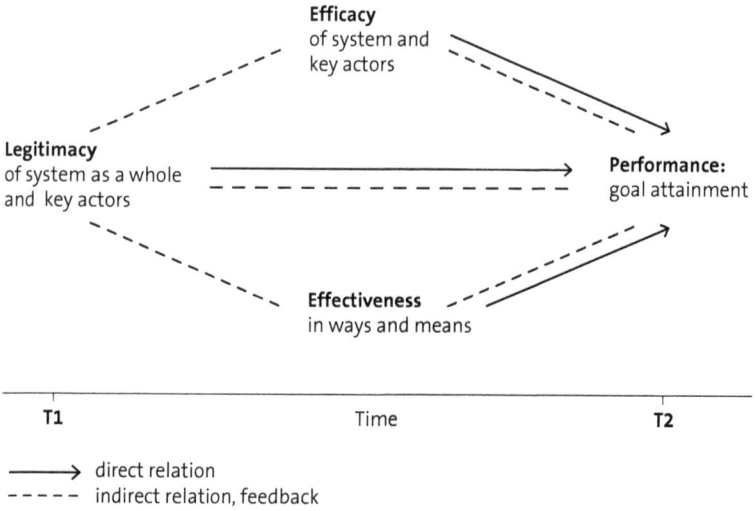

> **Kaul's Six Key Requirements for Global Governance**
>
> GR1: Averting the risk of dual (market and state) failure
> GR2: Correcting fairness deficits
> GR3: Strengthened externality management
> GR4: Promoting issue-focus and result-orientation
> GR5: Recognising and promoting synergies
> GR6: Active acceptance of policy interdependence
>
> Source: Kaul, I. (2013). 'Meeting Global Challenges: Assessing Governance Readiness', in Hertie School of Governance (ed), *The Governance Report 2013*. Oxford: Oxford University Press, 33–58.

ers?), efficacy (do they know what they are doing?), and effectiveness (do they achieve acceptable results with acceptable means?) in addressing and solving public problems (how do they actually perform?). The four components of this model, as illustrated in the figure, guided the development of a new generation of governance indicators that began with the first edition. Indicators are prominently featured in this edition as well, as the Report analyses the modern state's administrative capacity to find and implement solutions.

The first edition also introduced the framework of governance readiness, i.e. whether governance systems are ready to tackle the challenges confronting them. Inge Kaul introduced a set of six governance requirements that must be fulfilled in order to address public problems (see Box). While the requirements were developed with the provision of global public goods in mind, they are to a great extent also valid at the national and local levels and for state and non-state actors in governance systems, as we will see especially in this edition of the Governance Report. Averting the risk of dual failure, avoiding free-riding tendencies and moral hazards, for example, requires smart regulatory capacity, whereas promoting issue-focus requires significant coordination capacity.

The political economy lens highlights the practical and political trade-offs facing governance actors when presented with alternative solutions. In *The Governance Report 2013*, Mark Hallerberg and his colleagues used this lens to examine the financial crisis that began with the collapse of Lehman Brothers in 2008, among other financial and fiscal governance issues. Thus, for example, those involved in managing the crisis had to choose, or at least find a balance, between ensuring the liquidity of the financial system and the moral hazard that some actors might take greater risks knowing that they will inevitably be rescued. To understand where actors will come down on such trade-offs, we need information on their capacity to develop and implement innovative policies, the focus of this edition.

Beginning with the first edition, we also sought to wade through the 'cacophony' of new approaches to governance to identify (and eventually track) a set of promising or exemplary governance innovations. Our sample, albeit non-representative, revealed greater efforts toward improved efficacy and effectiveness (rather than systematic change) and the pronounced presence of non-state actors, in particular civil society, most often in partnership with other actors. (See the table for selected examples.) In this edition, which expands our collection, the governance innovations highlight the administrative capacity addressed by the new approaches and, in turn, what capacities these approaches require.

Finally, the Governance Report series seeks to provide the necessary evidence base for these various ways of looking at governance by developing a new generation of indicators. The dashboards in which we present data on a variety of variables either taken from existing sources or collected by our indicators team provide a wealth of information for policy-makers and researchers that can be extracted and analysed according to the issue or question at hand.

In the first edition, we offered the rationale for introducing a new set of indicators into a veritable 'indicators industry' and a sampling of the kinds of useful analyses that could be performed. In this second edition, Piero

Selected Governance Innovations 2013

Case	Challenge	Basic proposition	Key insight
Chiang Mai Initiative Multilateralisation	Providing liquidity to prevent financial contagion	Creating regional fund and ensuring surveillance via link to IMF	Two-tiered financial architecture to create nested institution to solve trade-off between liquidity and moral hazard
Hybrid Organisations: the L3C business entity	Stabilising co-producing, hybrid organisations that seek to combine social and economic returns	Providing a for-profit form with internal non-profit governance structure	Allow for diversity of incentives but create checks and balances to avoid goal displacement
Debt brake	Finding more effective ways and means for sustainable public finances	Recreating legal requirements and disincentives	Effective ex post control mechanisms via compensation accounts to take away incentives to overspend
mySociety	Promoting greater citizen engagement	Citizen-led creation and use of public websites	Increasing transparency on how public sector deals with 'everyday problems' reduces citizen-government gap

Stanig not only expands the set of dashboards, this time focusing on administrative capacity, but also again provides analysis to illustrate the many possible applications and uses of this new generation of governance indicators.

The Governance Report 2014, produced in large part by Kai Wegrich from the Hertie School and Martin Lodge from the London School of Economics and Political Science, sets the focus on administrative capacity in OECD countries. To be sure, much is expected of governments and their public administrations. How can they meet these demands? Specifically, how can they coordinate various branches of the state, regulate markets, deliver services and implement policy, and make sense of increasingly complex tasks through the use of knowledge and analysis? How much 'muscle' is left during the current 'age of austerity' after waves of reforms that have changed the architecture of the state? How can states usefully draw on non-state actors to act upon and address the pressing problems of our time?

By posing these and other central questions, and by addressing them in five of this Report's chapters, the authors summarise their findings with a set of recommendations in a concluding section. Among these are:

- Calls for a new realism in what actual capacities bureaucracies need to ensure governance readiness given resource levels;
- Attention to demand and supply mismatches and capacity bottlenecks in optimising administrative capacity;
- A move beyond checklists and scoreboard exercises toward adaptive learning approaches, combined with 'smarter' performance measures that include peer reviews;
- A debate on governance innovation that considers existing and future capacity when calling for, and implementing, new approaches, ways, and means of public administration.

While the 2014 edition carries forward the framework for studying innovations in policy solutions and governance institutions across a range of OECD countries, there are certainly many lessons that can be drawn for emerging market economies, even for developing countries in the Global South.

Onwards to 2015

The Hertie School's Mark Dawson, Henrik Enderlein, and Christian Joerges have already begun work on the 2015 edition, which will focus on Europe: The promise of an ever-closer union that has guided Europe from the Treaty of Rome to the present time rests on the evolution of democratic governance to meet the many challenges that European communities have faced in the past, are facing today, and will, undoubtedly, have to address in future. Like the American promise of 'more perfect union' and 'government of, for, and by the people', the distinct purpose of European governance of a closer union of and in Europe requires visions and innovations of many kinds; it requires new institutions and organizations and ways of doing things, and necessitates changes in the mind and hearts of citizens; it requires commitment and active participation across member states; and above all, in ways large and small, it requires the contributions of many actors. What can make Europe succeed, fail, or muddle through from a governance perspective? Is the European project a model to the world; should it be? Where are its limits and borders, both internally and externally?

As in previous reports, we will apply the governance frameworks for readiness and performance, identify innovations, track indicators, and make recommendations. And as before, we invite your comments and suggestions at www.governancereport.org.

    Helmut K. Anheier and Regina A. List
    Berlin, January 2014

Acknowledgements

Many people have been involved in developing this edition of the Governance Report, in addition to the authors of the various chapters.

First, we would like to thank the members of our International Advisory Committee who offered input at various stages of the project:

CRAIG CALHOUN	London School of Economics
WILLIAM ROBERTS CLARK	University of Michigan
JOHN COATSWORTH	Columbia University
ANN FLORINI	Singapore Management University & Brookings Institution
GEOFFREY GARRETT	University of Sydney
MARY KALDOR	London School of Economics
EDMUND J. MALESKY	Duke University
HENRIETTA MOORE	Cambridge University
WOODY POWELL	Stanford University
BO ROTHSTEIN	Quality of Government Institute, University of Gothenburg
SHANKER SATYANATH	New York University
JAMES VREELAND	Georgetown University
KENT WEAVER	Georgetown University
ARNE WESTAD	IDEAS, London School of Economics
MICHAEL ZÜRN	Wissenschaftszentrum Berlin

In the process of developing the Report, we convened a workshop in April 2013 of experts and contributors to the companion edited volume that will be published by Oxford University Press later in 2014. We are grateful for the inputs received from participants in the workshop, including Anke Hassel (Hertie School), Michael Hill (University of Newcastle), Jacint Jordana (Institut Barcelona d'Estudis Internacionals), Michaela Kreyenfeld (Max Planck Institute for Demographic Research), Nico Krisch (Hertie School), Andrea Lenschow (University of Osnabrück), Kira Matus (London School of Economics), Salvador Parrado (Universidad Nacional de Educación a Distancia), Eva Sørensen (Roskilde University), and Marco Verweij (Jacobs University).

We also thank the Hertie School community, especially the many faculty members who have contributed their ideas and constructive criticism. Working with the authors at various stages has been an active team of research assistants and associates including Alieza Durana, Mark Fliegauf, Sonja Kaufmann, Olga Kononykhina, Julia Kropeit, Dennis Mwaura, Christian Ruiz, Nathalie Spath, Ramsey Wise, and Christopher (CJ) Yetman. Thanks are also due to David Budde, Zora Chan, Magriet Cruywagen, Regine Kreitz, Iseult Rea, and Simone Dudziak.

We also wish to thank the Board of the Hertie School of Governance for encouraging this Report, and for providing critical feedback and direction.

At OUP we thank Dominic Byatt for seeing the promise in this enterprise and to Lizzy Suffling for guiding us through.

For the Report's look we are grateful to the team of Severin Wucher and Kilian Krug at Plural in Berlin.

Finally, we are especially grateful to the Hertie Foundation for its support, and to Evonik and Stiftelsen Riksbankens Jubileumsfond for providing the additional financial resources that made the Report's development and production possible.

I. Setting the Scene
Challenges to the State, Governance Readiness, and Administrative Capacities

MARTIN LODGE and KAI WEGRICH

How can states address future energy needs, communication patterns, or social integration? How can public services adjust to the challenges of changing demographics, of climate change, or, more immediately, of fiscal austerity? What kind of administrative capacities are required of the state to meaningfully contribute to tackling today's policy challenges?

These three questions are at the heart of debates about the contemporary state and are the focus of *The Governance Report 2014*. Though they are not of recent origin, they assume new urgency in a context in which not only the size, but also the role of the state are under scrutiny. States are said to lack the authority and capability to solve the many challenges facing societies today. Furthermore, in an age of international and national power dispersion, the idea that states are able to resolve the issues of ageing societies, mobile populations, climate change, and energy generation and transmission on their own is, at best, fanciful. These are genuine transboundary problems, if only because the decisions of one country are ever more likely to impact on others. Indeed, fundamental disagreements exist as to what the role of the state should be in addressing these challenges. This uncertainty about the state's role has also put the importance of cooperation among states and non-state actors into stark relief. States are in an interdependent relationship with non-state actors at the national and international level in addressing, or at least mitigating, contemporary policy challenges.

This questioning of the authority and capability of the state places the spotlight firmly on governance, the interdependent co-production of policies among state and non-state actors across different levels. Even when states and non-state actors operate in coordinated ways, the reliance on collaborative problem-solving at the transnational, national, and local levels is surely tested by today's challenges. As Kaul (2013) noted in *The Governance*

> *What kind of administrative capacities are required of the state to meaningfully contribute to tackling today's policy challenges?*

Report 2013, considerable capacities for good governance do exist, especially at the transnational level. However, much work is required to exploit these capacities for actual problem-solving and, ultimately, the exercise of 'responsible sovereignty' (Kaul 2013).

The Governance Report 2014 is about the way in which governance capacity can be realised to address core challenges facing states (and their populations), focusing primarily on OECD countries. The Governance Report emphasises the importance of governance readiness. It is therefore not about advocating any specific recipe (such as 'more liberalisation' or 'more performance management') to address contemporary challenges. Instead, the notion of readiness combines a number of dimensions. It is about issues of resilience and preparedness, it is about interdependency and coordination between state and non-state actors, and it is about the availability of tools to address policy problems in sustainable ways. Governance readiness requires the presence of agreed goals and objectives that inform the identification of problems and the type of responses to address these problems; the presence of appropriate tools to identify challenges and problems; and the presence of a range of resources to address these problems. Finally, it assumes that benevolent governance that is mainly concerned with addressing policy problems is possible and that governing is not merely about the expression of (short-term) political power and material self-interest.

Such an understanding of governance readiness raises a number of questions. First, how can systems of governing improve in terms of learning and cooperation, especially as the tried and tested ways of exploring and exchanging supposedly 'best practice' via international organisations such as the OECD have, at best, a mixed record? Second, what resources are necessary and available both to address the actual public problems and to enable the interaction among the various actors that is essential to doing so? Third, and even more problematic, how can contemporary states, in particular in OECD countries, contend with an ageing society and climate change while dealing with sovereign debt crises and depleted public finances? An emphasis on readiness, therefore, is concerned with the creation of conditions in which state and non-state actors achieve active problem-solving rather than politically astute deckchair arranging that postpones difficult choices. Indeed, to maintain governance readiness requires innovation.

> The Governance Report 2014 *is about the contribution of bureaucracies to governance readiness.*

The Governance Report 2014 is about the contribution of bureaucracies or public administration (the words are used interchangeably throughout) to governance readiness. In particular, we explore how contemporary states display problem-solving capacity through innovation and how different administrative capacities can contribute to innovation.

The Governance Report 2014 argues that:

- Any discussion about governance readiness requires a debate about the kind of actual competencies we expect bureaucracies to have. Such a discussion cannot be held at the generic level: A bland and abstract contribution that calls for public services to be 'fit for purpose', 'more responsive' to political and citizen demands, or more 'Weberian' is unhelpful. Instead, such a debate needs to be problem-centred. It needs to ask what the problems in contemporary governing are and what kind of administrative capacities might be required in different settings to address these particular challenges. In Chapter 2, four different administrative capacities are discussed: delivery, regulatory, coordination, and analytical. Delivery capacities deal with 'making things happen' at the policy frontline (i.e. the interface with citizens), regulatory capacities with oversight, coordination capacities with bringing dispersed actors together to achieve problem-solving, and analytical capacities with forecasting that informs decision-making.
- To contribute to discussions about governance readiness, it is important to have a closer look at the ways in which states have addressed contemporary governance challenges. In particular, the discussion needs to focus on how innovative policy solutions have utilised and depended on particular (mixes of) administrative capacities. Such learning from others' experience does not simply rely on a 'read across' of what today might be considered 'best practice'. Rather we need to look carefully at why and how certain interventions bring about change that is seen as beneficial and then explore how such experiences could be incorporated within the context of another system, what Bardach (2004) calls an extrapolation-based view on learning.
- We need to look at innovation in a way that systematically links innovations to administrative capacities, i.e. how certain innovations can address capacity limits, what kind of administrative capacities are required for making governance innovations work, and what the overall impact of governance innovations on administrative capacities is.
- We need to look for ways to evaluate empirically the central aspects of bureaucratic (administrative) capacity as conceptualised in this Report. To this end, in Chapter 5, we present a dashboard of indicators that address, from multiple perspectives, the four capacities we highlight. We move beyond the ranking approach adopted by many indicators projects, providing instead data that can be used to address the analytical and policy-relevant questions we raise. The data look at the existence of formal institutional provisions as well as at the outputs of the administrative process, and make it possible to detect patterns and possible links between those formal rules and administrative output.

- Any discussion about the future of administrative capacities has to understand the context in which bureaucracy operates. It should therefore avoid imposing overwhelming demands on bureaucracies that will only lead to disappointment. Innovation and capacity-enhancement have to take place in the context of a realistic understanding of what administrative systems are able to do. This requires taking into account the logic and rationale of bureaucratic action, which is about standardisation and routinisation of activities.

In this chapter, we explore the wider context of this Report. In the next section, we show why governance readiness matters. Then we point to four key areas that define contemporary statehood in our view and that are at the heart of ongoing and future public problem-solving. We then turn our attention to issues of capacity and innovation.

Governance Readiness and Why It Matters

Governance readiness involves preparedness and the ability to solve problems. In the Hertie School's *Governance Report 2013*, governance readiness was associated with six key 'governance requirements'. Though these six requirements were identified in relation to global public policy challenges (Kaul 2013), they ultimately can be applied to any level of governing. Table 1.1 translates them into administrative capacity requirements. All six emphasise the importance of mixing elements of predictability and discretion in administrative action. Indeed, they highlight the various types of administrative capacities that are at the heart of this Report, ranging from the analytical capacity to understand policy challenges in their transboundary setting, the coordination and regulatory capacities to bring together and control dispersed set of actors, and the delivery capacity to ensure that certain services are provided.

Governance readiness requires a careful discussion about how to adapt to contemporary challenges based on the notions of anticipation and resilience. Anticipation suggests that certain problems can be imagined and predicted. Actors, in turn, can mobilise resources to either prevent these events from happening or mitigate their impact. For example, flood barriers can be built, energy needs can be met by expanding generation and network capacities, or the effects of climate change can be at least mitigated or prepared for. Anticipation, therefore, assumes a degree of certainty about the likelihood of a particular event happening and what kind of impact it will have.

However, many, if not most, of the challenges that states face today are associated with uncertainty and disputes as to the potential severity of the problems and how to address them. Governance readiness is there-

Table 1.1 **Global governance requirements and administrative capacities**

Governance Requirement (GR) of Global Policy Challenges	Administrative Capacity Requirements
GR1: Averting the risk of dual—market and state—failure	Understanding the risk of both market and state (i.e. government/regulatory) failure
GR2: Fostering the fairness of international cooperation as a means of stimulating willingness to cooperate	Understanding the importance of collaboration beyond existing domain or national boundaries
GR3: Enhancing the management of cross-border spillover effects	Willingness and understanding of transboundary effects of national policy challenges and decisions
GR4: Promoting result- and issue orientation	Consideration of different administrative values—efficiency, fairness and resilience—in problem-solving that goes beyond turf-protection
GR5: Recognising the global public domain as a policy space that requires strategic leadership	Understanding that transboundary challenges require national *and* transnational analysis and action, i.e. also require administrative capacities at (sub-)national level
GR6: Recognising policy interdependence	Understanding policy interdependence and connectedness

fore about being 'ready' if an unexpected surprise occurs, not just when the expected happens. Thus, given conditions that put into question strategies based on anticipation, governance readiness is about resilience and adaptive capacities. Resilience requires actors to be sufficiently resourceful to be able to bounce back once a potential risk becomes reality. For example, energy systems can be brought back quickly after a disruptive storm, flood plains reduce the potential costs of storms, and communication flows are encouraged by allowing for diverse technologies to exist rather than putting one's faith in one single technology or provider.

The contemporary setting is particularly troubling for governance readiness when seen through the lenses of anticipation and resilience. Innovative solutions are called for given the prospect of exploding health care expenditures associated with ageing, mushrooming costs associated with the mitigation of severe weather events, challenges brought about by the potential spread of epidemic diseases, and the need to facilitate social and economic life by providing expensive infrastructure, whether this relates to energy, transport or information technology. We do know that ecological systems have deteriorated in the wake of resource depletion and/or pollution or where demography is likely to cause considerable burdens on welfare states. However, the consequences of the destruction of ecological systems or of an ageing society, the possibilities of new technologies, or the overall implications on future generations are less known. States are unlikely to have the resources to address these challenges on their own, even if they wished to do so.

These examples also highlight the centrality of uncertainty that underpins most contemporary governance challenges. No simple, uncontested decision rules exist as to what kind of resources should be devoted to any single problem. Uncertainty also exists about what kind of solutions should be pursued and what sort of evidence (and burden of proof) should be applied before commencing on any particular solution. Choices require trade-offs between different values, such as efficiency, fairness and redundancy, as the long-established literature on 'wicked problems' (Rittel and Webber 1973; cf. Verweij forthcoming) suggests. This is a problem given not only the considerable opportunity costs that are involved in the pursuit of any particular option, but also the risk that any solution may turn out to be a white elephant that will face widespread condemnation in the media, parliamentary accounts committees, and other public bodies. The search for agreeable problem definitions and solutions is even more problematic when transboundary solutions are required, given the frequent lack of political legitimisation of such decision-making.

Readiness therefore relies on resilience and adaptiveness: it is about creating and maintaining the conditions in which state and non-state actors are capable of developing problem-solving approaches.

> *Readiness relies on resilience and adaptiveness: it is about creating and maintaining the conditions in which state and non-state actors are capable of developing problem-solving approaches.*

It is a highly demanding condition: it demands openness to new information and actors, it needs established communication channels between state and non-state actors, and it requires agreement on the over-arching value of collaboration even when other values may be contested. In other words, governance readiness necessitates continuous updating or adaptation, and it also requires the resources to address multi-faceted problems. In addition, governance highlights that power and resources are, at best, dispersed. In short, governance readiness requires continuous adaptation, not only the application of grand, or not so grand, blueprints.

Why then does governance readiness matter?

First, governance readiness involves, as noted already, the creation of conditions in which problem-solving is possible as the resources of different state and non-state actors are brought together. One of the key functions of the state is generating the conditions that will allow its population a flourishing social and economic individual life. Such conditions have required states to engage in activities that nowadays are seen by many to be at the heart of statehood. These are the provision of welfare, infrastructure, sustainability and societal integration.

In the majority of this Report we concentrate on these four areas that, we contend, define statehood. They represent a particular cost driver and represent particular challenges for states, especially in the OECD countries that we examine:

- the **welfare state**: in particular, we focus on the health care costs associated with ageing populations;
- the **integration state**: in particular, the way in which the changing demographics and the official aim to encourage (selective) immigration are addressed;
- the **infrastructure state**: in particular, the way in which the provision of high speed broadband has been encouraged;
- the **sustainability state**: in particular, the way in which states have taken measures to deal with the challenges associated with different forms of energy generation.

Second, governance readiness matters in order to understand the continuing centrality of the state in constituting and facilitating governance systems involving non-state actors. It cannot be assumed that actors cooperate voluntarily against their short-term interest. States' resources to coerce, to allocate and extract resources, to mediate, and to control are as yet not matched by other organisations. However, under conditions of power dispersion, i.e. where power to do certain things (and therefore also the possession of resources) is spread across state and non-state actors that are located at different levels, governance readiness requires a differentiated view as to what states can do; most of all, it cannot assume conditions under which solutions can be imposed hierarchically, even if that might be seen as desirable.

Third, governance readiness is fundamentally about administrative capacities. In this Report, particularly in the following chapter, we ask what the role of public administration or bureaucracy is to enhance readiness. Suffice to say that such questions have much wider implications for public services. Expecting bureaucratic actors to have particular skills and competencies raises further questions as to how such skills and competencies should be attracted and on what terms, and to whom such actors should ultimately be loyal. Thus, reflecting on administrative capacities also raises wider debates about changing emphases within 'public service bargains' (Hood and Lodge 2006; Lodge and Hood 2012), i.e. the formal and informal understandings that shape the relation between politicians and bureaucrats, in particular concerning skills and competencies of bureaucrats, their loyalty, and their reward packages. We return to these questions in the concluding chapter of this report.

Fourth, readiness therefore is about establishing the conditions for enhanced governance performance. It contributes to legitimacy in the sense of political and societal actors being capable of and willing to play according to the rules in a climate in which citizens and other actors can place some confidence or trust in those involved in decision-making. Governance readiness is also about establishing efficacy and effectiveness by focusing on the required resources to enable decision-making and implementation. Thereby, governance readiness directly influences the likelihood that active problem-solving will be achieved (Anheier 2013).

Administrative Capacity and Governance Innovation

Innovation is defined as the intentional and repeated use of non-traditional ways of governing–or the 'generation, acceptance, and implementation of new ideas, processes, products, or services' (Kanter 1983: 20). Governance innovations, then, are novel approaches to address particular public problems in more efficacious and effective ways (Anheier and Korreck 2013). Positive side-effects of such outputs are improved outcomes, in terms of both achieving better 'results' and enhancing legitimacy.

Administrative capacities are required to facilitate governance innovation itself. In turn, governance innovation can advance administrative capacities. This raises three questions: How can innovation be understood and approached? What particular administrative capacities are required to encourage and maintain innovative practices when it comes to governance? What kind of implications do governance innovations have for administrative capacities? In this section we respond to each of these questions in turn.

Turning first to the issue of innovation itself, this Report offers examples of particular cases that could be defined as innovative in governance terms. That is, procedural or substantive arrangements were used with the intention to achieve particular outputs and outcomes. More generally, innovation can be looked at in the resource-use of the state: what kind of innovative resource uses do we find where states have sought to contribute to problem-solving in a multi-actor setting? We distinguish between four resources: finance (i.e. to pay or tax actors to do something); information (i.e. to inform actors about the consequences of some kind of behaviour and thereby shape future behaviours); organisation (i.e. to use the power to house and staff organisations directly); and authority (i.e. to use legal and quasi-legal means to shape behaviour). We can look across national and local examples of governance innovation by focusing on the way in which these four resources were creatively and innovatively brought to bear to solve problems. Again, we see this as a further way to advance the level of learning about innovation.

Second, for governance innovation to get off the ground and sustain its momentum, particular administrative capacities are required. To encourage particular forms of innovation, such as in financing or procurement, requires one set of capacities rather than others. Similarly, an innovation that involves extensive collaboration and decentralisation places a strong demand on coordination capacities. In short, to generate and sustain governance innovation depends at least in part on the presence of particular administrative capacities.

Third, innovation takes place within a certain 'possibility set' of options that are generated by a particular governance context. A perfect recipe for failure, disillusionment, and unintended consequences is the application of too highly demanding prescriptions to different contexts (see Andrews 2008, 2010). Innovation and a focus on administrative capacities are therefore not about asking for the impossible. It is far more important to consider examples of innovative practices and ask, first of all, what made a particular intervention so successful, and, second, how such a successful intervention could be made to work in a different context. Bureaucracy, after all, is about the routinisation of processes, the specialisation of labour in different branches, and the classification and allocation of specific events to bigger categories. These features, drawn from Max Weber's ideal-type bureaucracy, highlight how difficult it is for bureaucratic public administration to assume a more adaptive approach to problem-solving, since the two understandings about how to 'govern' are fundamentally at odds. Readiness, which emphasises anticipation and resilience leading to adaptive practices that solve problems, and bureaucracy, which emphasises predictability and routinisation, are not natural bed-fellows. The challenge therefore is to ensure that the conditions exist to facilitate readiness.

Measuring Governance and Administrative Capacity

One of the key themes in contemporary public management has been performance management. Organisations have used performance management to incentivise their employees, governments have tried to use performance management to generate improvements in public services through ranking and benchmarking activities, and transnational public and private organisations have also actively engaged in trying to put pressure on governments to reform aspects of their public services through ranking exercises. The debate about what governance indicators seek to achieve, whether they lead to undesirable 'Frankenstates' (Scheppele 2013) in that well-intentioned indicators are aggregated into an unholy mixture, whether they represent particular monocultural worldviews that are imposed on different cultures, and whether they reduce the complexity of actual practices in an undesirable way, is one aspect. The second debate concerns the extent to which, for example, administrative capacities can be measured through expert surveys or through reliance on output or outcome measures. A third debate focuses on the implications of such governance indicators for advocating particular capacity-enhancing strategies.

With its 2013 edition, the Governance Report introduced its own effort to develop a new generation of governance indicators that would take seriously the notion of governance as a multi-actor, multi-level system, address current governance challenges, and have an analytic and policy-oriented focus, i.e. be more than descriptive. The overall system, which seeks to measure and analyse governance readiness, governance performance, and governance innovation, builds on three dashboards: the Transnational Governance Dashboard, the National Governance Dashboard, and the City Governance Dashboard (see Anheier, Stanig, and Kayser 2013). For this edition of the Governance Report, we focus on the National Governance Dashboard and extend it to include additional variables relating to the public sector's administrative capacity. By presenting data on formal institutional provisions as well as at the outputs of the administrative process, the dashboards make it possible to measure efficacy, effectiveness and legitimacy, all elements of governance performance, and to detect patterns and possible links.

As we hope to show, these indicators provide a useful snapshot of the state of the administrative capacities that are the backbone of governance. The indicator set presented here is, to the best of our knowledge, the most comprehensive set of indicators related to administrative capacities, and the first one that systematically takes into account the governance context of bureaucratic activity. To complement the indicators, we advocate in-depth qualitative studies that go behind the scenes to highlight key bottlenecks and trade-offs in the practice of public administration today.

Of course, measurement, benchmarking and league-tabling have certain limitations. Indicators may reflect particular visions of what public services should achieve that may be more value-laden than is evident at first sight. Looking at observable outputs and outcomes is also difficult when measurement is inherently problematic. For example, it is easy to establish whether a country has adopted performance budgets or not. However, it is far more difficult to go beyond such a tick-box approach in order to find out whether performance budgets are operated in any meaningful way. Similarly, assessing ministries' competency requires an assessment of how ministries go about their job, not whether particular features appear on ministerial websites.

Despite these caveats, high-level indicators are indispensible. They allow for international comparisons as a first approximation that requires interpretation and sense-making. Such a 'hermeneutics of quantitative indicators' not only requires full transparency about methodological choices, it also suggests caution when it comes to aggregation of indicators into overall rankings (hence the dashboard approach to governance indicators followed here). Moreover, it is critical to combine indicator-based approaches with a perspective that explores how administrative capacities are used 'on the ground', i.e. in attempts to respond to governance challenges.

Conclusion

Governance readiness is about the problem-solving capacities that can be mobilised among state and non-state actors. It suggests that governments on their own or among themselves are not the sole site in which we can expect problem-solving to occur. In such a setting the importance of 'administration' has often been neglected; however, the questions as to what bureaucracy actually 'does' and what it 'should be doing' need to be addressed to develop a meaningful discussion about the future shape of public services. No report can offer a view of future public services that will please all interested parties. However, this Report offers a contribution to a more concentrated and meaningful discussion that is problem-centred. The following chapter therefore develops the notion of administrative capacity, as understood here, with the subsequent chapter illustrating the importance of these capacities through the lens of key governance challenges facing the OECD countries today. Next, we present a set of recent innovations that highlight the interplay between governance innovation and administrative capacity. Then, indicators relating to administrative capacity and some of the outputs of the process are presented and analysed.

Before pursuing these themes further in the following chapters, it should be stressed that this Report assumes that problem-solving seeks to deal with core governing challenges in a benevolent way. In other words, problem-solving is not about the imposition of technocratic rationality on disorderly politics and populations, it is about accepting the tensions that can exist between long-term planning, contested political values, and uncertainty about the future. We have no intention to commit the same mistakes as Beatrice and Sidney Webb who, after being shown select parts of Stalin's Soviet economy, declared that they had seen the future and that the (Soviet) future was bright.

> *The importance of 'administration' has often been neglected; however, the questions as to what bureaucracy actually 'does' and what it 'should be doing' need to be addressed.*

Furthermore, it is about encouraging responsive governing, namely one that incorporates the legitimate concerns of diverse parties that may be spread across jurisdictions. We also need to acknowledge the context of austerity currently experienced by most OECD countries. Demands for enhanced administrative capacity and governance readiness can always be accused of asking for more, whether this is more resources for learning, for supporting actors to participate in collaborative governance arrangements, for new technologies that will finally allow bureaucracy to 'break through', or for rewarding public servants better so that they will be more motivated. Any debate about administrative capacity has to take place in the context of limited resources, and even more so in the contemporary age of fiscal and financial austerity.

II. Administrative Capacities

MARTIN LODGE *and* KAI WEGRICH

Governance readiness involves a capacity to adapt, to bounce back and show resilience in the face of acute and salient challenges. Governance readiness raises questions about the resources that are required and available for problem-solving among highly dispersed systems, including transnational, national and local, state and non-state actors. Actors in such dispersed and diverse constellations operate sometimes in cooperation with each other, sometimes in competition against each other. Such varied configurations give rise to different expectations about the capacities required to bring about the intended interactions and, ultimately, desired outcomes. While much has been made of 'state capacity', less interest has been paid to the type of administrative capacities that are expected of bureaucracies to contribute to multi-level problem-solving in systems of dispersed governance. These capacities have a direct impact on the way in which states are evaluated by their citizens. In other words, administrative capacities directly influence issues of legitimacy, efficacy, effectiveness, and, ultimately, performance (Anheier 2013). This chapter looks at this often neglected ingredient in debates about governance and problem-solving capacities.

To address this gap, we pay particular attention to administrative capacities. Administrative capacities are defined as the set of skills and competencies that are expected of public bureaucracies so that they can facilitate and contribute to problem-solving. Administrative capacities therefore include, on the one hand, structural and procedural provisions that enable bureaucracies to perform particular functions. On the other hand, administrative capacities also embrace the individuals within these bureaucracies that are capable and skilful enough to meet the expectations of their political masters and the wider public.

> *Administrative capacities are the set of skills and competencies that are expected of public bureaucracies so that they can facilitate and contribute to problem-solving.*

A focus on administrative capacity directs the debate about governance readiness to the contribution of public bureaucracies to problem-solving. Such a focus on the demands and expectations placed on bureaucracies may be seen as limited. However, it is arguably particularly critical to do so in the contemporary age of depleted finances and other challenges that will have considerable budgetary implications (such as climate and demographic change). Then again, a focus on administrative capacities also expands established debates that usually concentrate on broad categorisations regarding bureaucratic types. Moreover, 'Weberianism' has often been used to denote the existence of merit-appointed bureaucracies, the assumption being that such bureaucracies will be more capable (i.e. qualified) and also less partisan in the execution of their functions. However, such accounts tell us very little about what kind of (technical, managerial, or other) capabilities these merit-appointed public servants are supposed to display. Indeed, the highly diverse ways in which 'merit' can be defined and assessed in light of potential cultural and other biases is often surprisingly underplayed.

The significance of administrative capacities for governance readiness emerges also from other developments. As noted in the previous chapter, it is widely acknowledged that national political systems have lost their capability to solve most of the important problems on their own. Furthermore, nearly three decades of managerialist reforms and privatisation are said to have 'hollowed out' the state and therefore reduced its capabilities by eliminating 'slack' (Rhodes 1997; cf. Lodge and Wegrich 2012c; Matthews 2012). The context of the financial crisis and the subsequent age of public sector austerity in most OECD countries has arguably further constrained the scope for ensuring a high-capacity bureaucracy. At the same time, attention to bureaucratic quality has mainly centred on the way in which national (and sub-national) administration works, but not so much on the context in which bureaucracies (have to) act today. In this chapter, and this Report, we aim to contribute to the understanding of administrative capacity that takes the dispersed nature of contemporary governance into consideration. The focus on administrative capacity as part of governance readiness is therefore about linking an interest in global public policy issues that has often underplayed the role of national bureaucracies, with an interest in national bureaucracies that has widely neglected the role of transboundary problem-solving and governance.

Administrative capacities represent the backbone to governance readiness, as noted in Table 1.1 in the previous chapter. It reflects on the wide-ranging demands placed on public bureaucracies in the diverse contexts in which governance is taking place. Given this diversity, the broad notion of administrative capacity needs to be differentiated further. Accordingly, we distinguish between delivery, regulatory, coordination, and analytical capacities. We will discuss these four capacities in more detail below. In brief, delivery capacities deal with affecting the frontline of policy, i.e. the kind of resources required to make sure that the rubbish gets collected, the water supplied or the post delivered; regulatory capacities are required to conduct oversight over activities (such as telecommunications, education or prisons); coordination capacities are required to bring dispersed constituencies together; and analytical capacities address demands on forecasting and intelligence that inform policy making. Governance systems require some mix of administrative capacities, and these four capacities feature in any system of governing, although how they are organised and deployed will differ considerably, depending on context.

To develop this understanding of administrative capacities and the contribution of such an approach to wider debates, this chapter progresses in three steps. First, it sets out the broader background to the discussion of administrative capacities. The second part discusses delivery, regulatory, coordination, and analytical capacities in turn. We justify the choice of these four capacities in that section. Third, we consider their implications for governance readiness and innovation.

Capacities, Governance, and Bureaucracy

Contemporary discussions about the state have emphasised a variety of understandings of 'capacity' (Evans 1995; Evans and Rauch 2000). Similarly, views about 'what is governance' have returned to well-established speculation about capacity in terms of 'infrastructural power' (Fukuyama 2013; Mann 1984). The traditional view about state capacity relates to the capacity to extract taxes and to conduct warfare. Others relate state capacity to the legal enforcement of contracts. Views as to how states managed to establish tax-raising or law-enforcing organisations range from those that are largely interested in the power of the state versus other sources of potential power (such as interest groups or public opinion) to those that are interested in the way in which states organise themselves to achieve developmental outcomes. Four particular perspectives can be distinguished.

The most traditional understanding of state capacity is, as noted, the view that bureaucracy can be examined in terms of its degree of 'Weberianism'. Whether Max Weber would recognise Weberianism is questionable given his concern about the undesirable side-effects of bureaucracy. However, Weberianism usually refers to the existence of a career bureaucracy where appointment and promotion are (broadly) on the basis of merit, i.e. not on the basis of direct patronage. Political influence is limited, thereby supposedly enhancing capacity: a bureaucracy that functions without any 'fear or favour' is more likely to be high performing than one that lives in permanent anxiety of dismissal by political masters, or disgruntlement over seemingly arbitrary personnel decisions. The Weberian image of bureaucracy is one that sees bureaucracy as separate from other (private) sectors and that performs according to consistent, impersonal, and predictable rules.

The connection between capacity and Weberianism has been made in a number of discussions. Evans and Rauch (1999), for example, have shown that, in comparative perspective, states with higher degrees of Weberianism are associated with higher rates of economic and social development, thereby implying that a reliance on markets alone will not lead to developmental achievements. Elsewhere, the work by the OECD's SIGMA group in advising bureaucratic development in Central and Eastern Europe has emphasised the importance of Weberianism as a pre-requisite for achieving capacity (see Meyer-Sahling 2012). In a more theoretical argument, Gary Miller (1992) has noted how autonomous (Weberian) bureaucracies offer a solution to what he calls the 'trust-honor game'. According to this 'trust honor game', 'agents' will not commit their full effort to their work if they are uncertain about being compensated for their efforts by their 'principal'. Creating an internal labour market with autonomy from political (and unpredictable) decisions is said to solve this uncertainty (i.e. the likelihood that the promise of reward is being honoured is increased as the political master is less able to cheat) and thereby bureaucracies will display greater effort.[1]

A second and related argument places its emphasis on the importance of consistent and predictable rules as an expression of 'quality of government' (Rothstein and Teorell 2008). Quality, which we equate with our understanding of capacity, is defined in terms of neutrality or impartiality; put differently, quality (i.e. capacity) refers to the way in which the institutions of the state act impartially (i.e. without any bias) in the execution of legislation. Citizens are therefore granted equality of access to the political process and receive equality of treatment by the state. This minimalist definition of capacity is based on the view that any other capacity-related aspects of bureaucracy are too broad, too functionalist, or seen through the exclusive lens of corruption (Rothstein and Teorell 2008: 167-8); impartiality, so the argument goes, is uncontested in both its universal appeal and its application. A separate literature that also emphasises the importance of consistent and 'neutral' rule application focuses on the 'regulatory state' (Majone 1997). The idea is that bureaucratic activity can be restricted to oversight functions, with appropriate institutional design facilitating private economic development, while keeping potential market (and other) abuses in check. A credible rule system sets the framework for private activity to flourish, limiting the scope for discretionary interference by political or administrative actors. The capacity of the state is limited to consistent rule application, without necessarily emphasising the distinctiveness of the public sector.

The third understanding of state capacity stresses the importance of markets and quasi-markets. According to this perspective, the state is primarily 'managerial' and 'entrepreneurial' with a reliance on markets and quasi-markets to deliver public services. To achieve high performance, incentive systems are focused on extrinsic individual motivation and rivalry. The state should treat private actors as motivated in and capable of controlling their own affairs; the role of the regulating state is to be capable of overseeing the robustness and validity of these self-controlling activities (instead of going in heavy-handedly and throwing highly prescriptive rule-books at regula-

Table 2.1 **Contrasting views on state capacity**

	Emphasis	Administrative Capacity
Weberianism	Distinctiveness and rule-boundedness of administrative action	Expert judgement, consistency and neutrality
Quality of Government	Impartial rule application	Unbiased application of legislation
Marketisation/ Managerialism	Enabling (quasi-) markets and discretionary judgement	Entrepreneurial ability to facilitate markets/resemble private sector management style
Public Value	Discretionary and collaborative judgement to facilitate distinct public value goals	Ability to identify public value of organisation to advance social welfare and to establish feasible administrative capacities and negotiate with environment to achieve outcomes

tees). In the public sector, organisations and individuals should be treated as profit-centres and provided with sufficient discretion to animate their managerial spirits. Control, at most, should be on the basis of outputs and outcomes. Thus, state capacity is about ensuring that markets are well-functioning and that public services follow a (quasi-)market logic of operation. The ideal of a capacity-rich bureaucracy lies in an organisational form that shows limited distinctiveness from the private sector and grants managerial discretion (and lack of 'red-tape'-ish rule-boundedness). High performance is achieved through creating market-type incentives and mechanisms.

The fourth view emphasises the importance of collaboration, networks, and negotiation in contemporary governing. Similar to the previous perspective with its emphasis on markets, this view is sceptical about the idea that bureaucracies are able to act on their own; high-performing and appropriate problem-solving is more likely to be achieved through collaboration with a variety of affected actors. Information asymmetries are seen as too high, while social differentiation has further decreased the societal acceptance of 'one size fits all' approaches. Accordingly, an important part of governing capacity is to establish collaborative settings to facilitate desired outcomes. Views informed by the 'public value' perspective (Moore 1995), for example, have increasingly paid attention to the significance of collaboration in governing in that managers are said to negotiate with and require support from their 'authorizing environment' (Moore 1995: 71ff; also Bennington and Moore 2011; Stoker 2006). At the heart of public value is a clear distinction between private and public sectors. Public value is about identifying the core activities that public organisations should be focusing on (their 'value'-driven mission is distinct from the profit-seeking motive in the private sector). In addition, public value emphasises the importance of managing and engaging with stakeholders (and politics).[2] Accordingly, capacity is understood here as capacity to mediate with groups to achieve outcomes.

Table 2.1 offers an overview of these four views of state capacity and their understanding as to how administrative capacity should be developed and deployed to achieve wider policy objectives.

Traditional Indicators of Administrative Capacities

These four images of capacity–the Weberian, the Quality of Government, the Marketisation/Managerialism, and the Public Value perspective–offer different views as to what administrative capacity is or should be. It is not surprising, therefore, that a variety of indicator sets exist that reflect these different understandings (although not necessarily acknowledging their underlying assumptions). Most prominent, arguably, are the World Bank Group's indicator sets such as the Worldwide Governance Indicators (www.govindicators.org) and the Doing Business (www.doingbusiness.org) datasets. The Doing Business indicator set seeks to pressure governments into rationalising regulatory burdens on business by focusing on the presence (or not) of particular procedures and their practical implementation in order to study their opportunity cost (Djankov et al. 2002). Among a variety of indicators, the Worldwide Governance Indicators rely on perception-based indicators, including enterprise, citizen and expert surveys, to examine aspects such as the rule of the law, the regulatory quality, and the openness of the democratic political process. These indicators have enjoyed much (ab)use and attention (Arndt 2008). They offer a benchmarking device for different governments to compete on 'quality' of government. Underlying the World Bank-sponsored indicators is a view that emphasises the market-enabling capacities of the state, rather than administrative capacities more specifically.

Although capacity relies on formal structural and procedural provisions, such provisions do not automatically generate particular outputs and outcomes.

As noted, the expert-survey based indicators, such as those that emerge from the Quality of Government initiative based at the University of Gothenburg, focus on the non-biased (impartial) execution of legislation, the perception whether governments recruit and promote on the basis of performance, and the existence of other government policies that are seen to be 'good'. Other indicators use broad institutional features that do not necessarily capture institutional practices and hence 'real' capacities. For example, the Bertelsmann Foundation's Sustainable Governance Indicators include a number of key governing issues, such as whether coordination devices exist within government and whether legislation and regulation are checked by particular institutional fixes, such as, for example, impact assessments and cost-benefit analysis. The presence of such devices is certainly interesting for public administration watchers. However, merely looking at the formal existence of devices is not actually evidence for capacity. Although capacity relies on formal structural and procedural provisions, such provisions do not automatically generate particular outputs and outcomes. Even though the argument has been made that 'institutional hard-wiring' can deal with capacity-low backgrounds and thereby establish certain degrees of certainty and thus development, more recent analysis has suggested that any formal institutional set-up requires essential informal understandings (see Fukuyama 2013; Levy and Spiller 1994, 1996). In other words, formal structures play some role, but to achieve anything, governance requires individuals who are able to meet the kind of expectations regarding skills and capabilities placed on them by their political masters and the wider political system.

The literature that focuses on capacity indicators along the lines of public value-related frameworks is linked to measurements of public service motivation (Perry 1996). This literature usually surveys employees and considers civil service attitudes towards 'red tape', managerialist initiatives that potentially conflict with professional self-understandings, and various audiences. It highlights the importance of intrinsic motivation among employees.

These diverse approaches towards developing indicator sets tell readers something about how countries are perceived by citizens, businesses, academia, and legal and public administration practitioners, as well as about the institutional arrangements that are in place. However, once such approaches are linked to ranking exercises, they become problematic not only because of a range of practical and technical problems related to data availability and quality but also because of the sensitivity of weighting of sub-indicators in the construction of aggregate ('rankable') indicators (Hood, Dixon, and Beeston 2008). Furthermore, such ranking exercises leave many questions unanswered because they rely either on perception-based surveys (which may not deal with biases such as different standards of assessment) or on some form of measurement of policy outputs or outcomes without necessarily considering underlying processes and mechanisms that may have contributed to those outcomes or outputs.

For example, to determine whether a country has a system of impact assessment or not is based on two (implicit) assumptions. It assumes, first, that the existence of such a device is a robust indicator for 'good government'. Second, it assumes that such devices do actually have an impact in the first place - and do so on a consistent basis. However, whether such devices are in themselves a robust indicator of 'good government' is questionable, while the actual value of such devices is often, at best, a matter of hope over experience. The UK's public administration is a good example here: it is regularly praised for its extensive impact assessment system, but its actual practice has been found to be far from systematic (NAO 2010).

Therefore, the desire to encourage a move to supposedly 'fit for purpose' bureaucracy via the pressure exerted by ranking exercises risks confusing the presence of institutional mechanisms with actual capacities. Measurement of appearances may be little else than a ritual of verification (Power 1997). It may constitute the application of programmatic ideas that are only loosely coupled to particular technologies of measurement, with the end result being placation effects. Furthermore, the assembly of perfectly reasonable individual indicators of 'good governance' into rankings may actually undermine 'good governance' where existing systems are over-stretched to comply with 'best practice' indicators or where the overall sum of reform initiatives leads to a dangerous cocktail of mutually contradictory initiatives (see Keberle 2013).

Moreover, it is not clear whether the measurement of initiatives in a particular area reflects actual action instead of mere activity. Initiatives to highlight particular reform aspects usually end up with slogans that are poorly defined. For example, the UK government in the early-to-mid-2000s emphasised the importance of 'delivery'. This was supposed to encourage a Blairite focus on 'making things happen'. One problem was that actual delivery at the frontline was often conducted by private providers. Another problem was that it soon became clear that the 'delivery' of politicians' wishes occurred in many different ways across different areas of government: As civil servants and their superiors struggled to identify their contribution to the delivery agenda, the 'delivery' notion came to be understood as more or less any activity. A simple, if not simplistic theme therefore became meaningless by being applied to ever more contexts.

Finally, the measurement of whether particular formal mechanisms are present should not be confused with actual practices and resources, especially at a time when public budgets are being slashed in a number of countries. Measuring perceptions, surveying agency staff, or ticking boxes whether institutional mechanisms exist or not is indeed interesting, but it does not offer insights into how administrative capacities are used, and which types of capacities are required or missing, in order to address governance challenges. In other words, to advance this state of affairs the discussion needs to move towards a more differentiated understanding of administrative capacity, especially in terms of the varied demands that are being placed on bureaucracy. The next section sets out such an approach.

Four Administrative Capacities

It is often said that governing has become 'more complex' as economies and societies are becoming more integrated, information flows are accelerating, and economic markets are becoming increasingly interdependent (Anheier 2013; Levi-Faur 2012). Governing is also said to have become more 'wicked' (Verweij forthcoming): the challenges of the financial crisis, of climate change, and of demographic change are of a multi-dimensional character that involve value choices. Any choice will require difficult trade-offs. It is further argued that governing has become more problematic due to changes in the architecture of the state over the past three decades or so (Matthews 2012; Lodge and Wegrich 2012a). These changes involve privatisation and outsourcing of public services, market liberalisation and thus loss of national economic boundary control more generally, and the dispersion of administrative and regulatory activities in quasi-autonomous bodies (as well as, in some countries at least, territorial decentralisation). These changes have further reduced the direct levers of states to impose their authority.

While it is difficult, if not impossible, to come to a conclusive argument as to whether governing has become more complex and difficult in comparison to a few decades or centuries ago, it is nevertheless pertinent to enquire more carefully into the different types of administrative capacities that underpin state action. A focus on administrative capacity highlights the varied expectations and demands regarding skills and capabilities and not only the presence (or lack) of institutions and practices. Such a perspective has the potential to contribute to more informed competency frameworks than those that usually populate human resource activities across national systems of public administration. This section looks in more detail at a number of distinct, but overlapping types of administrative capacities, namely delivery, regulatory, coordination, and analytical capacities.

These four capacities are at the heart of contemporary discussions about governance on the one hand, and civil service competency on the other (Levi-Faur 2012; Matthews 2012; Hood and Lodge 2006). Thus, as governance is defined by power dispersion among actors, one of the central competency requirements is coordination, i.e. the process of aligning dispersed actors. Second, the context of governance is also defined by uncertainty about future trends and developments, therefore highlighting the need for analytical capacities to offer knowledge to decision-makers. Third, governance among dispersed actors at various levels also leads to distinct challenges in terms of implementation. In particular, following decades of outsourcing and performance-related targets, the context of street-level bureaucracy has changed (Brodkin 2011; Hupe and Hill forthcoming), especially when public sector actors have to step in when private sector providers fail. This new context means that administrative capacity to deliver is

Table 2.2 **Four administrative capacities**

Delivery capacity	Regulatory capacity
Capacity to execute and manage policy requirements at the frontline	Capacity to provide oversight over heterogeneous private and public organisations
Coordination capacity	**Analytical capacity**
Capacity to mediate between and bring together dispersed actors to achieve joint action	Capacity to provide 'intelligence' and advice in conditions of uncertainty

even more important. Fourth, and finally, governance, and thus the growing heterogeneity of actors have placed a growing emphasis on oversight activities by state actors on private actors. Similarly, transnational state and non-state actors are involved in checking and inspecting. This demands greater regulatory capacities. Table 2.2 provides an overview of these four administrative capacities; the rest of this section explores these four capacities in more detail.

Delivery capacity

The capacity to 'make things happen' refers to the way in which states execute policy at the street-level. Such delivery activities include both service provision (such as the issuing of welfare payments, meals on wheels, etc.) and more coercive activities (such as policing). Delivery capacity relates to wider debates about how to achieve the implementation of policy goals or of compliance rates with the lowest resource use possible.

The context of delivery has substantially, if not fundamentally changed from the days in which the implementation literature of the 1970s explored 'top-down' and 'bottom-up' perspectives and considered how limited hierarchical intervention from a so-called 'top-down perspective' was in achieving intended policy objectives (Hupe and Hill forthcoming; Winter 2012). In contrast to the 1970s, the application of managerial doctrines, such as performance management, narrowed the scope for discretionary decision-making at the frontline. In particular, formerly discretionary judgement is now increasingly controlled through central indicators and the need to verify and record performance through audit trails and other checking devices (Hupe and Hill forthcoming; Brodkin 2011). For example, food inspections as well as social services, such as education, have witnessed an increased emphasis on recording performances so as to allow for external validation.

Furthermore, the societal context for delivery has arguably been altered as populations have become more differentiated and less accepting of discretionary decision-making by frontline bureaucracies. Contemporary society requires varied and bespoke forms of communication that go beyond the traditional government communication efforts that sought to broadcast their messages to their populations 'at large' (Hood and Margetts 2007). In addition, in an era in which populations can view local administrative performance in terms of 'crime hot-spot maps' or in terms of comparative performance data, the pressures on the frontline to 'deliver' in particular target-hitting ways have increased (Hupe and Hill forthcoming; Brodkin 2011).

Such demand for consistent country-wide 'target-hitting' competes with a potentially countervailing demand, namely one that emphasises the importance of 'localism'. According to this demand, delivery should reflect local preferences and therefore represent a result of local negotiation and deliberation. In other words, delivery capacity is exposed to competing demands, namely those calling for bespoke and tailored local adaptation on the one hand, and those following the logic of (inter)national benchmarking exercises, centrally imposed verification protocols, and target-hitting regimes on the other.

Moreover, widespread outsourcing, if not outright privatisation has altered the nature of administrative capacity requirements when it comes to delivery. Whereas in the past delivery was largely about the direct production of public services, a world of outsourced public services is one in which the public sector's role in terms of delivery capacity is one of inspection and 'provider of last resort' should private provision fail.

> The delivery capacity of 'making things happen' relies on a structure that is sufficiently resourced to give life to policy objectives.

So, what then, can be understood as delivery capacity? As the feasibility of hierarchical intervention is, at best, questionable, delivery capacity concerns the exercise of mediated authority, regardless of whether delivery activity involves services or coercive activities. Thus, it is about the capacity to ensure that policies are delivered, whether this includes policing, education, or child protection, and to be recognised by the target population as a legitimate provider of such services. Such legitimacy involves not only the appearance of professional expertise, but also the ability to engage with often diverse social groups and be accountable to diverse stakeholders, ranging from higher-level ministries to different communities among local populations.

In sum, the delivery capacity of 'making things happen' relies on a structure that is sufficiently resourced to give life to policy objectives. This happens in a context that is shaped by the competing demands of financial constraints, societal resistance to particular frontline activities (rather than others), the need to display discretionary judgement whilst hitting fixed targets and standards, and increasingly heterogeneous societies. This has direct implications for the measurement and the reward of performance (and what counts as performance), for the ability to run organisations and mediate with (potentially hostile) constituencies, and for the capability to navigate the tricky terrain between local demands, national priorities and organisational ambitions.

Regulatory capacity

Regulatory capacities are about control and oversight. They entail the presence of regimes that combine standards (i.e. statements, in more or less precise form, about what is to be achieved) with an apparatus that detects and enforces compliance. Considerations about regulatory capacity have arguably become more prominent over the past three decades as the 'regulation' word has become increasingly part of international governance discourse (Baldwin, Cave, and Lodge 2010; Lodge and Wegrich 2012b), but also because of recurring waves of concerns with 'too much' regulation and red-tape busting exercises (Lodge and Wegrich 2012d) as well as the large-scale failure of regulation in the financial sector (Baldwin, Cave, and Lodge 2010). This applies especially to the context of controlling (privatised) utilities and other infrastructure industries, but also to formally autonomous professions (such as medicine), and to governmental activities themselves (Moran 2003; Jordana and Levi-Faur 2004). Regulatory capacity is about the way in which coercive powers of the state are used to constrain economic and social activities.

In terms of organisation, regulatory capacity relates to debates about the way in which units tasked with 'regulation' are established. The late 20th century saw the rise of the argument that quasi-autonomous agencies offer a functionally superior way of organising control activities. The justification is that such bodies are removed from the immediate heat of political life and therefore promise more 'credible commitment' in terms of stability of regulatory objectives. This consensus has given rise to a much wider set of debates about, for example, how supposedly autonomous agencies are to be held to account, whether such agencies should be organised on a sector-, industry- or cross-sectoral basis, how such activities should be funded, and what kind of powers they should have. These debates link to much more fundamental concerns about the power of political and economic actors in shaping regulatory life. For example, the well-known concept of 'capture' refers to a world in which concentrated industries dominate (Stigler 1971), or where, over time, regulatory activities come to an accommodation with the interests of the regulated parties (Bernstein 1955).

Furthermore, regulatory capacity is about strategies or different modes. So-called 'command and control' regulation (legal provisions backed by mandatory sanctions), linked to formulaic inspection practices, is associated with suboptimal outcomes (Ayres and Braithwaite 1992): it creates adversarial relationships, requires formal enforcement action that depletes regulators' resources and can be frustrated through endless appeals by powerful economic interests, and it focuses on formal artefacts rather than real practices. In response, a number of strategies have emerged. These include those regimes that insist that regulated parties should control themselves in the first instance, whereas regulators should concentrate on the regulation of these 'self-regulatory' activities, either by focusing on observable performance measures or by checking on critical organisational processes.

Similarly, in enforcement, 'responsive' strategies, i.e. those that rely on advice first and deterrence later, offer advantages over 'pure' strategies that rely on either persuasion or deterrence alone (Ayres and Braithwaite 1992; Parker 2013). So-called 'risk-based' approaches offer a way to support decisions as to which areas of regulation are more critical than others (Black 2010). At the same time, context clearly matters: empirical studies have shown how the same domain in different national settings witnesses very different assumptions about effective control. For example, in the English and Welsh prison regime great emphasis has been traditionally paid to surprise inspections, whereas such unpredictability in inspection activity has been seen as an essential, but not necessarily informative part of the German prison regulatory regimes (Hood et al. 2004).

The structural organisation of regulation and regulatory strategies are but part of the picture. Regulatory capacities also require the appropriate personnel. For example, regulatory capacity raises issues as to what kind of expertise is required when it comes to decision-making about whether certain goods or practices can be considered as safe, and how such expertise is updated in light of changing technologies. Furthermore, it points to questions about whether regulatory expertise is aligned to, or in contradiction with, other logics that shape the domain, such as the demand to offer output-based performance assessments. Similarly, having regulators solely interested in 'econocrat' judgements about efficiency may make them less interested in other areas of regulation, such as consumer satisfaction or the provision of so-called universal services.

A focus on regulatory capacity also highlights issues about regulators' career structures, for example, whether so-called 'revolving door' career patterns (where staff move between the worlds of regulated and regulators) should be encouraged or discouraged, and how career incentive systems influence sanctions (Makkai and Braithwaite 1992). Finally, although regulatory capacities are inherently linked to a loyalty understanding that sees them as separate from the world of democratic politics, it nevertheless raises questions as to how regulatory activities can be made somewhat responsive to the wider world of changing societal preferences (Lodge forthcoming).

In short, regulatory capacity is about organisation and strategies that enable the control of particular activities. In addition, it requires the encouragement of expertise that sustains oversight over regulated activities in the light of perennial questions regarding the importance of what expertise is, whether autonomy and independence are important assets, and, if so, how autonomy and independence can be incorporated into formal arrangements and organisational practice. Finally, it is about the relationship between how those pursuing regulatory activities should be rewarded, as regulatory outcomes–such as the given degree of market concentration or levels of investment–will always be assessed differently by different constituencies (for example, those stressing efficiency and those emphasising equity-related values).

Coordination capacity

Most governing action is about coordination: problem-solving involves the interdependent actions of different, often dispersed, actors. Even where single organisational units are able to act on their own, their decisions and actions are likely to have effects on other governmental actors. Coordination, in all its varied configurations, is a perennial problem for governance, given the self-interest of different organisational units in not wishing to give up their autonomy for the 'greater good', distrust between actors, information asymmetries, transaction costs that impede communication, and value differences. Coordination has become an even bigger challenge as states have dispersed power through processes of 'agencification' (cf. for example Christensen and Laegreid 2006) and delegation to subnational and supranational levels of governance (Wegrich and Stimac forthcoming).

Fragmentation, however, is not inherently a coordination problem. Instead, problems emerge for at least three reasons. First, cooperation is shaped by decision-rules. Any rule system involves its own biases and gives particularly powerful (pivotal) positions to some actors rather than others. Systems that rely on extra-large majorities, for example, may prove particularly resistant to reform, while a lack of a need for consensus may breed dissatisfaction and opposition. Second, coordination may prove difficult as various parties are inherently autonomy-seeking and unwilling to share their turf with organisational rivals. In some areas, therefore, cooperative behaviour will be more easily obtainable than in more competitive settings, where any decision will establish administrative losers and winners. This leads to the well-known problems of over- and underlap (Wegrich and Stimac forthcoming). Overlap is defined as the problem where two organisations have a claim to be responsible for a particular issue, leading to duplication of services, competing claims for authority, and rivalry. In contrast, underlap, a word also used by the former British Cabinet Secretary Sir Gus O'Donnell, is the condition where no organisation wishes to take on responsibility, thereby seeking to avoid blame for when things go wrong. Coordination failure as a result of both over- and underlap can be seen as an outcome of the autonomy-seeking behaviour of organisations. Third, the diagnosed problem of achieving decisions among dispersed actors frequently gives rise to calls for centralised 'fixes'. However, this hope of being able to fix fragmentation through centralised units has been widely proven to be illusory as information asymmetries, time lags, and resistance undermine attempts at forcing coordination through top-down means.

Therefore, the search for solutions to coordination problems has proven as perennial as the discussion of coordination problems themselves. For example, these comprise recommendations to create over-arching bodies to coordinate dispersed actors or to establish procedural measures to facilitate joint-working among them. Such devices include joint performance targets, the installation of czars to bash (organisational) heads together, the existence of memoranda of understanding, and the creation of joint task forces and commissions to overcome turf-fights over organisational responsibility through joined-up working.

Furthermore, as the literature on collaboration and implementation has emphasised (Torfing et al. 2012; Winter 2012), in highly differentiated and often adversarial domains, governmental action takes places in a non-hierarchical network-type setting and is thus largely restricted to a mediating role between competing and rival perspectives (Stoker 1998; Rhodes 1997; Matthews 2012). A mediating role is not one that can rely on hierarchical intervention. Instead, administrative involvement relies on mutual acceptance among the different parties involved, and one that is able to safeguard the legitimacy of the agreed actions. In other words, what is required is the capacity to move between different systems, whether this involves, for example, different areas of science, business, labour, or various ethnic communities. This is the world of the boundary-spanner in government who is able to competently move across various settings and systems and is able to negotiate and mediate between them.

In sum, coordination capacity has considerable implications for bureaucracies, apart from the development of structural devices that seek to constrain turf and autonomy-seeking behaviours. First, coordination capacity relies on boundary-spanners in government. Such boundary-spanners require the development of skills in facilitating and moderating often highly contested negotiation processes. Second, coordination capacity also requires the ability to mediate between the need to specialise through dispersing functions within organisations and by creating new actors, on the one hand, and the need to keep a common interest among dispersed actors, on the other. Third, boundary-spanning and mediation between dispersed networks of actors has implications for rewards: an emphasis on collaboration challenges performance-oriented reward systems that focus on results in terms of outputs in particular.

Analytical capacity

Analytical capacities are required to understand how systems are performing, but also what kind of future demands and challenges are likely to emerge. Contemporary communications technologies have led to an explosion of information flows, although it is difficult to measure information flows and the utilization of knowledge over different periods in time. Furthermore, knowledge and expertise have become increasingly contested as societies have become less deferential towards traditional sources of authority (Fischer 2009). Finally, deliberating over more or less uncertain future social and economic developments is inherently tricky, especially when value conflicts and entrenched interests are involved. Therefore, making choices about future health care provision in the light of an ageing society, for example, involves highly political choices, as does the decision as to how to draw down natural resources (e.g. gas or oil), rare metals, or fragile eco-systems. Given such complexities and the often transboundary nature of such issues, analytical capacities are argued to be increasingly 'bought in' rather than assumed to be 'built-in' within bureaucracies themselves (cf. Parrado forthcoming; Döhler 2012; Raudla 2013).

The traditional image of expertise inside bureaucracy refers to the 'best in world' expert who assesses contrasting claims and develops well-informed policy approaches. This is the world in which civil servants have amassed not just *Dienstwissen,* i.e. on-the-job experience, but also *Fachwissen*, i.e. knowledge of the subject matter, and are seen as experts in their field. This know-how may be based on specific training (such as medicine or urban planning), but it may also be represented by more generic skills, such as legal or economic expertise. Such an image of 'the' expert residing inside as part of the sitting army of bureaucrats may have always been somewhat of a caricature. However, this image is most certainly no longer applicable to all areas of bureaucratic activity in the early 21st century: As 'best in world' knowledge cannot be said to naturally reside in national bureaucracies and as knowledge is contested, the nature of expertise in government is arguably about being an intelligent consumer of different claims and of different sources of advice and expertise rather than a (or the sole) producer of knowledge itself.

Analytical capacity, therefore, is as much about deciding 'whom' to ask, as it is about 'what' to know. Formulating the problem in terms of analytical capacity moves beyond the traditional discussion about the advantages and disadvantages of experts and generalists (Ridley 1968). According to this long-standing debate, experts are associated with knowledge and analytical skills, but they are also accused of being unable to look beyond their own patch and incorporate different demands that are involved in governing. Similarly, generalists, i.e. those that have no particular training for the specific position they are occupying, are seen as being able to look across government and pose challenging questions outside the consensus of the particular domain. At the same time, they are often also criticised as amateurs in not being sufficiently competent to offer advanced policy analysis and development skills. In other words, one needs to move the debate about analytical capacity beyond that of the 'generalist' versus the 'expert' (Hood and Lodge 2006; Page and Jenkins 2005).

The analytical capacity to collect, assess and advise on information can come in a number of ways. One is the political-advisory one that supports politicians in the handling of a media that is said to have become ever more invasive and headline-seeking in an age of rolling headlines on 24-hour news channels and the twittering worlds of social networks (Hood 2011). However, analytical capacity goes beyond sage-type advice on political tactics and scheming. It also refers to areas of specialist expertise in forecasting and evaluation. To advance governance readiness, states organise their 'knowledge' in different ways, whether in terms of in-house, blue-sky-thinking units, government-funded research institutions or 'think tanks' (for example, the blueprint of the radical state sector reforms in New Zealand was developed by an in-house unit in the New Zealand Treasury, see Lodge and Gill 2011).

How analytical capacity is organised and resourced is not just about the ability to detect future trends in politics. It has direct implications for the contemporary world of 'outsourced' governance. For example, analytical capacity is required when it comes to procurement decisions. As Patrick Dunleavy (1995) has suggested, a world in which public services are increasingly run by global private corporations (and consultants) presents considerable challenges for national 'dumb' bureaucracies who will be outgunned by the resources (and salary incentives) of these international corporations. Similarly, a decision to embark on, for instance, particular health care initiatives requires a view as to how care should be organised as medical treatments evolve, doctrines about 'proper' care fluctuate, and patient profiles change given demographic and lifestyle changes.

In other words, expertise is required across various areas of governing and problem-solving and can be organised in different ways. The varied demands on analytical capacity also have distinct implications for bureaucracies: it emphasises the need to address the tricky balance between maintaining in-house analytical skills to act as intelligent consumer and acting as 'networker' between different, and often competing knowledge systems. Related questions include what kind of expertise should be encouraged 'in house' and what kind of analytical expertise can be 'in-sourced' from whom and on what conditions. In addition, in an age in which no consensus exists among OECD countries as to the economic recipes to fix holes in public finances, the ways to address or mitigate changes in the global and local climate, or the ways to manage the implications of an ageing society, what could be an 'ideal' relation between the worlds of politics and bureaucracy on the one hand and the wider think-tank world on the other?

Table 2.3 **Overview of key aspects of administrative capacities**

	Delivery	Regulatory	Coordination	Analytical
Competency	Making things happen	Keeping actors under control	Bringing dispersed actors into harmony	Giving advice and informing about the future
Reward	Performance-related on output/outcome vs. performance non-related due to fear of incentive distortion	Achievement of regulatory objectives vs. judge-type predictable pay	Achievement of coordination outcomes vs. achievement of joint working vs. acceptance by diverse 'stakeholders'	Right predictions vs. power maintenance vs. stable pay to maintain expert neutrality
Loyalty	Towards profession vs. towards 'public service' vs. towards target population	Towards 'sector' vs. towards public interest vs. towards 'efficiency' vs. 'competition'	Towards 'stakeholders' vs. towards wider public interest vs. towards 'state'	Towards 'science' vs. towards political party in power vs. towards national strategic interest
Standard	How to set standard that describes 'effective' performance	How to set standards that define 'safe' or 'acceptable' or 'efficient' conduct	How to set a standard for degree of 'acceptable' level of coordination	How to establish what the important goals and time horizons for advice are
Detection	How to establish how services are delivered without creating distortion	How to establish whether behaviours are compliant with intended objectives	How to establish which areas require coordination and whom to include/exclude	How to ensure that advice is 'best in world'
Behaviour modification	How to set incentives to change behaviours among street-level actors	How to establish a sanctioning system that facilitates individual responsibility	How to incentivise/force actors to collaborate with each other	How to ensure that intelligence informs decision-making

Today's challenges also bring into question whether analytical skills in government should be about long-term trends or about the short-term political business cycle. Finally, analytical capacity raises distinct issues regarding reward: as analysis deals with areas of relative uncertainty, questions arise as to how to incentivise reward systems that encourage analytical capacities that are willing to 'speak (uncomfortable) truth to power'.

In sum, analytical capacity is about the organisation and type of advice that informs governmental policy-making. Analytical capacity is, therefore, partly about the kind of skills civil servants are supposed to have. The effects of skills on type of policy approach will matter as different academic dis-

Table 2.4 **Contrasting perspectives on administrative capacities**

	Delivery	Regulatory	Coordination	Analytical
Basic principle	Ensuring the production/execution of public services	Control and oversight	Bringing different units to work together	Accessing, analysing and advising on information
Weberianism	Stress on professional public servants	Stress on inspection, rules and procedures	Stress on procedural provisions and task forces	Stress on experts in government and government-financed think tanks
Impartiality	Stress on execution of policies in an impartial way	Stress on rule-based regulation with minimised discretion	Stress on procedural provisions	Stress on detached expertise and requirements to display balanced advice
Managerialism	Stress on market-type production and execution of public services	Stress on incentive-based regulation	Stress on individual incentives and benchmarks	Stress on ad-hoc procurement of advice
Public Value	Stress on co-production of public services in 'public value' entrepreneurial way	Stress on public value outcomes that go beyond pure efficiency considerations	Stress on ability to align various stakeholders	Stress on identification of 'public value' and strategies to achieve it

ciplines bring different priorities and approaches. Beyond the skill-base of individuals, analytical capacity entails decisions among different foci, ranging from those delivering long-term research-based perspectives, to those that seek to bring together contested evidence bases, to the more short-term political rune-reading skills associated with the world of 'spin' and public relations. Last, but not least, it raises the question of how to reward the exercise of analytical capacity.

Summarising the four administrative capacities

The above discussion can only offer a brief consideration of the key aspects of each of the four areas of administrative capacity that are at the centre of this Report. The four administrative capacities are overlapping and should not be seen as mutually exclusive. Indeed, all four relate to some key issues, raising questions about what the aim of the particular capacity is, how the need for a particular exercise should be detected, and the ways in which these capacities are being brought to bear in public problem-solving. As noted, each one of these questions raises fundamental issues about how administrative capacities should be organised and executed. These debates are summarised in Table 2.3.

Returning to the four perspectives outlined at the outset of this chapter, it is possible to extrapolate the way they emphasise different aspects. Table 2.4 illustrates how different ideas about particular administrative capacities would look. It also suggests that the application of the four perspectives leads to diverse recipes as to how certain capacities should be understood. It is therefore unlikely that there will ever be a single interpretation as to what different administrative capacities should be. Such questions reflect on much more fundamental views as to the appropriate relationship between bureaucracy and the wider social and political worlds.

Implications for Governance Readiness and Innovation

This chapter has offered a differentiated approach towards administrative capacity. In an age in which the challenges of the financial and fiscal crises, the sustainability agenda, and ageing societies are placing a considerable burden on the industrialised world's public sectors, it is critical to interrogate the demands and expectations that political systems have regarding the skills and competencies of individual civil servants and public organisations.

Any serious attempt at maintaining administrative capacity in government needs to consider not just the wish-lists reflecting the latest fads and fashions, but the actual demands that are placed on public servants. Furthermore, such efforts have to be explicit about the underlying assumptions that support any reform initiative: doctrines about bureaucracy's role vis-a-vis society and politics compete. A context of constrained resources and competing views about the role of bureaucracy at large means that such exercises need to consider the tricky trade-offs between potentially conflicting ideas about how to place particular emphasis on some set of skills and organisational features rather than others. However, this also requires that the wider organisation of public administration needs to develop a sense of purpose, or 'core competence'. Defining what the 'core competence' is has traditionally been something that has proven particularly difficult to do, whether this is because of political difficulties, competing demands by societal interests, or the generally uncertain nature of government business.

A focus on administrative capacity facilitates the understanding of the role of bureaucracy in the setting of multi-actor governance systems. It raises three issues of central concern for this Report more generally, namely the link to measurement, to innovation, and to the interaction with innovative strategies and instruments (which are going to be discussed in the next chapter). These concluding paragraphs consider each of these three points in turn.

Turning to measurement first, we have suggested that one cannot turn our ideas about administrative capacity into easily measurable numbers. The field of governance indicators is still young and developing fast, and this Report, as stated in the Introduction, seeks to contribute to its further advancement. We have learned that it is indeed feasible to offer summary indicators as to how different states deal with particular challenges. These might include indicators that look at the way in which countries utilise particular coordination devices rather than others, create and resource 'blue-sky-thinking' units in government, or rely on a wider think tank universe to deliver policy ideas. Similarly, there are now indicators to measure regulatory capacity, the independence of various agencies, or the reputation of agency competency. However, such indicators may say little about the actual quality of problem-solving in terms of governance readiness, as the 'causal chemistry' of effective and efficient governance remains to be explored: why does it come about in one setting but not in another, or why are some actors beneficial in some instances but not in others, etc.? We see a need to combine the development of indicators with comparative research about how various governments deal with particular problems, what kind of skills and demands are required in doing so, and how such responses differ across national contexts.

> *Without sufficient administrative capacities, it will be difficult for any state to facilitate and sustain its contribution towards solving contemporary policy challenges.*

Second, a focus on administrative capacity contributes to discussions about innovation in at least two ways. Without considering the kind of administrative capacities required, any innovative governance strategy to deal with one of the core challenges facing contemporary states will be bound to fail. To, therefore, sustain innovative practices requires a systematic consideration of the kind of facilitating role that public administration can play.

Furthermore, innovation is important in developing administrative capacities themselves. The problems of human resources systems in developing career and organisational development plans are well-known, whether they relate to the inevitable grade-inflation creep that affects all performance management systems, the problem of dealing with ambiguous goals and prescriptions, or the absence of predictable career ladders given the whims of political life. Thinking more carefully about the kinds of administrative capacities required to deal with the contemporary and future challenges to statehood confronts human resources systems with the need to move beyond well-sounding phrases and towards a more difficult conversation about incentive systems, loyalty understandings, and the range of skills and competency requirements that are viewed as critical for governance readiness.

Third and finally, administrative capacities are essential for the development of governance strategies that involve innovative uses of resources and instruments. Without sufficient administrative capacities, it will be difficult for any state to facilitate and sustain its contribution towards solving or, at least, mediating contemporary policy challenges. At the same time, administrative capacities require innovative resource use themselves. Innovation therefore needs to address the tricky questions as to how administrative capacities are organised and how they are financed, authorised to act, and placed within systems of governance. In other words, thinking about governance innovation without considering administrative capacities misses one central feature of governance itself.

Endnotes

1 Somewhat ironically, the principal-agent literature would come to the opposite argument, namely that bureaucratic effort will largely be a result of enhanced political control (McCubbins and Schwartz 1984; cf. Krause 2010 for a review of the wide literature).

2 Arguably, the success of public value as a concept has been its appeal to numerous audiences, ranging from those focusing on managerial-entrepreneurialism, those focusing on the hierarchically-superior role of bureaucracy, and those that focus on the community-based emphasis. We emphasise the third strain.

III. Governance Challenges and Administrative Capacities

MARTIN LODGE *and* KAI WEGRICH

As noted in the introductory chapter, widespread concern exists as to whether contemporary governance systems, especially in the OECD countries, are sufficiently capable and legitimate to address the challenges of financial crises, demographic developments, and environmental sustainability and climate change-related phenomena. For one, governments are widely seen as part of the problem, rather than as part of the solution. They are also accused of being pre-occupied by short-term electoral motives, captured by special interests, and unable to navigate veto-point rich political environments. Similarly, markets are regarded as another part of the problem rather than as part of the solution, especially after the financial market meltdown in the late 2000s. Market players are frequently seen as too short-termist, too interested in sweating assets rather than developing new infrastructures, and too keen on exploiting consumers.

It is fashionable to note that contemporary governance challenges represent 'wicked problems' (Rittel and Webber 1973). Wicked problems are characterised by contestation over the definition of the actual problem and over solutions that, in any case, do not address other ongoing problems or create new ones, and where the *sui generis* nature of the problem makes replication and 'learning from experience' difficult (March, Sproull, and Tamuz 1991). The standard academic recipe to deal with wickedness is to respond through complexity and 'clumsiness' (Verweij forthcoming), thereby seeking to deal with the value conflicts inherent in these problems through the incorporation of different interests and stakeholders.

> *One of the common problems is matching the demand for public goods and services with the actual capacity of governing systems to supply.*

However complex contemporary governance challenges are, one of the common problems across these areas is matching the demand for public goods and services with the actual capacity of governing systems to supply. This matching problem points directly to administrative capacities, for example, in managing the link between demand and supply, in shaping demand, in incentivising and regulating particular forms of supply, and so on. This chapter emphasises the importance of considering the implications for administrative capacity of governments' responses to governance challenges. It is essential to question what kind of bureaucracy is required to be able to adapt and respond in varied ways to governance challenges.

To illustrate the importance of administrative capacities, this chapter considers four key governance challenges facing OECD countries in particular, namely the issues of expanding broadband infrastructure, of changing the energy generation 'mix', of dealing with the problems of an ageing society, and of managing immigration. In the industrialised world, it could be argued that all four challenges represent a problem for which, in different ways, demands for a particular service outstrips, or is likely to outstrip, the contemporary capacity to supply services at the appropriate level of quality.

This chapter looks at these four policy challenges to consider in more detail the bottlenecks that contemporary policy problems face, what kinds of strategies have been adopted to address these bottlenecks, and, finally, what this says about the kind of administrative capacities required of contemporary states. This chapter does not suggest that one or the other policy approach is better in dealing with elder care or the need to replace energy generation capacity. It is solely concerned with the kind of administrative capacities required to address these questions in the first place.

Four Governance Challenges

As noted, in this section we consider in turn four governance challenges that, we contend, are critical for contemporary statehood. These are 'infrastructure' in terms of broadband networks, 'sustainability' in terms of the provision of energy generation capacity, 'welfare' in terms of dealing with the consequences of an ageing society, and 'integration' in terms of attracting and accommodating immigration. The provision of infrastructure, sustainability, welfare, and integration are, we argue, at the heart of statehood. Therefore, failure to deal with these issues or even the perception of a deficit in problem-solving capacity will have significant implications for the legitimacy of states in general. The intention of this section is not to consider all aspects of particular governance challenges (it is impossible to do justice to these challenges in one brief chapter), but rather to illustrate key areas in which administrative capacities are required or are likely to play an important role.

Infrastructure: Broadband provision

Broadband, broadly defined as access to transmission speeds higher than 256 kilobits per second for downstream or upstream connections or both (see Kim, Kelly, and Raja 2010: 7), is widely seen as a key resource for social and economic activity in OECD countries, especially also in economically less well-connected regions. The underlying problem of (potential) demand outstripping supply is a relatively straightforward one. On the one hand, the demand for broadband capacity is increasing as online services grow more extensive and complex, smart online devices 'eat' more and more capacity, and ever greater emphasis is placed on the digital economy, all leading to potential dividing lines between those living in remote areas and those more centrally located. This, therefore, raises further public policy issues as to what can be considered as a 'universal service' and how it should be delivered. The supply problem is about how to plan for capacity, the technologies involved to deliver high speed/capacity broadband, and the planning and financing of these infrastructures.

Among the technical aspects that shape discussions about broadband provision are speed and capacity. Other issues are of a regulatory nature, for example, how to ensure that actual speed reflects the advertised one, given that a recent European Commission study found that consumers could expect approx. 74% of advertised speed (EC 2012). Table 3.1 provides an impressionistic snapshot of different aspects that could be seen as indicators for broadband quality–namely, speed and quality (the 'R-factor' measuring the quality of voice over Internet calls; a higher number implies a higher degree of quality) as well as household access to broadband.

A further question involves the type of infrastructure technology. Much of contemporary broadband delivery is via DSL (digital subscriber line) that utilises the existing copper network to transmit communication. It is widely argued that DSL offers short-term benefits, but ultimately is not capable of coping with the kind of services that industry observers expect to emerge. Therefore, arguments are made in favour of establishing fibre optic cable networks in particular. However, such demands are problematic as existing (and usually dominant) providers rely on exploiting the existing DSL technology and often prove unwilling to invest in new technologies whose regulation (and commercial returns) may be uncertain.

Finally, there are issues about universal service. A key question is what minimum level of service every customer should expect in terms of broadband speed and coverage–and cost. These issues feature strongly in the various National Broadband Plans across OECD countries (OECD 2011), which vary in terms of their emphasis on availability and in terms of rate of adoption. To facilitate the roll-out of fibre optic cables, some states (for example, Switzerland and Denmark) stressed regulatory strategies (especially interconnection, local loop unbundling, and other infrastructure access provisions). New Zealand created a special 'crown fibre holding' (www.crownfibre.govt.nz/) to manage the government's financial support for the expansion of fibre optic-based 'ultra fast broadband' (the aim being to provide 75% of all New Zealanders with a service of over 100 megabits per second by 2019). The actual delivery was based on four contracts with a range of (private) providers. For its rural broadband approach (employing fixed wireless broadband and fibre optic cable technologies), New Zealand relied on tenders with two private firms (Vodafone and Chorus), but involving a further set of local providers.

A variety of approaches towards broadband provision exists across OECD countries. These reflect in particular the relationship between (central) governments and communication providers. In the UK, apart from the controversial rural broadband policy noted below, one of the major regulatory issues concerned the dominant position of British Telecom (BT) and complaints that it refused to grant its competitors equal access to its network. In 2005, the sectoral regulator Ofcom ordered an internal separation of the delivery and infrastructure services run by BT–but stopped short of calling for a complete separation. Furthermore, broadband access was made part of the universal service obligation, placing higher demands on providers and regulators alike ('Turf Wars in Telecoms' 2006).

In Germany, broadband policy has been shaped by a variety of initiatives since the early 2000s. However, it took regulatory action (in 2004, when Deutsche Telekom's DSL charges and its monthly local loop charges were reduced) to allow for competition for broadband services to emerge. Questions about how to encourage investment in high-speed networks triggered debates about whether Deutsche Telekom should be granted a 'regulatory holiday' for certain aspects of its business, though this option was dismissed by the European Union (EU). In 2013, debates and judicial reviews centred on Deutsche Telekom's controversial plan to limit the speed of broadband connection after a certain amount of data transmission. While a court ruling and political debates suggest that the Deutsche Telekom will not be able to proceed with its plans, the development highlights the capacity limits in broadband provision.

Sweden, by contrast, focused public funding on the fibre optic broadband development of local networks by providing grants and tax incentives. In addition, local governments were required to co-finance these investments. These local networks were run by local authorities and connected to the general 'backbone' infrastructure. Regulatory oversight was to ensure non-discriminatory access and therefore to enhance the potential for competition.

Across national experiences, the provision of broadband for rural areas has proven controversial. For example, the UK government announced an intention that 90% of the whole UK should have 'superfast' broadband availability by 2015 (above 24 Megabits per second). The UK's aim was to encourage local authorities to be in the lead on the programme, but to provide them with central funding. This programme was hit by delays (of nearly two years) and revised targets (95% coverage by 2017). The UK National Audit Office noted that this delay was not just caused by problems of complying with EU state aids laws. The complexity of the bidding process meant that

Table 3.1 **Comparative broadband experiences**

	Download Speed	Household Quality	Household Access to Broadband 2010† in %
Australia	13.49 Mbps	81.49	62.0*
Austria	20.27 Mbps	87.32	63.7
Brazil	8.92 Mbps	—	—
Canada	18.79 Mbps	83.96	72.2**
China	15.08 Mbps	—	—
Estonia	24.38 Mbps	87.86	64.5
France	24.37 Mbps	83.71	66.8
Germany	22.02 Mbps	79.46	75.2
Greece	7.61 Mbps	75.96	41.2
Hungary	23.45 Mbps	83.11	52.2
Ireland	15.71 Mbps	85.36	57.5
Italy	6.80 Mbps	86.54	48.9
Japan	38.84 Mbps	—	63.4
Mexico	10.75 Mbps	—	21.1
Netherlands	40.44 Mbps	85.93	79.5
Poland	15.67 Mbps	83.57	56.8
Russian Federation	20.19 Mbps	86.39	—
South Korea	45.34 Mbps	—	97.5
Spain	18.84 Mbps	86.50	57.4
Sweden	38.22 Mbps	86.70	82.6
Switzerland	32.29 Mbps	85.25	70.8*
Turkey	9.39 Mbps	77.31	33.7
UK	22.34 Mbps	87.88	69.5**
USA	19.20 Mbps	85.91	68.2

Sources: Net Index (2013) for download speed and household quality; OECD (2013d) Broadband Statistics for households with broadband access.

†Numbers for Japan, Korea, and Mexico also include fixed wireless and wireless broadband connections.
*Numbers for Australia and Switzerland from 2008.
**Numbers for Canada and UK from 2009.

the number of interested parties dwindled to one–only BT remained as active participant and therefore as winner of most projects under this initiative. Furthermore, the relevant government department was accused of having insufficient oversight of BT's implementation and cost programme–and led BT to make a lower than expected contribution to the project, namely 23% of the overall cost of £1.5bn (instead of 36%), while it had benefitted from £1.2bn of public money for the project (NAO 2013).

For its part, in November 2013, the German coalition government (CDU, CSU and SPD) declared in its contract its intent to connect all German households with Internet speeds of a minimum of 50 Megabits per second by 2018 (Deutschlands Zukunft gestalten 2013). As in the UK, the roll-out of rural broadband programmes in Germany involved the transfer of grants from the federal level to local governments as well as the use of more general competitiveness-related programmes to finance the expansion of broadband provision. This programme was criticised in media reports for its sole concentration on fibre optic cables and for being ineffective in setting incentives for sufficient investment to ensure rural broadband access, though as demonstrated by one of the governance innovations described in Chapter 4, local citizens and governments are developing their own arrangements. The rural broadband issue highlights the problems for governments when seeking to run public procurement programmes that are to succeed in transferring risks for cost inflation, introduce the intended changes on time, and are not attacked for either being too cautious or too risky or for being too lenient on dominant market providers.

In sum, then, the problem of demand for broadband services outstripping supply can be separated into a number of issues. One is the issue of defining and updating standards for capacity and speed that are likely to advance social and economic well-being. Another concern is to ensure that these standards are met through investment and oversight. This again raises issues about whether the financing should be carried by solely private, mixed private-public, or solely public sources and the extent to which cross-subsidising rural services should be encouraged.

Sustainability: Energy generation

Energy policy is at the heart of many contemporary debates at both global and national levels. These debates cover topics ranging from trajectories regarding future demands for energy (given, in particular, the rising need for data storage), the cost implications that arise from placing trust in particular forms of energy generation, and the way reserve capacities for times of low production from renewable sources can be provided. How then can competing demands for investment, CO_2 emission reduction, and low prices for consumers (and industry) be accommodated?

In terms of the problem of supply and demand, there is a degree of uncertainty about future demand (for example, whether an emphasis on efficiency will reduce overall demand or whether those reductions will be more than compensated by new devices), as well as about the requirements for 'smart networks' that are able to transmit increasingly volatile supplies. Furthermore, choices have to be made in terms of investments into new and 'old' technologies and the way in which back-up standby capacity is being organised, financed, and regulated. In other words, how can the demand for future energy needs be met with a different kind of supply; and how can the demand for network capacity be met by new forms of supply in terms of infrastructure capacity?

As shown in Table 3.2, the share of renewables (solar, wind, etc.) in energy generation increased in most EU member states between 1990 and 2010. At the same time, however, in several countries outside the EU, for example, China, Japan, and Switzerland, the share of renewables has actually declined. Thus, while energy generation capacity has expanded more generally, it has done so not necessarily on the basis of renewable energy forms.

> How can competing demands for investment, CO_2 emission reduction, and low prices for consumers (and industry) be accommodated?

A reliance on renewables is very much a value choice: it is about preferring one source of energy over another on the basis that the former appears more desirable, whether this is in terms of availability, cost, fairness, industrial championing, or environmental impact. Renewables clearly seek to develop an industry that appears attractive in terms of reducing the impact of CO_2 in the atmosphere, while also addressing some countries' concerns about the safe operation of nuclear reactors and storage of nuclear fuel rods. It is notable, for example, that the response to the nuclear disaster in Fukushima in 2011 was very different across countries (especially when comparing the UK and Germany), in terms of media interest, public attention, and political concern.

Once a choice towards a policy in favour of renewables (such as solar or wind) has been made, however, then other investment decisions follow, especially in terms of infrastructure capacity. Here, again, uncertainty reigns. For example, it is uncertain how renewable technologies will evolve in the future, how much renewable energy will largely be produced on a decentralised basis or by large-scale offshore wind farms, and how national and international governance regimes interact with these technologies. Different trajectories are shaped by and have implications for governance arrangements and administrative capacities (see Mautz 2012 for Germany).

Furthermore, questions as to how to establish a portfolio of different energy sources need to be answered, especially also in terms of investing in back-up energy supplies. Renewables are highly volatile and increase the

Table 3.2 **Contribution of renewables and nuclear to energy supply (in % of total primary energy supply)**

	Renewables 1990	Renewables 2010	Nuclear 2010
Australia	5.9	5.5	—
Austria	20.3	26.8	—
Canada	16.1	17.1	15.0
China	24.2	11.6	—
Estonia	1.9	15.3	—
France	6.8	8.0	74.1
Germany	1.5	9.9	24.5
Greece	5.1	7.7	—
Hungary	2.6	7.6	42.8
Iceland	67.0	82.5	—
Ireland	3.1	4.6	—
Italy	4.4	10.6	—
Japan	3.5	3.3	29.2
Mexico	12.2	9.8	2.6
Netherlands	1.1	3.8	3.2
Poland	1.5	7.2	—
Russian Federation	3.0	2.5	—
South Korea	1.1	0.7	32.2
Spain	6.9	11.8	20.1
Sweden	24.4	34.0	38.2
Switzerland	24.4	19.0	38.0
Turkey	18.3	11.1	—
UK	0.5	3.4	15.7
USA	5.0	5.6	20.3

Sources: OECD 2013a, 2013b

risk of blackouts as both solar- and wind-based energy sources are weather-dependent. Concerns about eventual blackouts may be less of a problem in the future when there might be more international transmission networks, but during a period of transition in which renewable energies are still emerging and old forms of energy generation are declining, the 'slack' in the system is decreasing.

Questions about the security of supply are pertinent especially at a time (such as at the time of writing in October 2013) when energy utilities in Germany were complaining about collapsing profitability of their gas-powered plants, which are considered an important source of reserve capacity. Along a similar vein, the UK government approved a £16bn deal to build a new nuclear energy facility with private energy firms (led by Électricité de France and backed by two Chinese nuclear firms) that guarantees a 'strike price' per unit of electricity produced at double the rate of the wholesale electricity prices in October 2013–for up to 35 years (BBC News 2013). Again, such deals may be seen as highly problematic; they are most likely to be shown to be too restrictive (leading to inevitable re-negotiation) or as too accommodating to industry interests (leading to political pressure on regulators and companies alike).

In general, countries have moved in a variety of ways to deal with the issue of establishing sustainable energy generation. For some, this has included the use of guaranteed feed-in tariffs, while others have relied on quotas for renewables that energy generation companies have to meet. Feed-in tariffs that offer cost-based compensation are considered to be effective in promoting the increase of renewables, but if and how cost-efficient they are in achieving this goal depends on the details of the policy design, i.e. in terms of the scale of the tariff and regional and technology-specific regulation (cf. Mendonça, Jacobs, and Sovacool 2009). The design of a feed-in tariff also can have unintended consequences when the policy is 'too successful'. In Germany, for example, the feed-in tariff was initially guaranteed for 20 years. However, the 2011 decision to accelerate the *Energiewende* ('energy turnaround') to phase out nuclear energy resulted in a substantial increase of the fee that consumers had to pay to compensate the difference between declining prices on the energy spot market and the guaranteed price for renewables (when provider companies choose to transfer the fee to the consumer).[1] Ironically, this development, together with the low prices for emissions certificates (see below), made older coal-based power plants more profitable than modern gas power plants. In 2012, when Germany experienced a particularly cold winter, CO_2 emissions actually increased despite a rise in the renewables share of total energy generated (BMU 2013).

Another policy trend has been the use of emission markets, with the European Emissions Trading System being the possibly most prominent example (see Chapter 4 for other examples). At the time of writing, the European system was suffering from low price levels due to the economic downturn and the inflow of certificates from Eastern European countries. More generally, the use of emission markets and trading schemes has generally been problematic, given the high prerequisites for such market systems to operate, and the considerable lobbying power of large energy users that undermined the functioning of the price mechanism in the first place (Baldwin, Cave, and Lodge 2012).

In sum, as sustainability has become a central theme in contemporary policy-making, questions about the environmental impact of energy generation have returned to the forefront. Old debates about nuclear energy have been recast in terms of CO_2 emissions, though the 2011 Fukushima incident added a new twist. Questions have been raised about the viability of a strategy that relies on renewable, but more volatile forms of energy generation, especially also in terms of providing for the appropriate infrastructure capacity. The core governance challenges therefore include considering future demands, addressing uncertainty about technological developments, steering investment through taxes and subsidies, and dealing with regulatory issues about pricing. Even for those that argue that states should not be directly involved in the generation of energy and the organisation of relevant markets, the inherent monopoly elements of the transmission network and the considerable (positive and negative) externalities of energy mean that the role of the state–and thereby also the need for administrative capacities–continues to be central.

Welfare: Care for the elderly

The welfare state, particularly in the OECD countries, is facing many challenges, among them spiralling medical costs as treatments become ever more expensive, and as demand for medical services is potentially unlimited. One particular cost driver is the demographic profile of populations. How such costs will affect different countries will, of course, depend on the generosity of their welfare states and their demographic profile. When looking at the projected share of the population of over 80 year olds in various OECD countries (see Table 3.3), states display different degrees of vulnerability.

Demographic trends do not necessarily have a negative economic impact. Indeed, one of the key initiatives in many countries to stave off the potential economic impact of an ageing population has been to enlarge the working population. However, even with such initiatives, states will still face rising health care costs as the share of the population that reach advanced old age is rising. And it is in this particular population group that costs are likely to feature very highly.

According to OECD estimates (Colombo et al. 2011), by 2050, over 10% of national populations in the OECD world will be over the age of 80. In three countries, Germany, Italy, and Japan, the share is likely to be around

Table 3.3 **Share (in %) of population aged 80+, selected countries**

	1980	2050 (projected)
Austria	2.6	11.5
Brazil	0.6	6.8
Canada	1.8	9.7
China	0.6	6.5
Estonia	2.2	7.8
France	2.8	10.7
Germany	2.6	14.4
Greece	2.3	11.7
Hungary	2.0	6.9
Ireland	1.9	7.7
Italy	2.2	13.8
Japan	1.4	15.6
Mexico	0.7	5.9
Netherlands	2.2	11.2
Poland	1.4	8.6
Russian Federation	1.4	4.7
South Korea	0.5	14.2
Spain	1.9	12.8
Sweden	3.1	8.8
Switzerland	2.6	9.8
Turkey	0.6	5.7
UK	2.7	9.5
USA	2.3	7.9

Source: United Nations, Department of Economic and Social Affairs, Population Division (2013).

15%. Indeed, estimates in Germany suggest that the number of individuals requiring care will rise by 50% between 2007 and 2030. Such trends are likely to have implications for public expenditures (the OECD estimates that these will amount to 20–25% of GDP in Germany and Italy by 2050, above 25% in France). These changes in demographic profile place a considerable burden on existing pension systems, especially those that rely on a 'pay-as-you-go' system. As a consequence, states have (slowly) responded by shifting responsibility for pension provision increasingly to the individual and by (gradually) increasing the age of retirement.

Apart from pensions (not covered in this chapter), one central cost driver is the need to care for an unprecedented rise in the number of elderly people. Long-term care policies have, traditionally, been far less generous than other policies of the welfare state as families have tended to provide most of the caring. Nevertheless, the rise of an elderly population places a considerable strain on the public provision of care, with annual care costs increasing substantially over recent years across national systems, in an extreme case (the US) by 24% between 2008 and 2013 (Ellis 2013).

A second key area is the extensive share of (usually) unpaid domestic care that is provided for elderly people. In Germany, for example, 69% of elderly people requiring care are cared for at home (BMG). They rely on unpaid care support networks of spouses, children, and the wider family. In England, current estimates suggest that 85% of the 1.4 million elderly people with disabilities receive unpaid care from family members (Pickard 2013: 2). While there is relative certainty about the rise in elderly people likely to require care (and especially those over 80 years old who are likely to require relatively costly care), less certainty exists about the availability and propensity of family members to provide unpaid care in the future. Pickard (2013) has suggested that demand for elder care will outstrip the availability of unpaid care in England by 2017. She argues that there is likely to be a shortfall of 160,000 unpaid carers in England by 2032.

Among the key governance challenges are those that involve both the demand for care and questions about who supplies care and under what conditions. It is unlikely that breakthrough technologies, such as care robots, telecare monitoring systems, or other devices will mitigate the increased costs and challenges of dealing with larger numbers of elderly people requiring care. Furthermore, it raises questions about eligibility for financial support, i.e. should the material circumstances of carers be assessed as to whether patients receive financial support and at what level. At the same time, elder care insurance is one area where individuals notoriously underestimate the potential costs of their later requirements; therefore a simple market system based on insurance is unlikely to provide for sufficient coverage. Furthermore, controversial issues include the question of the extent to which it is fair that patients' life-long savings and assets have to be used to pay for their care.

States have responded in different ways to these challenges, reflecting also different starting positions. One initiative has been to grant specific employment provisions for those caring for elderly relatives, as introduced in Sweden and Germany, for example. While granting special redundancy provisions to employees is one thing, wider debates as to whether care-giving should be financially rewarded (or acknowledged in pension schemes) are continuing.

Variations exist in terms of the reliance on state-provided services versus a reliance on private and unpaid care, often combined with a system of financial allowances and other support schemes. While Sweden and the Netherlands depend more on public provision, the key role is played by the family unit in Italy and Spain. The French system builds on more institutional care, whereas Germany and the UK, in different ways, place considerable emphasis on cash schemes that offer a choice between institutionalised care and financial support for family-based care.

Financing models differ between those relying on taxation and those that rely on insurance-based systems. Some reforms have focused on establishing specific insurance-based systems; for instance, Germany introduced such a public insurance system in 1995 as an additional pillar in the insurance-based welfare regime. Elsewhere, funding is provided by both 'users' as well as taxpayers. In Sweden, for example, 85% of the total is financed by local taxes; the rest is financed by patients and national grants (OECD and EC 2013).

Among the key governance challenges are those that involve both the demand for care for the elderly, and questions about who supplies care and under what conditions.

In the UK, the question about establishing a sustainable basis on which to finance future care costs was at the heart of the 2011 review led by Andrew Dilnot for the UK government (although its application was limited to England (Dilnot 2011). The resulting report suggested that future financing should be means-tested to people whose asset wealth was below £100,000, but capped at £35,000-50,000. The government would then provide for the care costs above a certain threshold. Local authorities would be able to take out loans against the value of properties owned by patients requiring institutional care. Subsequent debates in the media revolved around the level of income up to which elderly people were to receive financial support and whether patients' properties should be included or excluded in paying for care provision. Ultimately, in February 2013, the UK government set the cap at £75,000 to start in 2017, referring to the depleted nature of public finances as justification for the higher threshold (Papworth 2013).

Apart from financing elder care, the quality of the care provided is itself a major concern, often involving various levels of government. Debates have involved the rise of country-wide standards (of an associational, state, and private nature), even though the inspection and running of care homes has traditionally been organised at the local level (Appleby 2013; BMG 2013; Dilnot 2011). A reliance on local authorities in financing care facilities raises the spectre of a postcode lottery in that patients receive highly different standards of care purely on the basis of their address rather than their actual need.

The use of privatised systems of care for the elderly also raises problems regarding the extent to which risk is being transferred to the private sector.

Ultimately, many would argue, the state remains responsible for the well-being of elderly people. If, therefore, care home providers go bankrupt or fail in their duty to care for their patients appropriately, then there needs to be sufficient capacity in the public sector to absorb the needs of these patients.

Moreover, private elder care requires systems of consistent standards, detection, and enforcement. As noted by Braithwaite (2008) in the case of the private-public provision of prisons in Australia, the private companies' demand to be placed on a level-playing field meant that standards were also formalised for public institutions.

In short, the governance challenge of elder care centres on three issues we identify as critical. The first is about how to maintain a financially sustainable basis for the provision of care for elderly people. The second is how to organise the actual provision of care, whether this is operating through the state, through para-public bodies (such as religious and other charitable organisations) or through private providers. Finally, the challenge is about levels of government, whether, for example, financial resources and the organisation of services are provided or controlled at the local, regional, or national level.

Integration: Immigration

One popular theme in contemporary politics in many OECD countries is that an ageing population profile, like that described above, and the perception of increased international labour market competition make a selective immigration policy attractive. Such a selective immigration policy follows the path of classic immigration countries such as Australia and Canada (see Table 3.4). Without wishing to consider whether such a policy of 'handpicking' immigrant populations is feasible in the first place, among the key governance challenges of such an immigration policy is to establish incentives to attract skilled labour especially in those areas where domestic shortages are foreseen and where such shortages are likely to have repercussions for the coverage of public services (such as health) or for the development of certain industry sectors.[2]

Similarly, international migration between countries has implications for governance, especially in terms of making public services responsive to diverse populations, for example, by preparing street-level bureaucrats to engage with people from different cultural backgrounds. Of course, other policy aspects are also relevant (but are not considered further in this chapter): these include how to balance the demands of a more heterogeneous populace in the context of a welfare state that functions under the premise of solidarity (for a controversial contribution suggesting that welfare state solidarity is not necessarily in harmony with diversity, see Goodhart 2004).

Furthermore, contemporary immigration policies are developed and

Table 3.4 **Share of foreign-born populations in select countries (in %)**

	2001	2011
Australia	23	27
Austria	14	16
Canada	17.6	20
Estonia	18	16
France	11	12
Germany	n.a.	13
Greece	10	7
Hungary	2.9	5
Iceland	6	11
Ireland	9	17
Italy	4	9
Mexico	0	0
Netherlands	10	11
Poland	2	2
Russian Federation	8 (2002)	8 (2010)
Spain	6	15
Sweden	12	15
Switzerland	22	27
UK	8.2	12
USA	11	13

Source: OECD 2013c, Table A.4

implemented in the shadow of earlier immigration policies and debates about their outcomes. First, in many countries, the domain is characterised by a long-standing denial that immigration is or should be a policy field deserving dedicated attention, even where immigration has been a long-established and long-standing feature *and* where policies have been in place to attract immigration (if only temporarily). A key case here is Germany where a denial of inclusion- (or integration-)related policy activities was used as an electoral strategy in order to avoid having to confirm that it was an 'immigration country' (Triadafilopoulos 2012).

At the EU level, the development of a common immigration policy combined anti-discrimination measures with harmonised border controls (Guiraudon 2003). Recurrently, debates were framed in terms of limiting migration so as to avoid 'asylum shopping' (Guiraudon 2003). But these debates also showed evidence of pluralisation and partial reframing of the policy field. On the one hand, there was the perception of 'failed multiculturalism' (Banting and Kymlicka 2010) and of a failure of the more conservative guest-worker model. The latter, in particular, was seen to have created social disadvantages and discrimination and therefore, over the long term, aggravated larger social problems (Castles 2006).

On the other hand, the competition for 'the best and the brightest' among skilled immigrants resulted in an at least partial reframing of immigration policy (which was, in Germany, made explicit with the creation of integration-related portfolios in a number of sub-national governments). Such a reframing was also evident in the area of citizenship laws which made naturalization easier, even if only gradually and not without generating their own contradictions (see Triadafilopoulos 2012).

In the 2000s, most European countries claimed to engage in a global competition for workers by developing national and European level policies that aimed to attract a highly skilled workforce from abroad (Shachar 2006; Schittenhelm and Schmidtke 2010). The EU's Lisbon Agenda marked the beginning of a development that would evolve into the EU's 'blue card' initiative, a work-permit program for the EU that was passed in 2009 (Nielsen 2009). The 'blue card' permitted families to live in the EU but to also work and travel. However, decisions about social rights and quotas were left to member states, requiring some to reconsider their approach towards immigration policies in order to appeal to international labour (Michalowski 2004; Koopmans 2010). For example, the new French immigration law passed in 2006 'epitomises the general logic of Europe's current transformation of immigration and integration policy' by creating a three-year resident card for highly skilled migrants with post-graduation stay options for foreign students (Joppke 2007: 11). Similarly, Germany, in its Immigration Act in 2004, offered permanent residency in exchange for talent (Shachar 2006). Such trends contributed to the liberalisation of immigration policies in order to address domestic shortages in skilled labour so as to remain competitive (Castles 2006; Schittenhelm and Schmidtke 2010). At the same time, the German 2004 Immigration Act has been criticised for failing to attract the qualified workers that would indeed help mitigate labour shortages (Hoßmann and Karsch 2011). Other developments, such as the willingness of only a select few EU member states (especially Ireland and the UK) to lift their borders to new EU member state citizens, led to considerable population flows, especially before the financial crisis brought about a major recession.

A policy aiming to attract skilled immigrants faces a number of political and administrative challenges. Such a policy creates winners and losers, and the (potential) losers in the domestic arena will have institutional representatives in the national (and sub-national) bureaucracy (cf. Boucher 2013). Furthermore, immigration represents a cross-domain governance issue involving employment, education, housing, health, and public participation. The domain is hence shaped by the presence of a variety of actors and institutions that follow different rationales and agendas. Those responsible for migration control and 'homeland' issues take a policing and controlling perspective on immigration. Similarly, those that stress the need to develop a dedicated policy towards skilled immigration and those that emphasise social exclusion effects of existing immigration and citizenship policies have their own institutional representation in the debate about overall immigration policy. Aligning these diverse actors and rationales is not only a matter of technical coordination, but also one of balancing (if not integrating) contradictory values. Moreover, street-level immigration policy is shaped by the existence of a bureaucratic landscape that is not necessarily ready to deal with diverse populations, not just because of a lack of resources, but also because of limited integration of policy and administrative activity across organisational boundaries and the negative perception of the target population. In sum, governing immigration policy combines the challenges of making value judgements in controversial issues in a context of changing media agendas and political moods concerning immigration and asylum issues and of aligning different rationales of immigration and integration (or inclusion) policies.

Tools and Resources to Address Governance Challenges

Having pointed to some of the key governance challenges across four areas that are at the heart of contemporary statehood, we now turn to the different ways in which states have sought to address these challenges. Rather than offering a detailed discussion of various initiatives, we concentrate on the use of particular resources and strategies available to contemporary states. In this section, we use four resources, those of regulation, finance, organisation, and information, to consider to what extent the above-mentioned governance challenges have offered insights into the innovative use of any one (or more) of these key resources.

Regulation

Regulation is integral to attempts at dealing with the key challenges noted above. Regulatory agencies and regulation are used to manage conditions of access and to ensure particular standards. In broadband, for example, regulation has been employed to control dominant infrastructure providers, especially in terms of seeking to ensure fair access conditions for other providers. Similarly, the implications for investment are clear: the fewer the available economic rents and the more regulatory strategies seek to exploit efficiency savings, the less there will be invested in new infrastructure. Thus, in both energy markets and broadband, regulation has been highly invasive (e.g. threatening to split up companies) and has had an impact on the energy mix, as pricing and subsidised schemes for renewable energies have decreased the attraction of some forms of energy generation.

In the area of elder care, regulation has taken an increasingly formalised role, which involves the establishment of standards for nursing homes and their enforcement in the light of recurring scandals involving appalling care provision. In the area of immigration too, regulation plays a significant role, ranging from the granting of visas to the oversight of employers' compliance with workplace provisions and recruitment, which has involved the extension of regulatory activities into employing organisations. Here again, the measures have been highly 'invasive' in the sense of imposing considerable compliance costs on business and other organisations seeking to recruit internationally. Considerable regulation is also carried out by the regulated entities themselves across the four governance challenges under consideration in this chapter (see Power 2007).

The four key governance challenges also point to aspects where regulation has been seen to fail. For example, the failure of inspectors to detect the extensive neglect, if not abuse in various English nursing homes pointed not just to overstretch of regulatory oversight activities; it also illustrated the perverse incentives that govern the performance management systems of care home providers. Elsewhere, seeking to establish a calibrated system to attract the 'right' type of skilled labour has been problematic as such schemes face considerable administrative complexity (and political pressure). In broadband, the continuous challenge of tensions among regulatory instruments has also been noticeable: Should regulation be used in competition-enhancing ways or should it seek to encourage investment by dominant firms by granting a degree of regulatory 'slack'?

One of the standard recipes over the past three decades (and therefore arguably an innovation of sorts) has been the increased reliance on quasi-autonomous agencies to conduct regulatory tasks, especially in the area of economic regulation (e.g. energy and telecommunications). These agencies were supposed to advance the quality of regulation in that they were conducted by specialists in an organisational environment that was not directly coupled to ministerial departments and therefore electoral cycles. This was to offer 'commitment' to private investors in particular. In the light of the 'time inconsistency' problem (i.e. the preferences of governments change over time), regulated parties seek certainty that their initial commitment to invest or to locate in a certain place will not be punished later. This idea of detaching decision-making from politics and therefore to safeguard technocratic 'discipline' has come under challenge over recent years (Roberts 2010), as governments have undermined regulatory agencies or overloaded them with so many tasks that they have become mini-governments in their own right. It is, for example, questionable whether an economic regulatory agency is best placed to consider the very diverse issues of economic efficiency, social equity, security of supply, and environmental concerns, especially about climate change. It is also problematic to ask regulatory agencies to set prices as long as governments are involved in subsidising certain services, or when governments offer fixed prices for particular forms of energy generation (i.e. guaranteed prices for nuclear energy generation to attract private investment). Similarly, regulatory agencies have also regularly been accused (rightly or wrongly) of failing in their duties–with regulatory failures ranging from financial to health care to food safety.

Furthermore, there are trade-offs in regulatory decisions about what services should be universal, who should be compensated for providing such services, and by whom. As shown by the British story regarding rural broadband, overseeing (regulating) the delivery of a large-scale project is tricky, especially in a climate of budgetary cut-backs.

In short, for many, regulation and regulatory agencies are seen as technocratic remedies against irrational political decisions. The governance challenges discussed here highlight the limitations of an over-reliance on such strategies.

Finance

Many of the interventions described in this chapter are of a financial kind. Particular developments are facilitated or hindered through subsidies or penalty payments, or through tax incentives and penalties. This includes the co-funding arrangements for the expansion of fibre optic cables to municipalities and other regions, the support for alternatives to CO_2-emitting forms of energy generation, the support for particular integration schemes in education or housing, or the use of financial support (means-tested or not) to ensure care for the elderly.

A reliance on tax breaks and subsidies raises a number of well-known issues, regardless of whether the revenues are generated through user charges, general taxation, or insurance payments. One problem is to reveal the 'real' financial needs of target populations in order to achieve the intended effect without simply substituting private money with public resources. Mechanisms intended to establish 'true' market rates for the provision of public services, such as infrastructure or care homes, involve competitive tendering processes or auctions. However, as shown in the case of rural broadband projects in the UK, such tendering processes are marred by considerable administrative complexity and their outcome is not always certain, especially not in terms of escaping public criticism.

Furthermore, financial means of encouraging or deterring certain behaviours always face the problem of potential resource depletion. It is unlikely that states facing sovereign debt crises are able to finance themselves into a future of publicly financed broadband infrastructure or renewable energy generation and adequate infrastructure capacities. The subsidisation of particular technologies or devices is also problematic in that it is easier to initiate subsidy programmes than withdraw them, or even just to adapt or reduce them. For example, such tensions emerge in debates about how to adapt subsidies for solar energy given declining production and installation prices and questions about solar energy's overall potential contribution. Moreover, there are issues about selecting 'winners'. Indeed, the key challenge in financially supporting particular technologies is to allow for openness to technological innovation rather than foreclosing certain technological developments and changes by putting all the financial eggs in one basket.

Organisation

The state's use of organisation, i.e. the physical ability (staff, buildings, material, etc.) to provide certain services and goods directly, is similarly widespread across the four key governance challenges discussed in this chapter. Organisation is particularly prominent in the area of immigration policy, given its cross-cutting impact on issues such as housing, education, and visa and immigration control, which all heavily rely on the state's physical resources and raise the issue of how to coordinate diverse governmental organisations. Similarly, social movements have emerged that demand the 'nationalising' or 'communalisation' of infrastructure networks as private profits are seen to be incompatible with 'essential' services and where price increases are said to impact primarily on those most in need. In other words, the state's use of 'organisation' as a tool for providing these services is back on the agenda after a period of reliance on private provision. In New Zealand, the state has used organisation to arrange partnerships with private firms in the roll-out of the high-speed broadband network.

Moreover, organisation is not just prominent in the provision of certain services, but also in the creation of particular forums to negotiate and mediate between potentially competing views. Organisation, in this sense, is also about the creation of settings that allow individuals and organisations to span boundaries, as can be seen by the emergence of various 'immigration summits' or 'councils'.

A reliance on organisation is, of course, not without its problems. After all, the kind of effort that is involved in dealing with the processing of work permits, housing, and education is not associated with high-powered, high-commitment bureaucracies. Instead, these are areas that are traditionally poorly resourced and deal with unpopular tasks. Whether a reliance on private sector organisations is likely to lead to stronger motivation and commitment of providers is questionable. However, one argument in favour of contractualised, privately provided 'organisation' is that such devices have the potential to guarantee more funding stability and therefore also a better basis to offer services. Other views, in contrast, note that privately organised services, such as private prisons or nursing homes, are not necessarily better in terms of their standards of care (Domberger and Jensen 1997; Brown, Potoski, and van Slyke 2006).

General problems in terms of organisation in the sense of convening boundary-spanning forums are issues of access and decision-making rules. The challenge is to identify individuals or entities that are legitimate in the view of the population that they represent. It is also an open question whether such forums should decide on the basis of extra-large majority, if not unanimity votes. This again raises the issue of how adaptive the deliberative or consultative bodies are in light of solutions that may, in part, affect the self-interest of particular representative actors.

Information

Information has always been a key resource of governments. For example, the implementation of regulatory and financial policy instruments is usually accompanied by the collection and dissemination of information about regulatory requirements or qualifying criteria for subsidies. But information has developed into a policy tool in its own right (Hood and Margetts 2007; Fung, Graham, and Weil 2007). This claim builds on developments in science that emphasise the potential of packaged or designed information to influence the behaviour of target populations.

For the four governance challenges considered here, we can observe substantial variation concerning the use of information as a distinct policy tool. In the area of elder care, like in many other public service domains, information is used as a signalling device concerning the performance of service providers to (future) users. The German system of applying school grades to nursing homes and publishing those results on the Internet (pflegenoten.de) is intended to facilitate informed choice and hence competition for quality (that inspection-based regimes could not provide alone). In the domain of energy policy, information plays an important role in encouraging efficient energy use by households and companies. Examples range from classical information campaigns to social nudges, such as electricity bills that provide comparative information on energy consumption levels by comparable households and 'smart meters' that provide direct feedback on the effect of the usage of appliances on electricity consumption patterns.

The domain of broadband infrastructure could be considered an information-rich area, since provider companies advertise the speed of their connections and contracts include these specifications. Also broadband speed tests offered by private companies are mushrooming. However, targeted transparency policies that require that certain information be made publicly available are less widely used in this field than one might expect. Also in the area of immigration, information-based policy tools play a more limited role, most prominently as a tool to promote ideas of societal integration and in campaigns aiming to enhance interaction with migrant communities.

Information-based policy tools provide for a 'soft', non-intrusive alternative to regulatory and financial policy instruments (Fung, Graham, and Weil 2007). Information is, therefore, also regarded as enhancing the effect of other, more traditional policy instruments, for example in the area of food safety with various schemes that signal compliance with hygiene standards.

At the same time, information-based instruments are subject to various limitations. First, in addressing cognitive or/and motivational components of individual decision-making, information-based policy tools require knowledge about the factors shaping individual decisions and how to influence them. A website providing tips on how to save energy might be consulted by individuals with a high motivation to engage in such an activity, but may not reach those most in need of such information. Another critical issue in the use of information is the increasingly widespread use of these tools by public, private, and nonprofit organisations potentially leading to information overload and noise. Finally, in areas where access to the target population is difficult (due to language barriers, social biases, or other cultural differences), the use of information-based policy tools might be limited.

In short, information is a policy tool of considerable significance that has recently received increasing attention. Considerable innovation has taken place in the way information is packaged and distributed. However, it also comes with a high uncertainty as to the tool's actual effects. Moreover, it is often said that information is not only a 'soft' policy tool in that it is not particularly coercive, but that it is also 'cheap' in that it does not rely on potential coercive enforcement. However, given the administrative costs of determining how to package information and the knowledge requirements that are being placed on the recipients of information, then information is hardly a 'cheap' instrument at all.

Bringing in Administrative Capacities

So what are the implications for administrative capacities? As noted we are not suggesting that one particular remedy or set of administrative capacities is more likely to solve problems than others. We however do argue that one has to be clear about the implications for administrative capacities once the decision has been taken to pursue one particular policy path. Table 3.5 offers an overview of what role the four administrative capacities at the heart of this Report–and, we contend, governance readiness–could play in addressing the governance challenges we have highlighted.

The **delivery capacity** challenge across the four governance issues is that in most of these areas, states have moved towards a private model of public service provision. This means that communications and energy networks are in private hands, care homes are partly private, partly para-public and partly public, and immigration policy is largely still a matter of delivery by public actors, although private and para-public actors are engaged in various activities, such as security, the processing of particular claims, and the provision of certain services to facilitate integration. Furthermore, it is not just delivery that has become more diverse, it is also the population that receives policy that has become more heterogeneous. This raises issues about how to deploy information in a bespoke way to maximise dissemination without offending different cultural sensitivities.

Whereas the actual 'doing things' (such as laying cables) might be a private matter, delivery in this kind of model involves allocating funding, organising processes, and establishing frameworks that facilitate access for and to the appropriate target population. On the one hand, such delivery activities face resource limitations as demand almost always outpaces supply. On the other hand, delivery is inevitably about decisions of inclusion and exclusion–such as in the setting up of 'immigration councils'. Here the key delivery capacity question is how to get access to the 'right' people and ensure that they meaningfully contribute to problem-solving.

Finally, there is also the question of actual risk transfer. Even if states have delegated delivery to private actors, this does not mean that such activities can be easily abandoned should private provision fail. States thus require a residual delivery capacity to take responsibility for the running of particular services, where their private provision is seen to be falling short.

Regulatory capacity involves, as noted, oversight. The key administrative capacity challenge here is to develop instruments that facilitate information collection and enforcement under conditions of inherent information asymmetry between the regulated and those doing the regulating. This requires on the one hand approaches that reduce these asymmetries by incentivising regulated entities to reveal information about their conduct voluntarily (for example, by linking compliance with particular financial support systems). Technological devices might reduce this problem

Table 3.5 **Governance challenges and administrative capacities**

	Delivery	Regulatory	Coordination	Analytical
Broadband	Ensuring provision of high speed broadband	Oversight of concentrated private providers	Aligning providers of Internet services with providers of network capacity	Future demand forecasting
Energy	Provision of stand-by capacity and development of network capacity	Oversight of concentrated providers in a field characterised by multiple well-resourced actors	Aligning dispersed set of actors with conflicting time horizons and self-interests	Projecting energy needs, technological developments and prerequisites
Elder care	Ensuring decent level of care	Oversight of quality of care	Aligning dispersed and diverse set of actors	Projecting future demand on elder care, knowledge of effects of particular interventions
Immigration	Ensuring procedural processes that facilitate inclusion and fairness	Oversight of administrative processes related to visas and work permits, and the quality of inclusion programmes	Aligning dispersed and diverse set of actors; coordinating demand for and supply of skilled workforce	Sensitivity to cultural differences, understanding of competing demands and impact of interventions

in broadband quality, and performance information might allow for some comparison in areas of elder care, broadband provision, and energy generation. In immigration, the problem is one of highly dispersed sets of actors. In terms of a reliance on privately provided services, regulatory capacity faces limitations in changing behaviours as the ultimate 'penalty' (nationalisation or closure) is either very costly or unrealistic.

More broadly, regulatory capacity is constrained in terms of enforcement as more resourceful actors challenge decisions or capture the process more generally. This raises issues as to how to maintain regulatory capacity in the light of more powerful corporate actors, competing objectives (efficiency, fairness, and security of supply), and uncertainty about the effects of particular regulatory strategies.

In terms of **coordination capacity**, all four key governance challenges deal with dispersed sets of actors with different interests and time horizons. All four require coordination capacity so that information is exchanged to allow for more well-informed (i.e. calibrated) interventions.

At the same time, each one of these governance challenges represents a distinct type of coordination problem regardless of how and what kind of coordination devices are being established.[3] The case of immigration policy is one that Christopher Hood (1976) has called a problem of 'multi-organisational sub-optimisation'. Multiple agencies in different domains are involved without necessarily being informed about the decisions of the other agencies, or the concerns that dominate decision-making in these other areas. In contrast, the energy generation and broadband infrastructure examples are not just cases in which resources among actors are dispersed. They are also ones in which decisions are ultimately about benefitting some interests over others and have implications for decisions up- and downstream. Therefore, they are both cases of 'interest group politics' in which well-resourced interests are pitted against each other (Wilson 1980). This contrasts with the areas of immigration and elder care. In both of these domains localised, concentrated interests exist, but, in immigration, these interests are not necessarily aligned with the policy objectives of the state, and immigrant views are usually not well organised (or represented politically). Similarly, despite the rise of the 'grey' vote, people in elder care are unlikely to be politically vocal, and their representation will, at most, be undertaken by relatives.

The challenge for coordination capacity is therefore how to align and bring different interests together so as to achieve agreement on certain objectives, to communicate these objectives, and to ensure their acceptance by the target populations and those delivering the intended interventions. This bringing-together should not just reflect the extent to which different interests are well represented or well resourced. In short, it is about seeking to align state and non-state actors through the creation of understandings that responsibilities are shared, that information has to be exchanged, and that forums exist that reduce the likelihood of dysfunctional inconsistency. At the same time, the hierarchical imposition of coordination mechanisms and prescribed outcomes faces limitations ranging from inability to motivate actors to participate to suppression of small-scale local initiatives.

In terms of **analytical capacities,** the traditional bias has been to focus on the forecasting capabilities that inform decision-making about future trends and the challenge of how to have access to 'best in the world' information. As the four governance challenges have shown, such a task is highly demanding, as questions about future trends are clouded in relative degrees of uncertainty, whether this involves the availability of unpaid carer populations in the future, the trajectory of energy or broadband demand, or the need to address particular labour market shortages.

A different, often neglected analytical capacity is knowledge about the targets of particular interventions. Highly transient populations make steering of housing and schooling needs very problematic, for example. Analytical capacity is therefore about understanding the contextual conditions in which certain interventions might be more appropriate than others.

Across the four governance challenges, the demand of analytical capacity is also about creating forums that allow for the accessing and exchanging of information even in areas where some actors may dispute the legitimacy of claims made by others. Examples of such exercises include the various energy summits in Germany that were supposed to bring together (pro-nuclear) energy interests with those demanding an almost immediate withdrawal from nuclear energy. Another (German) example is the use of integration councils at all levels of government. In both of these cases, the actual analytical capacity is not simply to develop a better understanding of the various positions and thus be able to develop boundary-spanning analytical capacities (so as to access and communicate with different constituencies). Analytical capacity is also enhanced as it improves understanding of the likely implications of one set of interventions rather than others. At the same time, analytical capacity must be able to avoid being captured by the vastly superior resources of corporate actors.

Constraints to Exercising Administrative Capacities

The above may sound like a long list of wishful thinking. The typical challenge to such arguments is that it would be more useful to consider options so as to introduce such capacities into administrative life rather than come up with just another list of convoluted terminology. One response to this particular criticism is to look at the reasons why the exercise of the four administrative capacities is often impeded. It is only through a better understanding of the mechanisms that disable capacities that we can develop more sophisticated ways of enhancing administrative capacity. In this concluding section, we consider the kind of constraints that affect the exercise of particular administrative capacities.

Bottlenecks in the delivery capacities of the state are those that have been traditionally associated with the coping mechanisms of street-level bureaucrats (Lipsky 1980). Accordingly the key challenge is to accept that delivery is about negotiating between the 'real world' and the rule book and that actors are likely to filter out the difficult and disliked aspects of their work. The cases of immigration and care for the elderly are further characterised by a patchwork of different delivery capacities, as different professions and state and non-state actors are all involved.

Regulatory capacity is typically impeded by a lack of resources: it is not possible (or even desirable) to inspect every single activity. Furthermore, regulatory capacity is inherently about a trade-off between two types of potential errors. On the one hand, it might generally be desirable to operate a regulatory approach on the basis of 'innocent until proven guilty'–which means that in certain cases the 'guilty' will walk free as their guilt has not been proven (Type II errors or false negatives). However, in other areas, regulatory capacity might be more directed towards 'guilty until proven otherwise' potentially leading to over-inclusive regulation (Type I errors or false positives). Such a precautionary approach might be seen as highly interventionist and prone to incur high opportunity costs (Wildavsky 1988). Still, demands for more precaution are likely to occur where public and political pressure to do so are high, or where the reputations of those involved are at stake.

Similarly, there are also debates as to what regulatory capacity in the area of enforcement should constitute. Leaving aside the problems generated by long, drawn-out processes in which regulatory decisions are being challenged, it is a matter of dispute whether one sees regulatory capacity as high when enforcement follows a gradual sanctioning regime that, however, seeks to reduce the occurrence of formal enforcement action by aiming to settle cases informally, or one that imposes high sanctions and is able to develop a reputation for deterrence. Settling cases without formal court appearances may be seen as a sign of high regulatory capacity as it means that organisational attention can turn to more highly complex cases, but such an understanding requires political support.

One typical problem that affects coordination capacity inside government is the creation of performance-based incentives that focus on observable outputs and outcomes. Much coordination activity, however, is not measurable: for example, to create a roundtable between different parties interested in immigration or in energy might already be seen as an important achievement, even if tangible and measurable outputs or outcomes do not directly result from such forums. Furthermore, coordination capacity is also impeded by the dominance of organisation-centric loyalties and performance assessments. It is not likely that organisations will voluntarily give up their traditional privileges and share processes with others, even if this leads to supposedly better coordination. For example, the proposal that coordination among US intelligence systems would be advanced by the creation of the Department of Homeland Security has hardly been achieved, given the continued prominence of the CIA and FBI and their unwillingness to lose privileges and share information and staff resources (cf. Kettl 2013). Similarly, trying to advance coordination capacity among actors will be impeded if the achievement of coordinated outcomes is seen as less important than the achievement of other targets or objectives (for example, why would health and safety regulators wish to coordinate with economic regulators and thereby possibly discount their own organisational interest in achieving high compliance levels). Indeed, it might be argued that the provision of 'more' coordination capacity, such as through the creation of pooled or joined-up information systems, presents a challenge to the security of systems as breakdowns will have more systemic consequences.

Finally, bottlenecks in the area of analytical capacities are, in particular, about the trade-off between generalist knowledge and specialist knowledge. On the one hand, generalist knowledge is required in order to create consistency and challenge the established discourses within determined areas. On the other hand, specialist knowledge is required in order to allow for informed decision-making that is not decoupled from the 'real world'. More generally, analytical capacity is challenged by the emergence of an 'audit society': as distrust of discretionary expert judgement grows, there is greater demand for verifiable reporting of performance, which in itself creates distorting effects (Power 1997).

In other words, simply arguing that contemporary states in general and bureaucracies in particular should simply have 'more' capacity is intellectually dishonest. For one, 'more' capacity is inevitably a matter of resources, but more resources are never enough. More importantly, however, there is no agreed definition of what 'more' administrative capacity actually implies: whether it is in terms of delivery, regulatory, coordination, or analytical capacity. Each capacity points to considerable disputes about what kind of activities and practices represent 'high' capacity and how capacity should or could be enhanced. Furthermore, as noted in the discussion of the four governance challenges, what capacity requirements are is also a matter of understanding the issues involving particular governance challenges–for example, it may be possible to rely on private users to exercise certain oversight functions, but it is less likely that dementia-affected patients in care homes will be able to perform similar tasks. In short, administrative capacities are at the heart of developing answers to the problem of matching supply and demand. However, this requires not just an acceptance of the inherently contested nature of the governance challenge itself; it requires a differentiated understanding of administrative capacities that points to the inherent trade-offs, limitations, and resource constraints as well.

Endnotes

1   A further implication of guaranteeing feed-in tariffs that are above spot market rate is that it directly affects consumer prices. Consumers were, as taxpayers, subsidising energy generation, which they, as consumers, had to pay for again.

2   We do not wish to comment here on the feasibility (or desirability) of developing a policy that 'selects' attractive migrant populations and thereby excludes other immigrants. In general, despite many claims, there is no established evidence of 'migrant welfare tourism' in the EU.

3   This is, of course, a gross over-simplification. Each governance challenge is characterised by numerous different coordination problems. The point here is to emphasise that 'coordination' problems are multi-faceted and cannot be addressed through one-size-fits-all prescriptions.

IV. Governance Innovations

RAMSEY WISE, KAI WEGRICH *and* MARTIN LODGE

As noted in the previous chapter, administrative capacities are central to developing options that promise to deal with a mismatch between current and future demands and contemporary supply. This chapter analyses ten cases of governance innovations–as did the first Governance Report (Anheier and Korreck 2013)–in the four policy areas that are at the heart of this Report and explores how they are linked to administrative capacities. Administrative capacities are essential to the cultivation of governance innovations, and vice versa, governance innovations are essential for enhancing administrative capacities. The analysis of specific governance innovations is thus essential for exploring the 'interface' between governance innovation and administrative capacity.

Innovation in the Public Sector

The public sector is said to be in need of innovation (cf. Sørensen and Torfing forthcoming). Given the growing demands of contemporary governance challenges, simply continuing with business as usual does not seem to be an option. Not only are policy problems becoming more complex, and hence knowledge about them more essential, but the actual interventions of governance institutions are also becoming more contested and demand for the legitimisation of public action is increasing. Moreover, the financial constraints of today's age of austerity set strict limits to the use of 'treasure', or financing, as a tool for responding to policy problems; hence, the call for innovation in the public sector.

> *Administrative capacities are essential to the cultivation of governance innovations.*

At the same time, confidence in the ability of public sector institutions to innovate is said to be low. As highlighted in *The Governance Report 2013*, compared with the private and nonprofit sectors 'weaker signals demanding innovation reach public agencies from the outside, and weaker incentives for innovations operate within them' (Anheier and Korreck 2013: 84). Public institutions are supposed to provide stability. For Max Weber, bureaucracy was the key part of rational-legal authority, the most rational form of authority. For bureaucracies to be effective as carriers of rational-legal authority, modes of organisation and decision-making, which we today call 'bureaucratic', need to be present: Decisions need to be predictable and verifiable, which often implies standardisation and formalisation. These bureaucratic features are key for allowing accountability and impartiality in decisions, which should only be based on legal norms. In other words, one can argue that it is in the nature of bureaucracies to oppose, or at least not promote, change or innovation.

Confidence in the key players governing public organisations to provide a counterweight to the gravity of bureaucracies toward stability is also considered to be low. For example, higher-level bureaucrats are seen as motivated by concerns for organisational maintenance and possibly growth (Wilson 1989; Niskanen 1971; Dunleavy 1991). Politicians are locked in a short-term attention span that let them shy away from reforms (or innovations) that come with certain short- to medium-term costs (i.e. more conflicts, more resources required, temporary performance loss, etc.) and uncertain longer-term benefits (Scharpf 1986).

Given these conditions–high demand for, but low probability of innovation in the public sector–the debate and practice have turned toward the potential of opening up the public sector to various forms of boundary-crossing activities. The call is for collaborative or social innovations, or even various forms of 'co-creation' of innovations (cf. Torfing et al. 2012; Voorberg, Bekkers, and Tummers 2013; see also Anheier and Korreck 2013). What these notions have in common is that in order for public sector organisations and institutions to innovate, some form of collaboration across boundaries must first be established. These boundaries can be between public sector organisations from different domains, between public, private and/or nonprofit organisations, or through the involvement of citizens in participatory processes. The notion of 'social innovation' has resonated strongly in the policy world, with an increasing number of governments developing reform programmes and establishing organisational units under this name, such as the Danish 'MindLab'. The European Commission, in particular, has launched a strategy on social innovation seeking to engage citizens in the innovation process (cf. Voorberg, Bekkers, and Tummers 2013).

The diagnosis underlying the trend toward collaborative innovation has not gone entirely unchallenged. Some have argued that we are living in the age of 'hyper-innovation' of the public sector that has, since the 1980s, adopted a range of managerial innovations that has fundamentally transformed the state (Moran 2003). Others have stressed that the recent history of government reform has resulted in the decline of traditional bureaucratic forms of governance, with adverse consequences such as the loss of institutional memory (Pollitt 2009). Hence, some have called for a 'rediscovery of bureaucracy' (Olsen 2008).

Although these views on innovation in the public sector appear to be contradictory, those advancing the collaborative innovation agenda have not necessarily dismissed such arguments. Torfing et al. (2012), for example, share the view that managerial reforms have played a major role in shaping public sector organisations. And they agree with some other critical analyses that these reforms came with substantial unintended consequences, potentially undermining state capacity. However, the conclusion they draw is not that there has been too much innovation in general, but that the wrong type of innovation has proliferated. Hence they call for more 'collaborative' (as opposed to managerial) innovation (Sørensen and Torfing forthcoming).

> Administrative capacities are challenged by the changes in the architecture of the state and the squeezing of financial resources.

Independent from the questions of whether there is an element of overselling inherent in this debate on social and collaborative innovation and whether a thorough evaluation would confirm the high expectations that have been raised, the role of public administration seems to be limited to that of a factor constraining innovation. Clearly, the different work styles, the prevalence of entrepreneurship in the absence of bureaucratic constraints, and the skills of making use of the potential of new information and communications technology (ICT) and internet-based solutions in the private and nonprofit sectors demonstrate potential to innovate. But what then could or should be the role of public administration?

As highlighted in the introductory chapter, what is missing in these debates about bureaucracy's role is an understanding of the link between administrative capacities and innovation. In this Report, we have stressed that administrative capacities are critical for delivering (innovative) policy solutions to complex problems. At the same time, administrative capacities are challenged by the changes in the architecture of the state (resulting from waves of previous innovations in the 1980s and 1990s) and the squeezing of financial resources. This chapter hence explores governance innovations in the four policy areas covered in this Report with a specific emphasis on the link to administrative capacities. In exploring cases of governance innovations, the chapter analyses:

- What type of administrative capacity limitations do these innovations address?
- Which administrative capacities do these innovations require to be effective (i.e. capacity requirements)?
- What impact do these governance innovations have on administrative capacity (i.e. capacity impact)?
- How do innovations interact with existing governance systems?

The Governance Report 2013 already discussed governance innovations that are relevant to our concern with administrative capacities. Social impact bonds (SIBs), for example, seek to enhance the delivery capacity of social services, such as prison rehabilitation programmes, by drawing on a combination of market mechanisms with third sector service delivery and public sector performance measurement. To this end, SIBs require a number of other administrative capacities. A sound regulatory framework is the first requirement, but beyond this, strong analytical capacities are needed to allocate resources to selected social services as well as some degree of coordination between involved actors. The question is whether the analytical capacity to measure and monitor performance is present and feasible. Another example of delivery is seen in the case of Ushahidi, a project that has made use of mapping technology in order to provide timely and accurate information to rescue and relief personnel responding to violent conflicts or national disasters. The technology improves the analytical capacity to collect, visualise, and redistribute critical information sent by SMS, twitter, email, or directly through the website. A third example comes from mySociety, a civil society venture that creates an Internet platform to connect citizens with locally elected representatives via open source technology. Its primary aim is to enable citizens to actively engage in civic life by sorting relevant information and facilitating dialogue. This innovation thus addresses an important area of politics where coordination and analytical capacities are weak, and in doing so, also develops potential to improve upon the delivery of local public services through bottom-up, citizen-led participatory practices.

In Search of Governance Innovations

In *The Governance Report 2013*, governance innovations were defined as novel rules, regulations, and approaches that address a public problem in more efficacious and effective ways, lead to better policy outcomes, and enhance legitimacy (Anheier and Korreck 2013: 83). This broad definition was the starting point for our search for governance innovations.

The search involved a number of strategies. First, we explored documents from key (international) organisations, such as the OECD and the World Bank, as well as media, for examples of governance innovations in the areas of infrastructure, sustainability, integration, and welfare. Second, a graduate course at the Hertie School of Governance during the spring of 2013 was centred on the exploration of examples of governance innovations. Two examples from this course are included in this chapter. Third, we conducted an expert survey in April 2013, inviting some 270 scholars and practitioners to report developments in their fields. These three search strategies produced a list of 50 governance innovations. We then selected ten cases on the basis of six selection criteria. Accordingly, governance innovations had to:

- address a governance challenge in a novel manner
- be applied in at least one instance or context
- be implemented in the last 15 years
- demonstrate scalability and replicability
- hold promise for better policy outcomes
- provide enough information to make an assessment.

In addition, the cases present a diverse coverage of geographical regions, policy fields (i.e. infrastructure, sustainability, welfare and migration), leading actors (i.e. from state, market and civil society sectors), and administrative capacities (i.e. delivery, regulatory, coordination, and analytical). Each case is discussed by presenting the key policy challenge, solution and potential impact. The aim is not to offer an exhaustive discussion of the cases themselves and the particular circumstances that gave rise to them, but to illustrate how governance innovations interact with administrative capacities.

We are not suggesting that the selected examples are inherently desirable. The individualisation of welfare, for example, is a highly value-driven choice that has attracted considerable debate. However, we were interested in identifying innovation in terms of novel attempts at problem-solving. We therefore separate policy content from mechanisms. Such a separation is admittedly highly problematic as it suggests that political value choices can be separated from the 'technocratic' aspects of administration. We would not wish to be seen as advocates of such a separation. However, in order to show how governance innovations are based on particular administrative capacities, and what distinct administrative capacities are required to facilitate types of governance innovation, we need to make this simplification.

Governance Innovations 2014

The ten cases, summarised in Table 4.1, are taken from our four main policy areas, and they respond to different administrative capacity bottlenecks (and are presented according to which administrative capacity limit they address). The cases also differ in terms of the key mechanism deployed. Some are about engaging citizens and NGOs in the provision of public goods or delivery of public services, while others seek to make use of market mechanisms for the same aims. Several highlight new forms of governance to directly improve public services or policy-making systems.

Admittedly, many of these cases cannot be defined as first order innovations, i.e. governance decisions that fundamentally change the way in which both problems and solutions are formulated (cf. Anheier and Korreck 2013). They are primarily second order decisions that introduce an innovative element into existing organisational, policy, or regulatory design. In that sense,

Table 4.1 **Overview of selected cases (in order of appearance)**

Innovation	Challenge	Basic Proposition	Key Insight
Delivery Capacity			
Transportation 2035	Delivering efficient and sustainable transportation infrastructure increasingly contends with urban population growth and geographical constraints	Combines transportation infrastructure investment plans with performance-based project assessment processes that reflect regional policy goals	Requires strong analytical capacity to systematically support the region's land use strategy and deliver efficient transportation infrastructure
German Broadband Crowdfunding	Private companies may lack incentives to set up adequate broadband coverage in less populated areas where returns are not as large	Advances broadband expansion by allowing for a provision of broadband infrastructure *independent* from telecommunications service providers, allowing for citizens to become investors in broadband infrastructure	Requires coordination capacity to use community-based crowdfunding mechanisms to invest in broadband infrastructure
Barcelona Social Inclusion Plan	Nationalised social services may not effectively address diversifying local welfare needs	Provides a regulatory framework to strengthen the city's autonomy and an institutional framework that links local government, citizens, and civil society organisations	Requires strong networks and coordination capacity to build social capital
Personal Budgets	Budget cuts in social care may restrict nationalised welfare programmes from delivering adequate services	Gives individuals greater control over how they receive support, operating under a self-directed, state-approved budget of individual social care needs	Requires coordination and analytical capacities to offer differentiated funding schemes for care service provision
Regulatory Capacity			
Biodiversity Banking and Offsets Scheme	The conservation of biodiversity is not reflected in the market price of land use nor is strict regulation always feasible	Introduces a market-based, voluntary offsetting scheme that aims to counteract development activities that are detrimental to biodiversity by ensuring that they do not incur a net loss	Requires strong analytical capacity to accurately signal ecological value, monitor, and enforce biodiversity markets
Regional Greenhouse Gas Initiative (RGGI)	Strict regulatory solutions for sustainability are often in conflict with economic growth and therefore not always feasible	Introduces a cap and trade scheme to reduce GHG emissions and boost the economy by reinvesting revenue from auctions into clean energy programmes and jobs	Requires analytical capacity to effectively regulate and enforce the cap on GHG emissions

Innovation	Challenge	Basic Proposition	Key Insight
Coordination Capacity			
Climate Investment Programmes in Sweden	Local sustainability projects contribute to the transition toward sustainable societies, but may lack the resources to have a significant impact	Uses economic-based policy instruments to analyse and invest in local sustainability projects	Requires analytical capacity to efficiently distribute resources that will encourage the reduction of and reliance on fossil fuels
Mobility Partnerships	Labour-related migration policy is a transnational challenge that currently lacks cohesiveness as well as enforcement measures	Uses soft law based on bilateral country agreements to share responsibility and management of circular migration	Requires coordination capacity between sending, transition, and receiving countries
Analytical Capacity			
Toronto Region Immigrant Employment Council (TRIEC)	Insufficient immigrant skill assessment and the lack of professional networks create barriers for migrants to directly enter the labour market	Brings local leadership together through a multi-stakeholder approach to improve recruiting mechanisms, build professional networks, and engage in public awareness campaigns	Requires a combination of analytical, coordination, and delivery capacities to systematically and effectively match immigrant skills
Integration of Renewable Energies and E-Mobility (IRENE)	Decentralised energy supply is challenged by energy supply volatility and supply and demand mismatches	Uses smart grid technology to identify technical solutions and feed power from fluctuating, decentralised, and renewable energy sources	Requires strong analytical capacities to deliver, monitor and match renewable energy supply with consumer behaviour

they intend to supplement existing governance systems rather than replacing them. They do so by the two main mechanisms that have been defined in *The Governance Report 2013*, namely recombination (i.e. introducing 'borrowed' elements from one governance system to another) and refunctionality (i.e. the relocation of one proven principle into a new context).

Delivery capacity

Delivery capacity is perhaps the most visible and prevalent of the four administrative capacities, as the name itself implies an ability to directly act upon a pressing challenge or to meet a specific goal. For the purpose of highlighting key governance innovations that address areas where delivery capacity has been found lacking, four cases have been identified. The first showcases a novel approach for planning public investments in the transportation infrastructure in the San Francisco Bay Area, USA. The second illustrates citizen-led initiatives for delivering high-speed broadband Internet to rural areas in Germany. The next two cases address welfare service delivery, one at the local level in Barcelona, Spain and the other by means of user choice and flexible finance mechanisms as developed in the UK. Although these examples primarily address the need for delivery capacity, they are often supplemented by or require at least one of the other four administrative capacities.

Transportation 2035

While larger cities often have early incentives to invest in transportation infrastructure, rapidly increasing urban growth combined with geographical and resource constraints has proved challenging to even the more well-designed urban areas. Such is the case for the San Francisco Bay Area (USA), whose once considered well-developed transportation infrastructure was in great need of maintenance, repairs and expansion due to a projected 26% population growth by 2035 (MTC 2009). As a result, the Metropolitan Transportation Commission (MTC)–the transportation agency and planning organisation overseeing the Bay Area's nine counties–found its current Regional Transportation Plan (RTP) lacking a positive investment scenario that would improve upon its current infrastructure while at the same time addressing transportation mobility and accessibility needs, housing, and land development as well as the reduction of greenhouse gases (MTC 2013b).

In 2006, even before the 2008 passage of the State of California's Sustainable Communities Act, MTC began drafting its Transportation 2035 Plan, *Change in Motion*, to emphasise the immediacy and tangibility of the much-needed change to its current infrastructure. More than innovative public planning, it makes use of analytical capacities to improve its transportation infrastructure. The MTC conducted a detailed assessment of over 700 proposed projects, the selection of projects being based on a quantitative appraisal that includes a cost-benefit analysis in relation to the performance objectives and a qualitative policy assessment that reflects the broader Three Es and Plan Goals, as outlined in Table 4.2. This two-pronged method would provide investment feedback and allow for the prioritisation of projects and funding decisions. In total, the plan was to oversee the investment of 218 billion USD (approx. 169 billion EUR) in funding of projects between 2010–2035 (MTC 2009). Eighty percent of this budget would be spent on transit operations and maintenance and another 15% toward transit expansion and investment in bold initiatives that would improve transportation in the region (MTC 2008). More than 70% of the budget would be covered through revenues generated locally (e.g. through taxes or transit fare revenue) (MTC 2007).

Table 4.2 **Transportation 2035 goals and selected performance objectives**

Three Es	Plan Goals	Performance Objectives
Economy	Maintenance and Safety	**Improve maintenance** • Local streets and roads: maintain pavement condition index of 75 or better • State highways: distressed lane-miles no more than 10% of system • Transit: average asset age no more than 50% of useful life and average distance between service calls of 8,000 miles. **Reduce injuries and fatalities** • Motor-vehicle fatalities: 15% from today • Bike and pedestrian injuries and fatalities: 25% each from 2000 levels
	Reliability	**Reduce delay** 20% per capita from today
	Efficient Freight Travel	
	Security and Emergency Management	
Environment	Clean Air	**Reduce vehicle miles travelled** • Vehicle miles travelled: 10% per capita from today
	Climate Protection	**Reduce emissions** • Fine particulate matter (PM2.5): 10% from today • Coarse particulate matter (PM10): 45% from today • Carbon dioxide (CO_2): 40% below 1990 levels
Equity	Access	**Improve affordability** 10% reduction from today in share of earnings spent on housing and transportation costs by low and moderately-low income households
	Liveable Communities	

Source: MTC (2009)

In partnership with regional agencies, such as the Bay Area Air Quality Management District or Bay Conservation and Development commissions, the overall aim of this plan is to comprehensively address multiple policy goals related to the economy, environment and social equity. Through these innovative programmes, Transportation 2035 has attempted to revolutionise transportation in the Bay Area by developing and maintaining sustainable infrastructure. The Plan is both policy-oriented and performance-based, offering a systematic method for supporting the region's land use strategy in a way that should stimulate job growth by 'boosting the efficiency of the existing transit and road system' (MTC 2013a: 12). To this end, this innovation not only addresses delivery capacity, but it also develops the public administration's analytical capacity to assess individual investment scenarios, as well as its multi-level coordination capacity.

German broadband crowdfunding

High-speed broadband coverage, or lack thereof, is of both political and economic concern, affecting individuals as well as businesses, acting as a hindrance to development, and reinforcing competitive urban-rural cleavages (BBSR 2012). Yet, in cases where broadband coverage and structural expansion are completely managed by private telecommunication companies, there is a lack of incentive for investment in less populated areas.

Despite being one of the most economically competitive countries, Germany is surprisingly ranked 21st of 144 countries in Internet bandwidth coverage per Internet user, falling behind most of its European neighbours (Schwab 2012). Having adopted the EU broadband coverage strategy, Germany aims to expand 50Mbit/s coverage to all households by 2018. However, this goal will be difficult to achieve, as economic prospects for future network service delivery are insufficient for triggering network providers to install cost-intensive broadband infrastructure in sparsely populated, rural areas. For example, less than 42.3% of non-urban households had access to 16 Mbit/s as of 2012, whereas video applications, large data sharing, and cloud

Table 4.3 **Selected German broadband local and citizen initiatives**

Name	State	Year of Est.	Associates	Website
TeleKommunikations Gesellschaft Südwestfalen mbH	Nordrhein-Westfalen	2008	4 communities represented by local governments	www.tkg-hsk.de
Breitbandnetz GmbH and Co. KG	Schleswig-Holstein	2010	40 companies, 50 communities, individuals	www.breitbandnetzgesellschaft.de
BürgerBreitbandNetz GmbH and Co. KG	Schleswig-Holstein	2012	Over 850 independent partners	www.buergerbreitbandnetz.de

computing all require a minimum of 10Mbit/s (TÜV 2012). From a capacity perspective, the federal state cannot deliver broadband infrastructure on its own, nor has it seemed to have or use regulatory capacity to provide better broadband coverage equally to all regions of the country. Although the state does offer funding for feasibility studies, consulting, credit provision, and grants (BMWi 2012b), the financing options only target the provision of broadband connections up to 2 Mbit/s (BMWi 2013).

From this backdrop emerged several citizen-led initiatives for the expansion of broadband coverage, independent from private telecommunications service providers (see Table 4.3). These initiatives are based on bottom-up financing and crowdfunding schemes that operate under different organisational models in order to develop the infrastructure (BMWi 2012b). Local governments, individuals, businesses, and other legal entities can become partners of such initiatives and hold equity shares. As a key principle, provision of infrastructure and telecommunication services is kept separate: The involved actors are owners of the infrastructure, renting out the cables to a selected service provider for a usage fee, but they do not receive revenues from service provision. Over time, investment costs are financed via the rental fees, with any profits going toward further network expansion.

One of the largest examples of such initiatives was launched in Nordfriesland (Schleswig-Holstein) by Breitbandnetz GmbH and Co KG in 2010, totalling 70 million EUR in investment and covering 50 communities. As of 2013, fibre optic cable installation was completed in two of the 50 communities, was on-going in seven others, and was scheduled to be completed by the end of 2016. The minimum investment sum of 10,000 EUR yields a guaranteed interest of 3%, and up to 5% depending on the profit scenario, which will be paid out after a period of 30 years. The majority of its partners are local small and medium-sized companies, particularly renewable energy firms, but also local governments and individuals. A second initiative, Bürger-Breitbandnetz GmbH, was introduced in neighbouring communities of Schleswig-Holstein aiming to increase the number of private households as investors, as its minimum investment sum is only 1,000 EUR.

In order for the broadband grid to be expanded to a community, at least 70% of the inhabitants must sign up for a connection to ensure that the infrastructure can later on be rented out to a service provider (Breitbandnetz 2011). In particular, local businesses have been shown to be key drivers behind investment decisions and represent the largest portion of shareholders.

Thus, in the absence of the German federal state's capacity to deliver broadband infrastructure to underserved areas, citizens, businesses, and local governments have stepped in to fill the gap with creative financing and organisational arrangements. The concept is gaining interest from those lacking broadband access both elsewhere in Germany and in the US (e.g. Crowdfiber.com) and the UK (e.g. Broadway Partners). In addition, the notion of citizens as investors has been spreading to other areas of public good provision as well, such as in energy. Even in such cases, where actors other than the federal state have taken on delivery, strong state administrative capacities are needed, especially in terms of regulation to ensure fair and open processes and coordination to exchange information, mobilise actors, and foster collaboration.

Barcelona Social Inclusion Plan

Local governments everywhere play a key role in addressing the social, economic, political, and cultural complexities that contribute to diverse welfare challenges. Many social services are delivered at the local 'street-level', and local governments are increasingly called upon to bear the financial burden of welfare spending–in particular in times of austerity when the national government cuts support for local services. In cities where diverse social problems crystallise, innovative solutions are in high demand. The challenge is then to deliver welfare services effectively and efficiently, while also contributing to greater social inclusion. Yet, social problems are 'adaptive' in that they are ill-defined, involve multi-layered challenges, and therefore require solutions that go beyond purely technical ones (Barcelona City Council 2013: 11). While local authorities may have better knowledge of local demands for specific public services, they may lack the resources needed to gather, analyse, and manage information, act in an autonomous capacity, or provide the services at a sufficient level of quantity and quality. Moreover, a number of aspects of social services are in many ways co-produced, i.e. they need the active and supportive involvement of the target group. Within this context, social services delivered at the local level present a way to translate social conflicts into creative opportunities.

One exemplary case of governance innovation in delivering social welfare services is the Barcelona Social Inclusion Plan, the first for 2005–2010 and the more recent plan for 2012–2015. Barcelona (Spain) is a dynamic, metropolitan city that 'translates into a mosaic of citizen needs, problems and expectations [that] challenge the local authority and call on it to provide answers that are local, responsive, creative and innovative' (Eurocities 2011: 2). For many years, Barcelona has engaged in participatory approaches to welfare provision involving its large and vibrant civil society. The Plan has built these elements into a novel strategic regulatory and institutional framework that both strengthens the city's autonomy so it can be more responsive to the needs of its own citizens and creates mechanisms for cooperation between the City Council and other nongovernmental actors. The framework assists not only in the implementation of the Plan, but also guarantees and prioritises a local strategy for social inclusion (Barcelona City Council 2013).

The institutional framework consists of many levels. First, upon the City Council's resolution to create a Plan, public agencies prepare a draft based on its analyses. The draft is subject to an extensive public consultation process involving, among others, working groups of the Municipal Social Welfare Council composed of numerous public and private agencies and the action networks organised under the Citizens' Agreement for an Inclusive Barcelona, a product of the 2005-2010 Social Inclusion Plan that has since evolved into a separate entity. The various inputs from the working groups,

Table 4.4 **Networks comprising the Citizens' Agreement for an Inclusive Barcelona**

Network	Date	Number of Organisations	Purpose
Network for assistance to the homeless	2005	25	To help homeless persons regain autonomy and social relations
Network of centres for children and teens	2006	17	To improve the city's responsiveness to children and adolescents in situations of social risk
Support network for family caregivers	2006	18	To promote entities that support family caregivers assisting persons with illnesses that lead to the loss of autonomy
Network for the reception and support of immigrants in Barcelona	2007	89	To aid recent immigrants in taking up residence in the city by sharing information, providing counselling, and covering the basic needs of new immigrants
Inclusion housing network	2010	40	To reflect the work of a significant number of social organisations focused on residential inclusion
Cultural network for social inclusion	2010	23	To fight against inequalities in access to cultural and educational capital
Network for children's rights	2011	19	To strengthen the city's ability to defend and promote the rights of children
Network for co-existence and prevention	2011	11	To prevent social conflict and aggression toward individuals and public and/or private property
Network for social economy	2012	80	To coordinate the efforts of public authorities, local businesses and other social agents in local social responsibility projects

Source: Teresa Montagut, University of Barcelona

action networks, public sector professionals, and citizens are then incorporated into the final Plan.

A key element in the Plan's development and its implementation is the Citizens' Agreement. As noted above, the action networks are organised under its umbrella (see Table 4.4) to promote cooperation, share responsibility, and exchange information and resources. Within its first year of existence, 235 private social welfare agencies, charities, businesses, and universities signed the Citizens' Agreement, with the number doubling within five years. An Annual Meeting provides space wherein participants provide an account of their work and agree on next steps. During the preparatory process for the 2012-2015 Plan, the city administration and the Citizens' Agreement reached a consensus that allowed for the formulation of a joint strategy to strengthen the capacities of social associations and charities and collaboration between public and private agencies.

The Barcelona Social Inclusion Plan and the Citizens' Agreement for an Inclusive Barcelona are the result of the joint work of Barcelona's City Council, local public agencies, citizens, and civil society organisations. The efforts of the Plan have been recognised by the Eurocities CASE Project (Cities Combat Against Social Exclusion) and later recommended as an example of best practices by the European Anti-Poverty Network (EAPN).

Since the first Plan and the Citizen's Agreement that emerged from the process were so strongly promoted by the city's government of the time, there was concern that the whole framework might be undone when a new government came to power in 2011. Given that the 2012-2015 Plan follows essentially the same path and even includes a joint strategy with civil society, it appears that there is no intention to reverse course soon from a political perspective. From an administrative capacity perspective, the Plan demands high levels of delivery, analytical, and coordination capacity on the part of the city government (one could add, also on the part of the Citizens' Agreement's signatories). The impact of this multi-level, multi-actor initiative on social inclusion in Barcelona and whether such local mobilisation, commitment, and coordination are transferable to other settings remain to be seen.

Personal budgets

In addition to increasingly diverse welfare needs, welfare provision is further challenged by an increasing emphasis on improvements in performance despite cuts in expenditure (Fox 2012). The UK's response was to promote personalisation, defined as 'the process by which services are tailored to the needs and preferences of citizens. The overall vision is that the state should empower citizens to shape their own lives and the services they receive' (HM Government Cabinet Office 2007: 33). In terms of governance, this agenda shifts responsibility of social care from the state to the individual through different forms of cash transfers as put forward by early initiatives under the Labour government in the late 1990s. The personal budget agenda took off in 2006 when first pilots were carried out in 13 local authorities in England over a six-month period, during which 959 persons received funding through direct payments to the individual, service provider, or a third-party broker. In 2008, personal budgets, which may cover the cost of services ranging from cleaning and shopping to job training and transportation, were formally introduced so as to save on costs, promote choice, and expand the competitive market for social care services (Leadbeater, Bartlett, and Gallagher 2008). They offer a change not only in how services are funded, but also in how they are designed and delivered, encouraging people to self-manage their own care (Dayson 2011).

As part of the process of self-directed support, personal budgets are provided through a resource allocation system, a point system for measuring a person's level of dependency and awarding a monetary value accordingly

Table 4.5 **Other examples of personal budget programmes**

Country	Programme (Date Initiated)	Eligibility	Use
Australia	Consumer Directed Care (2010)	Elderly and disabled persons	Personal assistance, transport, emotional support
Austria	Cash Payments (1993)	Persons requiring 50 hours of care or more per month due to physical or mental disability	Compensation for families providing informal long-term care
Finland	Home Care Service Vouchers (late 1990s)	Elderly with long-term care needs	Personal assistance and related care services
Germany	Personal Budgets (2004)	Persons in considerable need of care for a minimum of six months due to physical or mental disability	Personal assistance, transport, therapy cost, support equipment, and other related services or activities
Sweden	Assistance Allowances (1993)	Persons requiring 20 hours of care or more per week	Personal assistance, related care services, support equipment, transport, and therapy costs
United States	Self-Directed Care (1998)	Elderly with long-term care needs	Personal assistance, related health services, support equipment, and rehabilitative therapy costs

Source: Gadsby 2013

(Slasberg, Beresford, and Schonfield 2012). Planning and delivering stages are based on the seven-step approach designed by the UK nonprofit organisation, In Control. First, the local authority asks the individual to complete a self-assessment, allowing for the individual to control his/her own needs evaluation while also reducing the administrative burden of local authority staff. Once eligibility is met, an estimated budget or indicative budget is allocated, upon which users develop a support or care plan, which outlines the individual's goals or expectations, how support will be arranged and managed, as well as risks that may impact how support is delivered. Individuals have the option to design their plan independently or in consultation with a third party, be it a social worker, family member, or professional brokerage service. Finally, the plan is submitted for approval to a local authority, which also monitors and reviews the plan and its management on an annual basis (Tarr 2011).

Personal budgets have also been taken up in other OECD countries (see Table 4.5), although the extent of their usage is perhaps nowhere as far-reaching as in the UK. For example, Austria introduced cash payment schemes in 1993, covering home care for the elderly and persons with physical disabilities or mental illness by compensating family members for informal care. Cash payment schemes were also introduced in Germany as early as 1995 in order to increase choice, competition and cost savings and may be, therefore, used for a wide variety of needs, such as transportation, nursing, therapy and other support equipment. Australia set up a more recent consumer-directed care programme for the elderly and persons with disability in 2010, and by 2012 most US states offered self-directed care options for Medicaid recipients so as to expand long-term home care options. Although self-directed care is not formalised in the Nordic countries, there are examples of service vouchers in Finland as well as assistance allowance in Sweden.

Despite their wide uptake, those concerned about personal budgets argue that the risks of implementing choice in other policy areas (e.g. health and education) outweigh the benefits. Tummers, Jilke, and Van de Walle (2013) highlight potential risks, such as lack of real choice, increased inequality, worsened work conditions for caregivers, and problems associated with using performance information. Moreover, the workforce assessing the budgets must be highly skilled and capable of calculating accurate and fair budgets. Therefore, necessary preconditions for the success of personal budget implementation include a high degree of analytical capacity to accurately assess individual social needs and costs as well as some degree of regulatory capacity to allow for the direct deposit of social care funds. Effectiveness also depends on whether individuals can influence the options available to them and whether clients are skilled choice-makers (cf. Tummers, Jilke, and Van de Walle 2013). Indeed designing choice is critical in this context, but when implemented well, it could cover a range of social needs, especially for the elderly and persons with disabilities or mental health problems.

Regulatory capacity

A growing body of research demonstrates a compelling need for sustainability regulation in order to minimise long-term, harmful effects from human activities that contribute to environmental deterioration. The development of regulatory capacity in this area is hampered by the risk that sustainability regulation might disrupt economic growth, as the two policy aims often exist as trade-offs. Still, a range of regulatory measures have been employed, including: (i) reporting and disclosure measures; (ii) development regulations (e.g. green development certification and codes or environmental impact reviews); and (iii) market-based instruments (e.g. carbon tax, cap and trade schemes, or voluntary markets) (cf. Whitten et al. 2007). The first two measures are more prevalent but may not be adequate for inducing significant impact, as their primary aim is to deter negative human and/or business behaviour. Therefore, the two cases selected as innovative governance solutions to challenges in this area focus rather on the third type of measure. These cases, the Biodiversity Banking and Offsets Scheme (or BioBanking) in Australia and the Regional Greenhouse Gas Initiative (RGGI) in the US, are novel approaches to sustainability and are estimated to have significant effects. Both address the absence or lack of sustainability regulation by implementing market-based solutions for biodiversity conservation in the first case and greenhouse gas (GHG) emissions and climate change in the latter.

Biodiversity Banking and Offsets Scheme

Biodiversity serves many necessary functions, such as the purification of water and air sources, the detoxification of waste, and the stabilisation of the biosphere (UNEP 2000). Yet, these benefits are treated as externalities and are generally not accounted for in market prices. Regulation that could prohibit development contributing to biodiversity loss is not always feasible or sufficient in some cases or as efficient as it would be to internalise externalities as offsetting does. However, offset schemes require processes to quantify the environmental value of biodiversity loss.

Within this context, biodiversity offsets emerged as a means to counteract activities that are detrimental to an area of habitat by (re)creating a habitat elsewhere to offset the loss, thereby preventing a net loss to the environment (ten Kate, Bishop, and Bayon 2004). They are different from other ecological compensation mechanisms, however, in that they require demonstration of measurable outcomes. In this sense, they are unique because they have the potential to address drivers of biodiversity loss while also creating incentives for conservation by discouraging activities that reduce biodiversity and by creating a demand for land conservation (Blom, Bergsman, and Korteland 2008).

Figure 4.1 **Life cycle of a biodiversity credit**

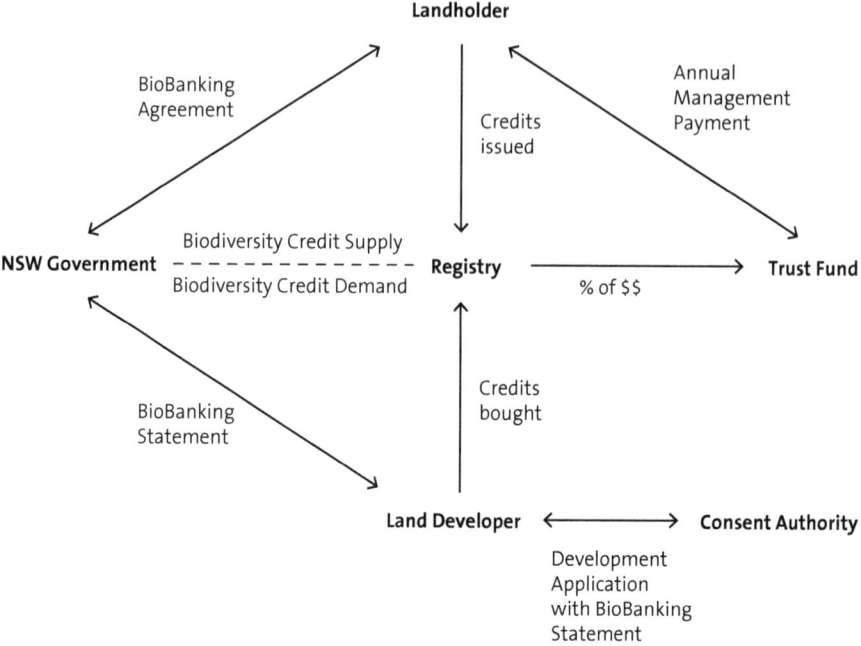

Following early international examples, such as the 1976 German Impact Mitigation Regulation, 1985 US Wetland Mitigation, and 2000 Brazilian Project Developers Offsets, BioBanking was formally introduced in New South Wales (NSW), Australia in 2006 via an amendment to the Threatened Species Conservation Act of 1995, and commenced two years later in 2008. Within this framework, land developers can voluntarily purchase biodiversity credits through a biodiversity conservation banking system. Unlike mandatory biodiversity offsets and environmental impact assessments, voluntary programmes like this are not required under legal or planning provisions, but still allow developers to respond to growing public pressure for corporate social responsibility and demonstrate their commitment to addressing the environmental impacts of land-use activities (Darbi et al. 2009).

Within this framework (see Figure 4.1), the credits are created through voluntary, legally binding BioBanking agreements between the NSW government and private landholders. Once the agreement is made, the land will be registered as an official biobank site, wherein the agreed-upon management activities for the conservation or enhancement of biodiversity will be upheld even if the land is later sold.[1] Significant tax advantages incentivise landholders to enter into such agreements. The price of the credits are set by the market, taking into account the cost of management actions, establishment of conservation agreements, land acquisition, obtaining expert advice, compliance, and reporting. To purchase biodiversity credits, developers must obtain a biobanking statement, which details the number and type of credits required to offset the impact of development and ensures greater certainty of the project's biodiversity loss impact. Credits can be purchased from the landholder (or other credit holder), with a portion of the proceeds of the first sale deposited into the BioBanking Trust Fund that is used to assist the landholder in conservation management. Once a statement and credits are secured, the developer can incorporate the statement in its development application to be considered by the appropriate consent authority (see DEC 2006a). A central element in the process is the BioBanking Assessment Methodology (BAM), which provides a set of rules to determine the number and type of biodiversity credits that a biobank site can create and sell and that a development site will require to offset impacts. The aim of BAM is to achieve a 'like for like' basis to ensure 'no net loss' (ten Kate, Bishop, and Bayon 2004). The NSW government manages the public register of biobank sites, biodiversity credits and agreements, oversees the BioBanking Trust Fund, and ensures compliance (DEC 2006b).

By combining soft regulation with market mechanisms, BioBanking seeks to improve or maintain biodiversity while also avoiding barriers to economic growth and creating incentives for individuals, companies, and organisations to voluntarily take part in conservation efforts. The multiple tasks and multiple stakeholders involved require significant coordination on the part of the NSW government BioBanking team. Indeed, both regulatory and coordination capacities are essential for establishing, monitoring, and enforcing biodiversity markets (Hanley, Shogren, and White 2001). Analytical capacity is also required so as to accurately assess the ecological value of credits and the potential biodiversity loss of land site development, especially over time.

Despite uncertainty in predicting gains or losses, biodiversity offsets and other mitigation schemes are increasingly popular instruments that have been widely adopted in some 40 countries worldwide and are currently being developed in 27 others (Madsen, Carroll, and Moore Brands 2010).

Regional Greenhouse Gas Initiative

Another growing sustainability concern is the increasing levels of greenhouse gas (GHG) emissions as they contribute to climate change and global warming. Although these consequences have become widely apparent and well researched, the slowing down of global warming is not easily achieved due to the heavy reliance of developed countries (and increasing reliance by emerging economies) on fossil fuel use. Moreover, the harnessing of GHG emissions is predicted to have a tremendous effect on national economies and their growth. For this reason, the US, widely recognised as one of the largest contributors of GHG emissions (accounting for 36% of global GHG emissions in 1990 and 20.6% in 2000–see Dessai 2001 and Baumert, Herzog, and Pershing 2005), signed but never ratified the Kyoto Protocol.[2]

In the absence of national regulation, the Regional Greenhouse Gas Initiative (RGGI) emerged in 2003 as the first mandatory, market-based system to reduce GHG emissions in the US. The objective of this initiative is to reduce emissions by 10% before 2020 by capping power sector emissions at 2000-2002 levels between 2009 and 2014 and further reducing levels by 2.5% per year between 2015 and 2018. Initially agreed upon by ten US states of the New England Region, the number was reduced to nine when New Jersey pulled out due to political pressure spurred by concerns over higher consumer costs.[3]

RGGI is essentially a supply-side, cap and trade scheme that aims to cut CO_2 emissions by regulating over 200 power plants in the region. Under this regulatory framework, power plants within cooperating states must obtain an emitter's permit, which guarantees them a sufficient number of allowances or carbon credits (which may vary between states) over a three-year period. An emitter's permit application will also include an Emissions Monitoring Plan, designed to disclose information about the plant's energy output and monitoring procedures to ensure compliance. Tracking and monitoring emissions data are supported by the US Environmental Protection Agency (EPA), although state agencies are responsible for monitoring compliance as well as designing and enforcing penalties in the event of non-compliance. The control of CO_2 emissions is then facilitated through a quarterly auction mechanism, differentiating RGGI's approach from the EU Emissions Trading Scheme's (ETS) original 'free' allowances. Participating states have committed to selling the majority of their carbon budgets through these auctions, where 65% of revenue is invested in energy efficiency and clean energy resources (Ramseur 2013: 12). Power plants then buy emissions allowances from states for every ton of CO_2 they emit. Hence, the more CO_2 a plant emits, the more allowances it has to purchase, the price being newly determined at each auction in response to current demand for CO_2 allowances. The total number of available allowances is designed to decrease as the overall cap is lowered, thereby raising their price and providing an incentive for power plants to invest in clean technologies to avoid the higher cost of polluting.

To provide for flexibility and shelter power plant operators from adverse effects of steeply rising prices, RGGI also includes a safety valve mechanism as well as a carbon-offsetting scheme, similar to BioBanking. Unlike the EU ETS, RGGI has been able to adjust rather quickly to market developments, in particular the natural gas boom. In 2012, for example, only 91 million tons of CO_2 were emitted despite the regions' allowance of 165 million tons. As such, the overall cap was adjusted to 91 million tons starting in 2014, while maintaining the plan for additional annual reductions of 2.5% (Daley 2013). Not only is the auction system a fair and effective means for allocating emission allowances, but also its proceeds are strategically invested in complementary programmes targeting energy efficiency or providing direct bill assistance to low-income families and qualifying small businesses. What is more, with the investments made in new green technology, the same amount of energy can be produced while emitting less GHG, at which point consumer prices are expected to go down again.

Theoretically, cap and trade schemes can be an efficient and cost effective means of encouraging lower emissions. Moreover, empirical evidence shows that each RGGI participating state demonstrated positive gains to the economy. Total revenue from allowances was 1.1 billion USD (approx. 860 million EUR), 900 million USD of which was shifted back to consumers' utility bills. Moreover, the minor increase in the price of electricity also had the effect of decreasing consumer demand, which rendered a decrease in total cost across the ten states by 2 billion USD (approx. 1.56 billion EUR) during the first three years of the programme (Hibbard et al. 2011). This success can, in part, be attributed to the strong regulatory, coordination, and analytical capacities that accompany it. Thus, RGGI demonstrates that well-designed cap and trade schemes that are supported by administrative capacities can potentially provide the private sector with more flexibility than other sustainability solutions.

Coordination capacity

While many governance challenges require top-down, regulatory capacity development, other challenges may require a more coordination capacity approach. This is often the case when involving diverse groups of stakeholders or complex multi-level organisations. Policy implementation may not suffice, but rather, solutions are based upon the interaction and contribution of individual actors. Two cases have been selected to demonstrate the importance of this capacity. The first case continues with sustainability challenges and exhibits alternative local investment programmes in Sweden. The second case then jumps to EU migration regulation challenges, an area in great need of greater coordination capacity between the EU immigrant-receiving member states and respective home countries in order to develop more cohesive policies and better mechanisms for enforcement of labour-related immigration.

Climate investment programmes

Following the ratification of the Kyoto Protocol, the EU launched the first large-scale emissions reduction scheme in 2005, which operates under a cap and trade principle similar to RGGI. Activities contributing to climate change are often local in nature, and thus, arguably require local solutions. Indeed, addressing sustainability at the local level could further contribute to the reduction of GHG emissions in ways that are not addressed under larger scale operations. The challenge is that local authorities often lack the resources to undertake activities that would have any actual significant impact, and therefore, may require an overarching investment strategy for local sustainability projects. To do this, a regulatory approach may be insufficient, or even unfeasible, as projects are likely to extend beyond the public sector alone. Instead, local sustainability investment requires the contribution of and coordination between private actors, civil society organisations, and local authorities.

One front-runner example of climate investment programmes emerged in Sweden. With the overall goal of sustainable development, the Swedish climate strategy emphasises three areas: protection of the environment; the efficient use of resources and reduction of reliance on fossil fuels; and the assurance of a sustainable supply of resources. To this end, Swedish climate policy is based on broad programmes with cross-sector and sector-specific financing instru-

Table 4.6 **Selected examples of Swedish local sustainability projects**

Municipality	Total Number of Projects	Total Funding (in SEK millions)	Total Investment (in SEK millions)	Total GHG Emissions Reduced (tonnes/year)	Sample Project Activities
Helsingborg	22	41	171	17,410	Biogas production and partnership between food, agricultural, and recycling companies
Linköping	22	35.8	19.8	15,006	Public Education Project TEMP (transport, energy, environment project), plus several related campaigns
Stockholm	26	107.8	603.4	74,546	Expanding capacity for district-wide new cooling systems to reduce CO_2 emissions
Mölndal	9	5.9	27.1	2,269	Replacing electric boiler model housing with geothermal heating, which stores solar heat to use during energy shortfalls in the winter, reducing consumption by half

Source: Swedish Environmental Protection Agency (2009)

ments that fit into these overarching frameworks. The result of these objectives manifested in three consecutive subsidy programmes from 1998 to 2012.

In economic literature, subsidies are often viewed as inferior to taxes because they give potential incentives for rent-seeking behaviour; however, these Swedish local investment programmes entail a solid review process that acts as a safeguard against such behaviour. In the first stage of this process, grant applications are ranked along several criteria, such as the quality of their strategy, distribution of knowledge, and planning of follow-up work and evaluation. Experts then examine and assess projects based on cost efficiency. Proposals with the highest ranking are then allocated grants, which are monitored by regional state agencies and overseen by the Swedish Environmental Protection Agency in cooperation with local municipalities and other local stakeholders, usually private actors and/or local civil society organisations. Many of the investment projects (see Table 4.6 for a selection) are implemented in sectors that have the greatest impact on the climate, namely transport and energy use, and are expected to cut GHG emissions by 4% (compared with 1990 levels) by 2012 and 40% by 2020 (Swedish Environmental Protection Agency 2009).

Local investment programmes contribute to reducing GHG emission in several ways: directly (via investments that cut energy use), through increased collaboration within the municipality and between other local stakeholders, and by increasing knowledge among other actors and the general public. Moreover, these programmes offer measurable results and have clear impact targets. These programmes are embedded in a holistic view of overall sustainability goals, exemplify a bottom-up process via local authority priority-setting, are results-focused, and embody competition and joint financing. Local climate investment grants thus appear to be able to produce results where other climate policy instruments are too weak, unfeasible, and/or ineffective (e.g. for sectors that have low taxes on GHG emissions). Other countries (e.g. the Netherlands, Denmark, Germany, and the UK–see Keskitalo 2010) have since implemented similar environmental grant schemes; however, the Swedish case is unique in terms of the amount of funding (180 million EUR) and its specific aim (i.e. greenhouse gas reductions) (Johansson, Samakovlis, and Treich 2011). Its combined approach of decentralised regulation and collaborative management demonstrates how sustainability projects at the local level can be effective, when proper analytical and delivery capacities are also in place.

Mobility Partnerships

In response to changing population demographics in Europe, circular migration, or the temporary movement of individuals between home and host area, has become an important focus of EU external policy-making, primarily as a means to address worker shortages. While human rights-related immigration policy has become internationally institutionalised, labour migration-related immigration policy remains a competence of individual states. Circular migration 'usually occurs through informal channels and outside of inter-state labour agreements' (Maroukis and Triandafyllidou 2013: 4). In practice, migrant workers, at least in Europe, often fail to complete the circle by actually returning to their country of origin. Moreover, if such irregular migrants have not gone home first, their legal readmission becomes problematic for many EU member states. In part, this can be explained by the lack of a cohesive policy and mechanisms needed to regulate the cross-border mobility of individuals.

In 2006, the European Council stressed the issue of legal migration opportunities and called upon the European Commission to present a concrete proposal for what would become the parameters of Mobility Partnerships. Essentially, the partnership entails a soft law approach via a signed memorandum of understanding, i.e. an agreement between EU member states and interested third countries, which would enable non-EU citizens to have better access to work opportunities within the EU (CEC 2006). In particular, the programme encompasses a cohesive migration approach between receiving, sending, and transit countries within Europe, Africa, and along the Mediterranean, with the word 'partnership' referring to the mutual commitments and shared responsibility, management, and ownership of the initiative for all parties involved (Cassarino 2009). By 2008, the first two agreements were signed with the Republic of Moldova (one of Europe's poorest countries, which is highly dependent on remittances) and the Republic of Cape Verde (a high-emigration island off the coast of western Africa) as pilot runs. In 2009, Georgia became the third country to be included in the initiative, partly as a political response to the country's conflict with Russia. Armenia followed in 2010. Negotiations have also taken place with Ghana since 2010 as well as Egypt and Tunisia in light of the Arab Spring. The fifth and most recent partnership was entered into with Morocco in 2013 (see Table 4.7).

Following the first pilot runs, the Commission established a set of criteria for selecting partner countries based on third-party interest, cooperation readiness, and capacity for internal coordination to negotiate and implement the partnership (CEC 2009). The pre-selection process begins with exploratory talks to ensure that these criteria are present before moving toward an intermediate stage, which entails stock-taking of existing or planned initiatives as well as needs assessment, before making a final decision. These periods of consultation aim to identify shared strategic objectives and to avoid mismatches of expectations. The final adoption phase and identification of cooperative activities are then 'shaped on the basis of these shared objectives' (CEC 2009: 4). Mobility Partnerships are next formulated as declarations of intention and signed by the Community, the Presidency of the EU, interested member states, and the respective partner country. The agreement is written in non-binding terms, ensuring that the arrangements are flexible and adaptable and remain open for additional parties to opt-in at a later point. Within these declarations, a division of competences is made surrounding three central themes: mobility, legal migration and integration; migration and development; and border management, identity and travel documents, and the fight against illegal migration and human trafficking (Carrera and Hernández i Sagrera 2011; Reslow 2010). In the Moldovan case, for example, 64 actions were proposed, such as the EC providing assistance on biometric passports and Moldova strengthening its information centres for Moldovan migrants.

Mobility Partnerships create new multi-level regulatory and structural institutions of labour migration governance that before did not exist. They give citizens of non-EU countries legal access to work within parts of the EU, while also addressing areas of worker shortage in the EU and decreasing the potential risk of immigrant-receiving countries. Its soft legal framework allows for addressing circular migratory issues by establishing agreements among interested countries in an attempt to share responsibility and management (Carrera and Hernández i Sagrera 2009). While the current pilots are still much too new to realise their direct impact and long-term effects, the EC's preliminary evaluation of the Mobility Partnerships' pilot phase in 2009 called them 'the most innovative and sophisticated tool to date of the Global Approach to Migration' (CEC 2009: 4). Although the challenge that this innovation addresses is a very complex one, it is one of the few cases selected that does not appear to require additional administrative capacities beyond coordination and regulation.

Table 4.7 **Mobility Partnerships**

Partner Country	Date	Participating Member States
Cape Verde	2008	France, Luxembourg, the Netherlands, Portugal, and Spain
Moldova	2008	Bulgaria, Cyprus, Czech Republic, France, Greece, Germany, Hungary, Italy, Lithuania, Poland, Portugal, Romania, Slovenia, Slovakia, and Sweden
Georgia	2009	Belgium, Bulgaria, Czech Republic, Denmark, Germany, Estonia, Greece, France, Italy, Lithuania, Latvia, Netherlands, Poland, Romania, Sweden, and the UK
Armenia	2010	Belgium, Bulgaria, Czech Republic, Germany, France, Italy, Netherlands, Poland, Romania, and Sweden
Morocco	2013	Belgium, France, Italy, the Netherlands, Portugal, Spain, Sweden, and the UK

Analytical capacity

Analytical capacity is commonly associated with policy advice, although the definitions provided for in the first two chapters of this Report go well beyond this understanding. The governance innovations selected for this section demonstrate situations wherein information is a key component of developing successful solutions to some of the most challenging problems to date. Both cases are sub-national examples of market failure due to a lack of information. The first case addresses the issue of immigrant skill-matching and underutilisation, which in this context was solved by building analytical and coordination capacities. The second case is a local-level pilot project for a much larger national initiative, the German transition to renewable energy, or *Energiewende*. For this purpose, analytical capacity enhances decentralised energy grid systems by implementing smart grid and energy metering technologies so as to improve energy supply and demand matching.

Toronto Region Immigrant Employment Council

Many have argued that skilled immigrants bring creative and entrepreneurial capacity, competitiveness, dynamism, and innovation (Gertler 2004). Despite their potential value to employers, skilled immigrants are often prevented from entering the labour market due to barriers such as: difficulty obtaining local work experience; lack of recognition of international education, training, and experience; insufficient information about employment opportunities and requirements; lack of professional networks; lack of occupation-specific terminology in national language; and lack of targeted training programmes to bridge gaps in qualification (cf. Teelucksingh and Galabuzi 2005). In the Toronto (Canada) region, whose economic growth relies heavily on the recruitment of skilled immigrants due to its large ageing population and declining birth rate, the underutilisation of immigrants' skills, education, and experience is one of the most important challenges.

Indeed, 2001 census data show that 43.7% of residents in the Toronto Region were foreign born, the highest proportion for any major city in the world and still growing (by 2006, this number reached 50%). Other estimates expect immigrants to contribute to 80% of Canada's overall population growth (Cohen 2012). Yet, little on the part of the federal, provincial, or local government has been done to seek out effective solutions for skilled immigrant labour market integration. As a result, the creation of the Toronto Region Immigrant Employment Council (TRIEC) was proposed in the Toronto City Summit Alliance's 2003 report 'Enough Talk: An Action Plan for the Toronto Region' as a means to improve access to employment for immigrants in the region and to foster a coordinated and collaborative approach to integrating newcomers. Within the same year, TRIEC was officially launched as a multi-stakeholder council of both public and private institutions and supported by the Alliance and the Maytree foundation. In 2007, it became an independent nonprofit organisation.

The Council is comprised of a board, working groups, and a secretariat. Council members represent various interest groups, bringing together key stakeholders, such as employers, regulatory bodies, professional associations, educators, employees, community groups, government, and immigrants. TRIEC's objectives include: (i) convening and collaborating with partners to create opportunities for skilled immigrants to connect to the local labour market; (ii) working with stakeholders to build their awareness and capacity to better integrate skilled immigrants; and (iii) working with all levels of government to enhance coordination and effect more responsive policy and programmes for skilled immigrant employment. To this end, TRIEC connects companies to programmes that help improve recruitment and retention of immigrants by developing and distributing learning tools and curriculum; helps immigrants build their professional connections through mentoring and professional immigrant networks and mentoring programmes; and engages in public awareness campaigns and policy development (see Table 4.8).

According to its website, TRIEC has matched over 5,000 skilled immigrants through its Mentoring Partnership, from which 70% have found employment within six months of completion of the mentoring programme. In this sense, TRIEC is essential in that it fills a governance void and necessary demand for matching skilled immigrant labour with employer needs:

Table 4.8 **Selected TRIEC programmes and initiatives**

Programme	Description
Mentoring Partnership	Links skilled immigrants with established professionals in their field to discuss the nuances of the Canadian workplace culture and create professional networks and contacts
Professional Immigrant Networks	Links skilled immigrants to employers and employment resources and services, building the capacity of the networks and their leaders and making connections with key stakeholders
Career Bridge	Helps organisations find educated, experienced and pre-screened talent while adding skills and diversity to their workforce and helping highly qualified and motivated individuals gain meaningful work experience
Intergovernmental Relations Committee	Brings together representatives of ministries and departments from all three levels of government to share information and explore key policy and programme issues related to immigrant employment

'TRIEC recognises that there are gaps in government policy and practice as regards the integration of immigrants into the labour market and has set itself the task of identifying these gaps and of articulating solutions' (OECD 2006: 125). It does so by engaging a variety of actors and stakeholders that have developed a number of innovative, efficacious, and influential programmes that have demonstrated a strong potential to enact structural change where no such structures before existed. As it fills a gap in analytical capacity, strong coordination and delivery capacities are also required.

Integration of Renewable Energies and E-mobility

As part of the 2011 German *Energiewende* agenda and transition to renewable and efficient energy, the national government has made efforts to decentralise its energy supply in order to increase its renewable energy share to 80% by 2050 (BMWi 2012a). Instead of relying on large-scale energy plants, Germany hopes to increase its renewable energy provision through small-scale electricity plants (e.g. biomass-fuelled power plants), wind turbines, and individual households via photovoltaic panels. However, the change is accompanied by increasing volatility, as most renewable energy sources cannot offer consistent supply and current national grid systems are not sufficiently developed to store and allocate energy resources to match demand. Therefore, the success of renewable energy deployment is reliant upon the development of current energy infrastructure so as to allow for additional (mobile) storage capacities (e.g. electric cars) as well as improve data and information flow (Horenkamp et al. 2007). To this end, new 'smart grid' technology enables energy to pass in two directions and incorporates intervention and steering devices to more effectively match supply and demand (Metzger et al. 2012). A smart grid is essentially a new form of electronic grid that integrates the behaviour of both energy generators and consumers through intelligent monitoring, information and communications technologies, also referred to as smart metering technology.

As the first large-scale, real application of smart grid technology and development of smart metering technology in Germany, the Integration of Renewable Energies and E-mobility (IRENE) pilot project was launched in 2011. The location of its launch, Wildpoldsried (2,500 inhabitants) in the state of Bavaria, was selected due to the town's large volume of decentralised electricity provision, mainly through photovoltaic panels and wind turbines. Overall, Wildpoldsried resembles the energy scenario expected to prevail in many German communities in 2020 and therefore allows for real-life applications of Germany's future smart grid technology (Müller 2012). Supporting the project is the German Ministry of Economics in cooperation with private corporations, such as the regional electricity supplier, Allgäuer Überlandwerke GmbH (AÜW), and Siemens AG, the developer of

Figure 4.2 **Smart metering technology**

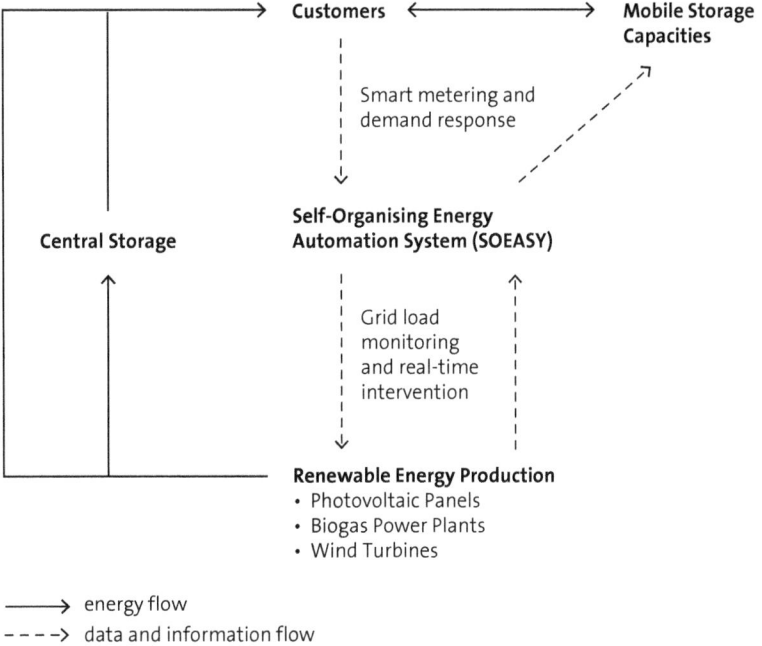

German smart grid and metering technology, as well as Kempten University and RWTH Aachen University, both of which offer expertise in forecasting models related to renewable energy sustainability. By combining forecasting models with realistic feed-in and energy consumption data, it is further possible to identify any additional network upgrading work or smart network integration concepts required.

The project aims to identify solutions to enable distribution network operators to feed power from fluctuating decentralised renewable energy sources into the grid. It serves as a platform to operationalise a pioneering, self-organising energy automation system (SOEASY). This optimises the timing of power generation from small-scale energy producers, aligns consumption patterns with energy availability, and stores any surplus of generated energy by involving both a newly developed stationary battery and 40 mobile batteries contained in electric vehicles distributed to private and business customers (see Figure 4.2). Smart metering technology further enhances data collection of power consumption patterns and enables grid load monitoring and real-time intervention (Köberle et al. 2012). The total cost of IRENE is 6 million EUR, of which both Siemens AG and AÜW contribute one million and the Ministry of Economics finances the remaining four million (Müller 2012).

While the energy grid in Germany will still require fundamental investments and expansion in order to comply with the goals of the *Energiewende*, information provided and employed by technologies such as this may help to decrease the costs of energy grid expansion substantially by allowing for a more efficient expansion of the grid that facilitates decentralised energy production and consumption (Metzger et al. 2012). While the project is too new at this point to comment on its success or performance, it is clear that decentralised energy solutions are of high interest and demand, but rarely practiced on such a large scale as this. Furthermore, the technological advances made from this study will be valuable and likely transferable to other contexts (Wohlgenannt 2012). However, the application of a large-scale project like IRENE is extremely costly and depends on a strong state that is both willing and able to coordinate relevant actors and incentivise participation. Although IRENE presents an innovative solution to significantly increase analytical capacity that is in high demand, and likely to become more so in the future, the replicability of such a project in other cities in Germany as well as throughout the world, will require a great deal of coordination and regulatory capacities in addition to a large amount of funding.

Conclusion

Continuing the analysis of the relationship between the ability of states to respond to key governance challenges, on the one hand, and the availability of administrative capacities, on the other, this chapter has focussed on ten selected cases of governance innovations. Focusing on the four policy areas explored in this Report, these cases explore the extent to which such innovations respond to capacity limits. The cases also point to which kind of administrative capacities are required for such solutions to be effective. Thus, in answering the first two questions posed at the beginning of this chapter, the empirical presentation of cases attempts to address a substantial void in academic and policy debates on governance innovations.

While all ten governance innovations address some type of administrative capacity bottleneck, and frequently demonstrate a combination of various capacities required to make a solution work, they do so for two main reasons. The first rationale for the innovations is the decline of the capacity of the state, or the state in its 'status quo ante'. For example, the crowdfunding initiatives to expand broadband coverage are responses to the state's inability to provide such services on its own (delivery capacity) or to regulate private providers who do. Inclusion initiatives, such as TRIEC, also suggest weakness in the state's ability to appropriately analyse and assess the diversifying needs of their populations. The San Francisco Bay Area Transportation approach is another example where the limits of traditional state infrastructure provision and planning are the starting point for an innovative process that addresses the issue of sustainability in recognition of limited financial resources. This case is also an example of the second rationale behind these innovations, namely the emergence of new policy problems and governance challenges. The IRENE case, which came about in an effort to manage and match energy supply and demand with renewable energy resources, also exemplifies the need to find solutions to emerging challenges.

Possibly not surprising, but widely ignored in the debate on (collaborative) innovations, all cases heavily rely on administrative capacities, and in some cases, not all administrative capacities can be considered as belonging to the traditional capacity stock of the state. Some of the cases are basically innovations of traditional tools of government, such as the Swedish Local Investment Programmes or the Bay Area Transportation planning, yet they strongly rely on highly developed analytical capacities within the public sector in order to conduct option analyses and cost-benefit assessments, performance measurements and other policy analysis and management tools that do not necessarily belong to the established skill set of bureaucrats, even after decades of reforms that call for such skills.

> *The many instances of governance innovations that work with market mechanisms or civil society organisations also require the state's strong administrative capacities to function.*

But the many instances of governance innovations that work with market mechanisms or civil society organisations also require the state's strong administrative capacities to function. The personal budget agenda for care services, for example, calls for the extensive involvement of public authorities as regulators and advisors. Although based on market principles, BioBanking relies on its state environmental department to oversee and quantify credits, and is therefore dependent upon the state's development of analytical capacities. The crowdfunding initiatives for broadband Internet connection require more than just a regulatory framework for market activity; they also entail the active involvement of the state as a coordinator. Capacities required for these governance innovations are both the skills and competencies of civil servants, in particular analytical and boundary-spanning skills, but also structural capacities, in particular monitoring and regulatory capacities as exemplified in the RGGI and Mobility Partnerships cases.

As to the third question we set out at the beginning of this chapter pertaining to the innovations' impact on administrative capacities, the governance innovations here cannot be regarded as enhancing them. Some of them fill in the void of lacking administrative capacities; others are state-induced innovations to respond to new governance challenges, but they are not in themselves a means to re-charge administrative capacities. Possibly, this is to be expected from innovations that are motivated by external governance challenges and stress the role of non-state actors and alternative governance mechanisms. At the same time, the strong reliance of these innovations on administrative capacities suggests that there is something missing in the debate on innovations and in public sector innovation policies.

In other words, our analysis of governance innovations calls for a public sector reform policy that takes into account the critical role of the public administration for making governance innovation work. Considering bureaucracy and politics only as barriers to innovation is as unhelpful as it is misleading. Instead we need policies that enhance administrative capacity to steer, facilitate, and coordinate governance innovations–which is something very different than calling for an increasing speed of innovation of the public sector. One entry point for such a policy lies in the skills and competencies of public servants.

Finally, the fourth question we posed at the outset considers how innovations interact with existing governance systems. Our analysis suggests that in particular analytical and coordination skills are in high demand, especially given that many of the cases demonstrate a strong presence of local, community-led projects or at least projects that involved strong community involvement. In line with *The Governance Report 2013*'s findings, this suggests that there is a strong need for a multi-actor, multi-level governance approach to providing solutions to many of today's governance challenges. Indeed, innovations for each topic exemplified a variety of community, market, and state-led solutions and occurred at various levels of governance. This conclusion does not suggest a complete reform of the public sector itself, nor do any of these innovations rival existing governance systems. Many of the challenges addressed in this chapter, such as in areas of welfare and sustainability, are adaptive in nature, and therefore, public sector reform should aim to nurture capacities that allow social innovations to function in a way that mutually supports capacity building and innovation across sectors.

We need policies that enhance administrative capacity to steer, facilitate, and coordinate governance innovations.

In conclusion, our analysis points to the fact that the public sector is more adaptable to change and innovation than it tends to be given credit. Already, the many examples of experimenting with funding mechanisms as well as the coordination and collaboration between sectors suggest a wider momentum toward innovating. The more difficult question to answer is whether innovation is actually improving policy outcomes and levels of public welfare. As most of the cases selected in this chapter are biased toward being fairly recent, it is not possible to make any general assessment as to the overall impact of the innovations. What is clear is that many of the governance challenges they address are not local in nature, and thus, the degree of scalability and replicability is crucial and likely to depend upon a number of conditions, particularly of an administrative capacity nature, required for the implementation of these governance innovations within other contexts.

Endnotes

1   This type of agreement was available even before the BioBanking initiative was launched. By 2005, 182 sites had already been created, demonstrating this model's potential for success (DEC 2006b).

2   Although the US was involved in early stages of the Kyoto Protocol's development following the 1992 United Nations Framework Convention on Climate Change (UNFCCC), President Bush withdrew US endorsement of the Kyoto Protocol in 2001 for economic reasons. Had the US ratified the treaty, it would have been required to reduce its emissions by 7% below 1990 levels between 2008 and 2012. The US approach to climate change has been to develop energy-efficient technology, market-based incentives to encourage the reduction of emissions by companies, and other conservation programs (see Fletcher 2005).

3   The original Memorandum of Understanding was signed in 2005 by seven states (Connecticut, Delaware, Maine, New Hampshire, New Jersey, New York, and Vermont) with Rhode Island, Maryland, and Massachusetts signing in 2007. New Jersey pulled out in 2011.

V. Governance Indicators

Piero Stanig

The field of governance measurement has been developing at a very fast pace over the past decade and a half. As detailed in Stanig and Kayser (2013), there is room for improvement, and the Hertie School Governance Indicators are an attempt in this direction. In particular, the indicator dashboards presented in *The Governance Report 2013* provide a contribution that takes seriously the multi-level and multi-actor nature of governance in a globalised world. In addition, given the distinction between formal institutions, actual administrative behaviour, and outcomes and the difficulties associated with establishing causal connections between them (see Anheier, Stanig, and Kayser 2013; Stanig and Kayser 2013), the indicators presented here try, as much as possible given the constraints one inevitably faces in empirical work, to provide information on all three aspects. This information makes it possible to address empirically many questions about the possible relationship between institutional design, the functioning of bureaucracies, and governance output.

As noted in Lodge and Wegrich's introduction to this Report (Chapter 1), the ranking of countries has received an excessive amount of attention. Ranking countries should not be the priority in empirical work on governance, and ranks in themselves (in particular, but not only, when insufficient attention is given to the margins of error that are naturally associated with any estimates) contain very little information, and much less than the disaggregated information contained in the variables. For this reason, and as described in more detail in Stanig and Kayser (2013), the focus here is more on reporting dashboards, i.e. sets of key indicators related to a broader concept of interest–in this case, governance and administrative capacities–rather than creating yet another aggregate 'governance index'. These dashboards acknowledge the inherent multi-dimensionality of the broad phenomenon of governance.

> *Our dashboards acknowledge the inherent multi-dimensionality of the broad phenomenon of governance.*

Aggregate index estimation assumes that trade-offs between different aspects of governance are clearly understood, and this assumption is in most cases untenable. In substantive terms, ranking countries is not possible in many cases because one country might be good at performing some governance-related tasks well (say, providing primary education) and bad at others (say, regulating utilities); another country might display the opposite pattern. And if we do not have a strong theoretical reason to believe that utility regulation is more important than primary education, or vice versa, it is impossible to decide which of the two countries displays 'better governance'. In the dashboards and sub-dashboards presented here, aggregate indexes are estimated only when they involve medium-range phenomena about whose definition there is sufficient agreement in the literature.

The disaggregated strategy gives a more nuanced picture of the state of governance, and makes it possible to highlight interesting patterns and developments that aggregation might mask. In other words, an index at a high-level of aggregation is very likely to yield results that are far from original or novel: on average, the 'usual suspects'–developed, high-income, democratic countries located in Western Europe, North America, and East Asia– are going to receive higher scores, and, similarly, less developed countries are going to receive lower scores. For this purpose, there would be no need to engage in yet another empirical effort related to governance: any aggregate index would probably correlate quite strongly with existing indicators of governance and prosperity, for instance the World Governance Indicators or the Human Development Index, thereby missing several somewhat surprising patterns that emerge in terms of countries and regions that display quite good performance on at least some dimensions.

Furthermore, there are different purposes of a governance measure, each permitting and possibly requiring different combinations of components. The estimates of individual aspects in the dashboard can be used to assess, at a glance, the comparative performance of different countries in each aspect, and can also be used as inputs, if needed, in the construction of indexes that are more aggregated than the ones we present.

Creating a dashboard of indicators of administrative capacity is not an easy task. In particular, two main problems face the researcher. The first problem is related to the fact that, to a certain extent, the conceptual framework introduced in this Report requires a combination of both a more direct analysis of how governments draw on administrative capacities in responding to governance challenges and the development and analysis of high-level indicators. While the first perspective allows a description of how administrative capacities work in practice, indicators are required to engage in large-scale comparisons.

The second problem has to do with the complex interconnections between institutions (de jure), their actual functioning (de facto), and the outcomes of bureaucratic performance. As pointed out in Chapter 2, the fact that a country has a certain legal provision (that, for instance, prevents regulators from getting a job in the industry they regulate) does not say much about whether that provision is actually respected: in low-enforcement settings, formal institutions can be poor predictors of actual administrative behaviour. In addition, regulation might be of poor quality even if the provisions that prevent revolving-door phenomena are de facto enforced: there are many ways in which regulators can 'shirk' that are unrelated to revolving doors. And poorly designed regulation might be counterproductive regardless of the probity and effort of the agents in charge of its implementation. Conversely, there might be functional substitutes for a given institution: a country might not have independent regulatory agencies, but, using some other device (say, the public-spiritedness of the regulators themselves, or an active civil society that keeps them under control), it might be able to achieve good regulatory outcomes. We address this problem as well as possible within the framework adopted in this report.

At the same time, it has to be recognized that in order to gain greater leverage on the issue of the interconnection between formal institutions, policy implementation, and policy outcomes, the focus on administrative capacities can and should be further developed and combined with approaches that incorporate also policy discretion and bureaucratic autonomy (Huber and Shipan 2002; Huber and McCarty 2004; Fukuyama 2013) as important moving parts in the framework. The framework should also make it possible to understand which characteristics of a given administrative apparatus might act as substitutes, for instance, for the traditional 'Weberian' characteristics. These concerns should inform the future development of the Governance Report indicators.

Unlike the dashboards presented in *The Governance Report 2013* (Anheier, Stanig, and Kayser 2013), the collection of indicators presented in this edition focuses exclusively on the national level, following the approach of the rest of the Report. Some of the indicators presented in the 2013 National Governance Dashboard are updated with newly-released data, and many other indicators and medium-range aggregate indexes that follow the quadripartite taxonomy of administrative capacities proposed by Wegrich and Lodge in Chapter 2 have been added. The next section describes the key components of this year's Administrative Capacity Dashboard and is followed by a sampling of the kinds of analyses that can be conducted using the data assembled therein. We refer the reader to the Governance Report website (www.governancereport.org) for the complete data, additional information (including estimates of the indexes using a more complicated methodology), more technical details, methodological notes, and variable lists.

To my knowledge, the data presented in this Report comprise the most comprehensive 'snapshot' collection on administrative capacities available. At this stage, due to data limitations beyond my control, it is not possible to produce time-series data, with the exception of the updates of some of the indexes presented in last year's edition. Thus, the indicators provide a record of bureaucratic capacity as of the time of writing.

The Dashboard: Four Administrative Capacities

As detailed in Chapter 2, one possible way to analyse governance, in its meaning of bureaucratic capacity, is to classify administrative activity, and therefore administrative capacities, in one of four categories. These are delivery capacity, regulatory capacity, coordination capacity, and analytical capacity (see Figure 5.1). As it becomes apparent when discussing actual indicators and specific variables, it is often difficult to allocate a given phenomenon to one (and only one) of the categories defined by the taxonomy. This said, in order to be consistent with the approach adopted in the rest of this Report, the classification proposed in Chapter 2 is followed as closely as possible.

For the purpose of measurement and in order to organise the material, some simple working definitions of the capacities were adopted. Clearly, these are not meant to be substitutes for the conceptual framework introduced in the remainder of the volume, but they illustrate, informally, the guidelines along which the data collection and data analysis were organised.

Thus, **delivery capacity** relates to the execution and management of policy requirements 'at the frontline'. In other words, delivery capacity is related to the direct provision of services by the government apparatus. A government has delivery capacity if it can provide, at a minimum, those goods and services that would be undersupplied if their production were left to private agents. These include goods and services that involve positive externalities (e.g. education), services whose provision requires the use of coercion (e.g. crime control and contract enforcement), pure public goods (e.g. transportation infrastructure), and other 'frontline' services (e.g. revenue collection).

Regulatory capacity relates to the provision of 'oversight over heterogeneous private and public organisations' (see Table 2.2). In other words, regulatory capacity involves primarily the government's use of its coercive powers to limit the autonomy of private agents and induce them to choose some course of action. Many of the activities that can be performed as part of the regulatory tasks of the government, and that require regulatory capacity to be performed, are attempts to solve market failures, but some of them might simply aim at achieving outcomes also in cases in which a market failure is not present. Regulation, in fact, need not be welfare-improving, and one can think of many types of regulation that benefit special interests while causing a net damage to society overall.

Coordination capacity is 'the capacity to mediate between and bring together dispersed actors to achieve joint action' (see Table 2.2). In other words, coordination capacity is related to the ability of a government to align its various branches in order to design and implement policy coherently. Individual agencies might act in ways that are inconsistent with the main policy objectives that the administration has set for itself. Coordination prevents opportunistic behaviour on the part of agencies. The government, as an organisation, must be able to monitor whether or not its branches are engaging in self-serving behaviour and prevent conflicts or disagreements that lead to disjointed policy design and implementation. Lack of coordination capacity implies that conflicts between ministries and within specific agencies limit the ability of the government to act effectively and that incoherent policies are developed and executed. For instance, lack of coordination might have the consequence of a plethora of rules and regulations, or requirements and procedures, that burden citizens.

Finally, in the framework outlined in Chapter 2, **analytical capacity** is related to the provision of 'intelligence' and advice in conditions of uncertainty. In other words, analytical capacity has to do with the ability of the government to mobilise resources to generate ideas and insights in order to address challenges. In particular, governance innovation, as argued in Chapter 4 and in Anheier and Korreck (2013), requires that new ideas and solutions to new challenges are proposed. The resources to generate policy and governance ideas can be located within the government itself, or might be non-governmental resources, in terms of a vibrant marketplace of ideas from which the government can draw. The dashboard tries to measure both aspects.

Whenever possible, multiple measures of the capacities, from different angles, are provided. In particular, we try to link the existence (de jure and de facto) of specific institutional provisions to observable consequences of that capacity. So, for instance, measures of the impartiality and autonomy of regulators, as codified in the law and as perceived by experts, are provided alongside measures of outcomes of the regulatory activities in which the government engages. The outcome-based measures provide information that can be interpreted from two different points of view. On a first, more basic level, they tell us about bureaucratic *performance* rather than bureaucratic *capacity*. Knowing about performance is interesting in itself, from a scientific and policy-evaluation point of view. For instance, one can use the outcomes-based indexes presented here as dependent variables in regression models to look at how variation in some country-specific characteristic predicts variation in outcomes. Along the same lines, later in this chapter, we look at how variation in our measures of institutions predicts variation in outcomes.

Nevertheless, at a deeper level, the outcome-based measures can (and should) be considered as indirect measures of capacity itself. This is the main reason why they are included here. Namely, good outcomes (for instance, good test scores in the PISA data) reflect the underlying (and not necessarily directly observable) presence of capacity within an administration (in this example, delivery capacity in the field of public education). Hence, it is reasonable to use quality of outcomes to infer capacity. Still there are reasons why one can doubt that outcomes of the same quality reflect the same level

Figure 5.1 **Administrative capacity dashboard overview**

Delivery Capacity

Effectiveness/Effectiveness+

Effectiveness

Bureaucratic professionalism

Bureaucratic impartiality

Researchers in government

Statistical capacity

Effectiveness+

Bureaucratic professionalism

Bureaucratic impartiality

Researchers in government

Statistical capacity

Meritocracy in public sector (3 indicators)

Outcomes

Education

Expenditures on education

Teacher salaries

PISA (2 indicators)

Enrolment (11 indicators)

Education quality (4 indicators)

Crime

Crime control (10 indicators)

Criminal justice (7 indicators)

Security (3 indicators)

Civil Justice Provision

Civil justice (15 indicators)

Revenue Collection

Taxes as % of GDP

Efficiency of tax administration (4 indicators)

Other Public Services

E-Government

Environment & sanitation (6 indicators)

Healthcare (2 indicators)

Infrastructure (3 indicators)

Legitimacy

Legitimacy

Regulatory Capacity

Impartiality/Autonomy

Impartiality

Impartial application & enforcement

Due process in administrative proceedings

Anti-revolving door, judges (2 indicators)

Anti-revolving door, civil servants (2 indicators)

Corrupt officials termination (2 indicators)

Central Bank Independence

Independence

Governor turnover rate

Expert opinion

Quality

Quality

Regulation, effective enforcement

Prompt proceedings

Regulatory Quality Index

Investor protection (4 indicators)

Time spent for regulation

Regulation is obstacle

Environmental protection (4 indicators)

Regulatory Outcomes

Price Regulation

Energy prices (3 indicators)

Telephone prices (5 indicators)

Broadband internet prices

Medicine prices (2 indicators)

Shadow economy

Size

Environment

Forest loss

Overfishing

Particulate matter

CO_2 emissions

Inflation

Inflation rate (2 indicators)

Coordination Capacity

Self-Monitoring

Monitoring

Nongovernmental checks

State-owned enterprises oversight

ACA (10 indicators)

Whistle-blowing protection

Conflict of interest law

Freedom of information law

Anti-corruption strategy

Independent police monitoring (2 indicators)

Coordination Quality

Quality

Coordination between ministries

Coordination within administrations

Coherence of public policies

Divisions within state apparatus

Outcomes

Business Procedures

Starting a business (3 indicators)

Construction permits

Electricity connection

Property registration

Export

Import

Analytical Capacity

Efficacy/Efficacy⁺

Efficacy

Economic departments (2 indicators)

Research funding (2 indicators)

Number of policy schools

Number of researchers (2 indicators)

Think tanks (5 indicators)

Efficacy⁺

Economic departments (2 indicators)

Research funding (2 indicators)

Number of policy schools

Number of researchers (2 indicators)

Think tanks (7 indicators)

Analytical Capacity

Expert Evaluations

Policy adaptation

Policy evaluation

Long-term strategic vision

Stakeholder coordination

Vision for human capital

Vision for territorial planning

Vision for environment protection

Vision for international integration

of underlying capacity. Some further considerations about the relationship between administrative capacities and outcomes are discussed in the conclusion to this chapter.

Thus, the Administrative Capacity Dashboard (see Figure 5.1) consists of four sub-dashboards, i.e. one for each capacity, with raw indicators and some thematic indexes and sub-indexes that are based on weighted averages of the standardised values of the raw scores.[1] Since indicators that draw from multiple sources are more precise in statistical terms, all else being equal (including the quality or signal-to-noise ratio of the indicators), the dashboard is composed of different types of data taken from different organisations and data providers, whenever possible. The very few exceptions are noted.[2]

Delivery capacity

Under the header of delivery capacity, we group some indicators that capture the ability of the administrative apparatus to directly deliver services to the governed, as shown in Figure 5.1. These variables can be subdivided in three groups: one on the overall Weberian nature of the bureaucratic apparatus; a second on outcomes of service provision in different policy fields; and a third on citizen evaluations of the quality of service delivery (what is called 'legitimacy' in Anheier, Stanig, and Kayser 2013).

The first group of variables focuses on the **effectiveness** of state administration, that is, its capacity to implement the strategies, policies and measures formulated by those charged to do so, with legitimate means yielding desired results (Anheier 2013: 27). The collection is aggregated into two indexes, effectiveness and effectiveness+. The effectiveness index, introduced in the first edition of the Governance Report (Anheier, Stanig, and Kayser 2013), relies on measures of the professionalism and impartiality of the bureaucracy (Teorell, Dahlström, and Dahlberg 2011), the presence of expertise in the administrative apparatus, and statistical capacity (The World Bank 2013), all elements considered essential for consistent, impersonal, and predictable implementation.[3] The effectiveness+ index adds information about the careers of bureaucrats and civil servants drawn from the Institutional Profiles Database, or IPD (CEPII 2012).

The **outcomes** part is comprised of a quite large set of variables that cover most of the main tasks that are entrusted for delivery to public administrations. These variables are aggregated in five thematic sub-indexes: quality and coverage of education provision; crime control; civil justice and contract enforcement; revenue collection[4]; and a residual category for other types of service provision, which includes a broad set of phenomena ranging from e-government to basic healthcare and sanitation, to public transportation and infrastructure. The sources used include UNESCO, the PISA project

(OECD), the World Justice Project (Agrast et al. 2012-2013), the above-mentioned IPD, the World Bank's Doing Business data, Enterprise Surveys, and Development Indicators, the WHO Global Health Observatory Data Repository, Eurostat, the Environmental Performance Index (EPI) (Emerson et al. 2012), and the World Values Survey.

Finally, the **legitimacy** indicator, which reflects the population's trust in the administration's capacity to deliver, is based on an array of cross-national surveys and aggregates individual responses to self-reported confidence in the police, the civil service, and the public education system. The most recently available information from the survey collection was used. See the Methodological Notes (Stanig forthcoming; available at www.governancereport.org) for a detailed list of sources.

Regulatory capacity

The regulatory capacity indicators are similarly grouped under three sub-dashboards, as depicted in Figure 5.1. The first includes measures of the impartiality and autonomy of regulators, the second looks at the quality of regulation, while the third focuses on some important regulatory outcomes.

The first group of variables under the regulatory capacity header addresses the **impartiality and autonomy** of regulators, which should ensure the credibility and stability of regulation. They combine information on de jure provisions and de facto implementation that promote effective regulation from expert surveys (Global Integrity and the World Justice Project) covering legal provisions that guarantee impartiality in regulatory activities and autonomy of regulators from special interest and political pressure. It is worth noting that 'autonomy' is used here in a narrow sense. Bureaucratic autonomy, meant as either delegation of decision-making discretion (Huber and Shipan 2002) or as the ability of an agency to set and pursue its own policy goals (Carpenter 2001), is a more complicated concept than what we measure here. By autonomy, we mean that regulators are not improperly influenced, due process is respected, and provisions exist that prevent corruption and regulatory capture. As suggested in Chapter 2 and discussed in Stanig and Kayser (2013), regulatory capture and phenomena like the 'revolving doors' are a very serious challenge to the capacity of the government to regulate private activity to correct market failures.

Also included under the heading of impartiality is information about central bank independence: the discretion allocated to central banks is probably the most important instance of delegation of policy-making to an agency staffed and directed by personnel recruited with meritocratic criteria. We rely here on some of the available indexes (Fry 2000; Crowe and Meade 2007), as well as an item from the Institutional Profiles Database about central bank independence.

The second sub-dashboard tries to capture the **quality of regulation**. By combining measures of regulatory quality from different sources, and for different policy areas, any aggregate of these measures should provide a picture of regulation that is not by construction tilted in favour of or against regulation. Thus, to depict the general quality of the regulatory framework, the sub-dashboard draws data from the World Justice Project (whether regulations are effectively enforced and whether administrative proceedings are conducted without delay) and the regulatory quality index from the World Governance Indicators project (Kaufmann, Kraay, and Mastruzzi 2010). Looking then more specifically at economic regulation, we rely on some items from Doing Business about the stringency of investor protection rules, and country-wide averages of two items in the Enterprise Surveys, i.e. the time spent by firms dealing with regulators and the perception that regulation is an obstacle to business. Ideally, regulation should affect individual behaviour and correct market failures, but it is not desirable for it to lead to an inefficient use of resources (time spent by firms to comply with regulation) or to create undue obstacles to private activity. Hence, more time spent dealing with regulation, holding the stringency of regulation fixed, is an indication of poorly designed regulation. Similarly, holding the amount (or stringency) of regulation constant, better regulation creates fewer obstacles to private activity, hence more obstacles indicate a lower quality of regulation. Finally, to measure the quality of environmental regulation, we use data assembled by the Environmental Performance Index (EPI) project on quality of regulation regarding pesticides, marine protection, biome protection, and critical habitat protection.

The capacity to perform a task can be inferred from the quality of the outcomes. For regulatory capacity, the **regulatory outcomes** sub-dashboard includes variables that capture several different phenomena for different policy fields and reflect the extent to which an administration is able to use regulation to achieve desirable outcomes. The first set of indicators is composed of utilities prices drawn from various sources, including the World Development Indicators, Eurostat, and international and nation-specific sources. Also included in this category are the consumer prices for generic medicines in relation to their international price, from data reported by the WHO.[5] The second set of indicators is the size of the shadow economy as a share of GDP, which captures the capacity of the government to prevent economic activity from escaping its reach and avoiding being regulated and taxed (Schneider, Buehn, and Montenegro 2010; Schneider 2013) While doubts about the validity of shadow economy estimates in general have been raised (Breusch 2005; see also Stanig and Kayser 2013), these estimates are commonly recognised as useful approximations that capture the ability of the government to tax and regulate economic activity. The third set of variables measures pollution levels and environmental degradation, based on the data published by EPI.

Finally, the last phenomenon that enters the regulatory outcomes sub-dashboard is the inflation rate. In particular, we include two variables: one is simply the inflation rate, the second is the inflation rate adjusted by subtracting the regional mean, so that countries are evaluated to effectively control inflation when they are able to keep inflation below the level of other countries in their region.[6] The inflation level captures (by proxy) the ability of the government, through independent economic regulators such as central banks, to effectively regulate economic activity. While inflation in itself is not a 'regulatory' outcome, a poorly-managed monetary policy indicates that either the central bank is subjugated to political will, or it has little capacity. This lack of capacity might affect both the quality and soundness of its monetary policy, but also the quality of its oversight of economic activity in general (on the role of central banks as regulators of the financial and banking system, see Goodhart 2005).

Coordination capacity

It is quite hard to address empirically a complex, and somewhat protean, concept like coordination capacity. In particular, as argued in Chapter 2, coordination capacity is not synonymous with the institutional provisions that might promote it. For this reason, the coordination capacity sub-dashboard tries to provide a limited, but informative, portrait of some aspects of governance related to the existence of coordination capacity. It does so by including measures at three levels (see Figure 5.1): measures that capture the formal existence of certain institutional provisions; those that capture the extent of coordination within the government apparatus; and those that try to detect lack of coordination from the outcomes of administrative activity.

The first set of measures capture the institutional infrastructure required to promote the **'self-monitoring' capacity** of a government apparatus. Does an administration put in place provisions that guarantee the oversight of its various branches? The task involves creating ex ante mechanisms to prevent conflict of interest and regulatory capture and setting up 'police patrol' and 'fire alarm' oversight mechanisms (McCubbins and Schwartz 1984). Such ex-ante mechanisms include legislation that regulates potential conflict of interest and financial disclosure requirements. Police patrol oversight involves surveillance of administrative activities 'with the aim of detecting and remedying any violations' and 'by its surveillance, discouraging such violations' (McCubbins and Schwartz 1984: 166). Fire alarm oversight, on the other hand, entails the establishment of 'a system of rules, procedures, and informal practices that enable individual citizens and organized interest groups to examine administrative decisions' and possibly challenge them. Among the fire alarm oversight mechanisms, one can ask, for instance, whether legal provisions exist to protect whistle-blowers, and whether there exists an independent commission that investigates civilian claims about police misconduct. As for the police patrol mechanisms, one can also ask whether there are specialised anti-corruption prosecutors, what their budgets are, and how many prosecutors they have.

The information we use comes from the World Justice Project, the Global Integrity Report, and the Anti-Corruption Authorities (ACAs) diagnostic survey, developed by a World Bank team, which gathers basic, factual information on each anti-corruption agency and its institutional setup. It is worth noting that some of these institutional provisions (in particular, independent anti-corruption agencies) are more common in countries that might have experienced more corruption incidents in the recent past. Hence several advanced countries (that tend to have lower corruption incidence) score lower than some developing countries (that tend to experience higher levels of corruption).

The conceptual scope of this 'self-monitoring' capacity is admittedly narrower than the concept of coordination as outlined in Chapter 2. These institutional provisions are put in place to prevent the most blatant instances of 'runaway' agencies pursuing goals that are against the law. Coordination capacity, on the other hand, involves also the ability to induce various agencies, that might be operating within their legally-allocated ranges of discretion, to pursue policy implementation in a coherent (and, indeed, coordinated) way.

The second sub-dashboard uses evaluations of **coordination quality** as found in the IPD project. In this case, the measures address directly the concept of coordination capacity along the lines discussed in Chapter 2. While these measures of coordination are relatively coarse, they make it possible to carry out comparisons among the existence of formal provisions, outputs, and perceived degree of coordination and collaboration, following the model briefly described above. Specifically, the coordination variables include four items in the IPD project about the degree of coordination between ministries and within administrations, the overall coherence of public policies, and whether the capacity of public authorities is hampered by divisions within the state apparatus. Given that all these variables come from a single source, one should exercise some caution when using the aggregated indicator.

The last sub-dashboard looks at the output side of coordination: again, we try to address the lack of coordination within an administration by measuring its consequences (**coordination outcomes**). In particular, relying on data collected by the Doing Business project, the European Commission, and surveys of entrepreneurs, we can estimate the extent to which lack of coordination manifests itself. One of the observable consequences of lack of coordination (under the condition of 'overlap', see Chapter 2) is the accumulation of administrative procedures that burden citizens and, in particular, those who more often need to deal with the administration, namely entrepreneurs. Governments with non-coordinated agencies are unable to implement more efficient ways to interact with private sector agents (by, for instance, introducing simplified procedures and 'one-stop shops' to start a business). For this reason, the number of procedures or documents required in order to start a business, obtain a construction permit, register property, or engage in international trade are informative about the amount of coordination capacity on which a government can draw.

Analytical capacity

Analytical capacity is measured here first in terms of **efficacy**, i.e. the capacity to find solutions to problems that have been identified (Anheier 2013: 26). The efficacy sub-dashboard (see Figure 5.1), introduced already in *The Governance Report 2013* (Anheier, Stanig, and Kayser 2013), relies on a set of empirical observables related to the existence and quality of an active marketplace of ideas for policy-making and experimentation on which public administration can draw. Thus, the original set, indicated in Figure 5.1 under 'efficacy', includes variables that measure the ranking of academic departments of economics[7], research funding, the presence of graduate policy programmes, and the number and quality of think tanks. All the values used for this year's edition are updated with the most recent data, with the exception of the graduate policy programmes information. Note that we do not assume (or believe) that these think tanks provide unbiased information to governments. Indeed, many of the most prominent in many countries are linked to political parties or support specific views or ideologies. Still, a vibrant think tanks scene might improve the analytical capacity of a government because their existence leads to a fact-based debate on policy alternatives, and factual information is released as a *by-product* of the policy debate. New variables related to think tanks, namely, an item from the Institutional Profiles Database (IPD) on the existence of public or private think tanks and an additional measure of think tank vibrancy based on rankings of think tanks in specific policy areas (McGann 2013), are included in the efficacy+ sub-dashboard, which is used for the analysis later in the chapter.

The efficacy measures are complemented by a set of variables from IPD that examine **analytical capacity within public administration**. In particular, we include information about authorities' capacity to adapt policies to changes in economic and social contexts, whether policy evaluation is a common practice, whether authorities act in line with a long-term vision, and whether the government does have a vision or not in a host of policy fields.

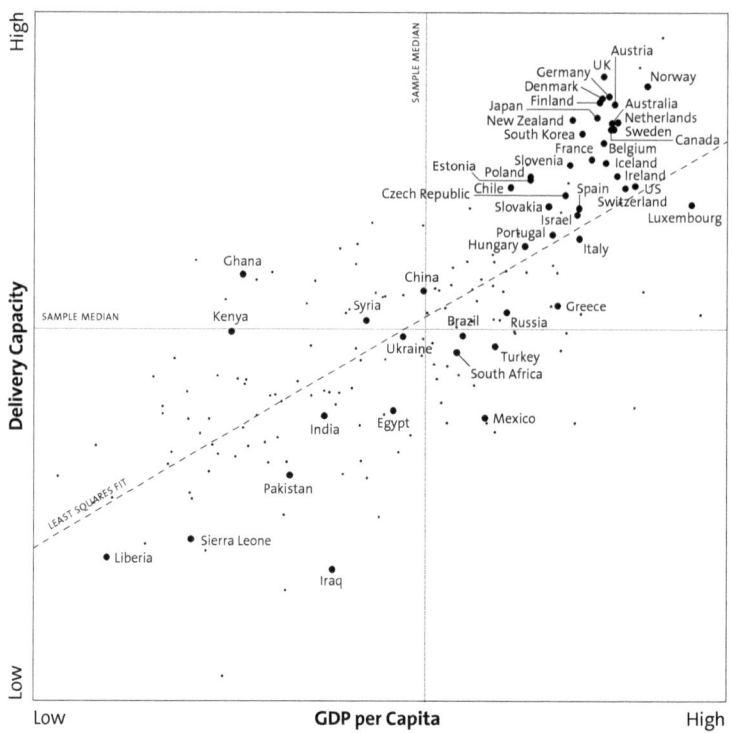

Figure 5.2a–d **Administrative capacities and GDP per capita**

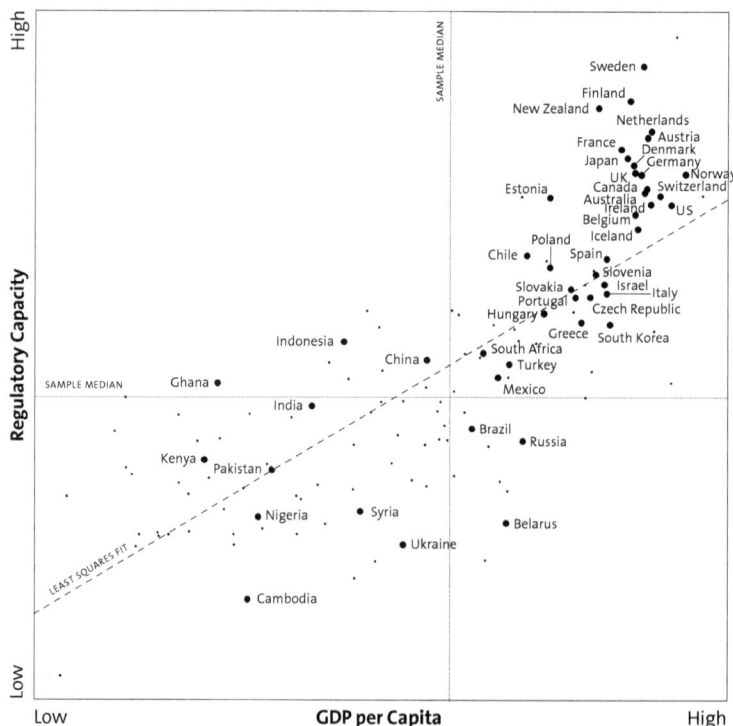

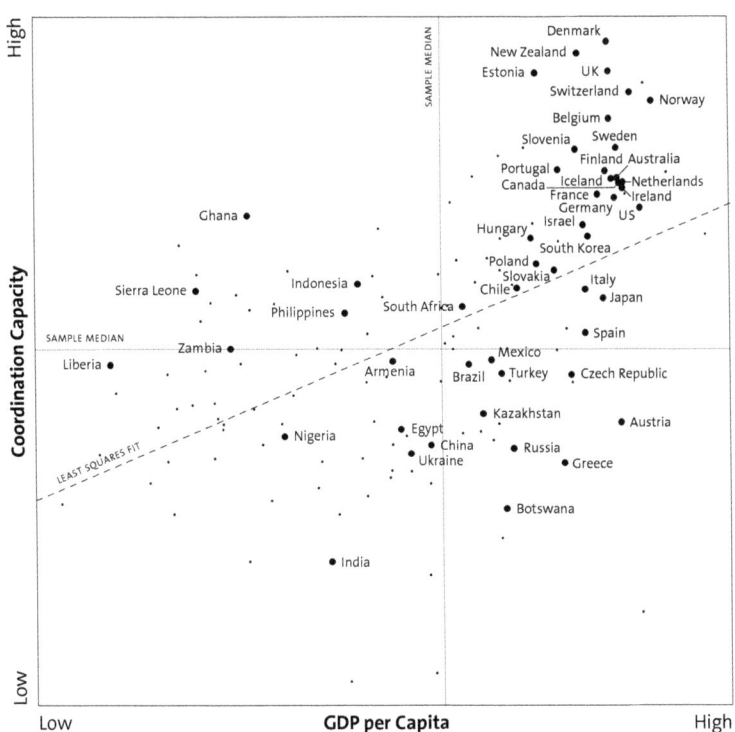

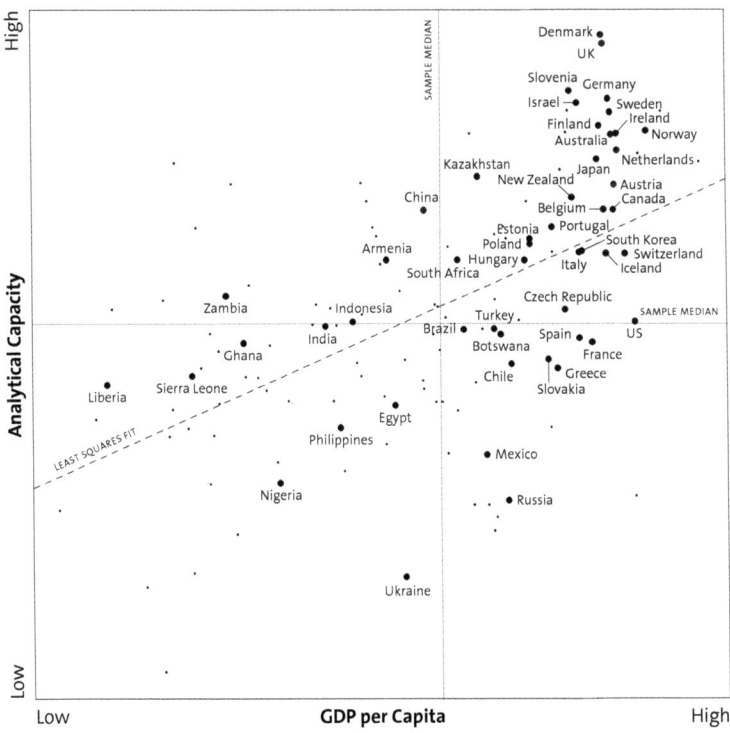

Administrative Capacities: Patterns and Relationships

Having described in some detail our contribution to the systematic measurement of the four administrative capacities, including the measures, their sources, and their relevance, we now turn to a brief overview of several of the interesting patterns we have found in the data. We deliberately do not report tables with countries sorted by their scores. These tend to distract from the main purpose of a project of this type, which is to make it possible to detect empirical regularities and also notice noteworthy outliers whose administrative and bureaucratic structure might be worth investigating in detail.

The four plots in Figure 5.2 (a-d) show the relationship between level of development (measured as GDP per capita) and the aggregated measures for the four administrative capacities. There is a clear positive association between administrative capacities and development. Indeed, most OECD countries are located in the top right quadrant for all four capacities. Yet, there are some notable exceptions: Turkey and Mexico, for example, score below the median in three cases out of four. Some other OECD countries have lower than expected performance for specific capacities: Greece, the Czech Republic, and Austria[8] in coordination capacity; Spain, France, Slovakia, Chile, and Greece in analytical capacity. It is also worth noting how some non-OECD emerging economies display performances comparable, when not superior, to those of OECD countries: for instance, South Africa performs above the median in coordination, regulatory, and analytical capacity, China in delivery, regulatory, and analytical capacity, and Russia in delivery capacity.

Weberian structures and their relationship with delivery capacity

Is the Weberianness of a given state apparatus, i.e. its professionalism and impartiality, related to its ability to deliver services to the population? Is a Weberian bureaucracy a necessary prerequisite of delivery capacity? Can some countries deliver services in the absence of what are often considered necessary requirements for effective administrative performance? Based on the indicators presented here, one can give some empirical answers to these questions. Though it is impossible to give causal answers to these questions using data like those presented in the indicators dashboards, the correlational evidence can make it possible to gain significant analytical traction in this setting.

The plot in Figure 5.3 displays on the vertical axis the aggregated scores of the delivery outcomes and on the horizontal axis the scores on the aggregated sub-index of effectiveness+ ('Weberianness'). Countries located in the top right quadrant have high effectiveness and good performance in terms of delivery-related outcomes, while countries located in the bottom left quadrant have low effectiveness and poor outcomes. As Figure 5.3 shows, first of all, institutions predict outcomes: the quadrants with high effectiveness and poor outcomes and with low effectiveness and good outcomes are less populated than the other two quadrants. Yet, there is a non-negligible set of countries that display outcomes that are significantly better (or worse) than one would expect based on their level of effectiveness (or 'Weberianness').

This information cannot be used to infer that one factor has a causal effect on the other. Indeed, while the positive relationship between a Weberian state apparatus and good outcomes is an empirical regularity, it is not an iron law: some countries perform much better than one would expect based on their institutional characteristics, and some much worse. Compare, for example, the case of two countries, India and Singapore, that receive

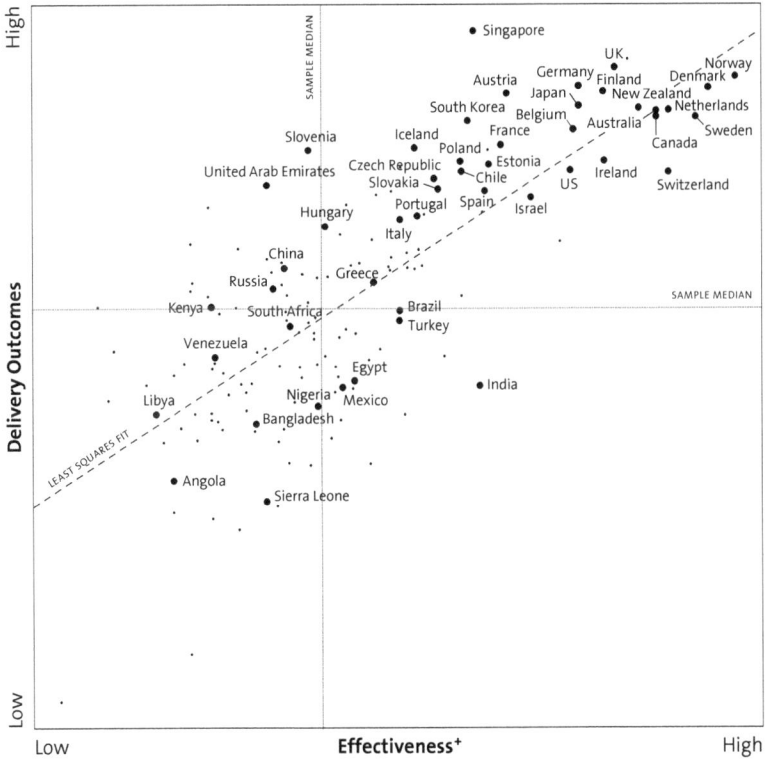

Figure 5.3 **Delivery outcomes and effectiveness+ ('Weberianness')**

approximately the same score on the effectiveness+ index. In terms of outcomes, Singapore is the best performing country, while India's performance is much worse than one would expect based on its effectiveness+ score. In fact, India performs below the overall average on each of the delivery outcomes sub-dimensions. But its effectiveness+ score is high, thanks to high scores in professionalism, statistical capacity, and impartial selection of senior officials, and a slightly below average impartiality score. Singapore ranks somewhat above average for the number of government employees with advanced degrees, and quite high in terms of career advancement in the public administration.

The case of China might also be of interest, as it is a mild outlier: its effectiveness+ score is somewhat below average, while its performance is

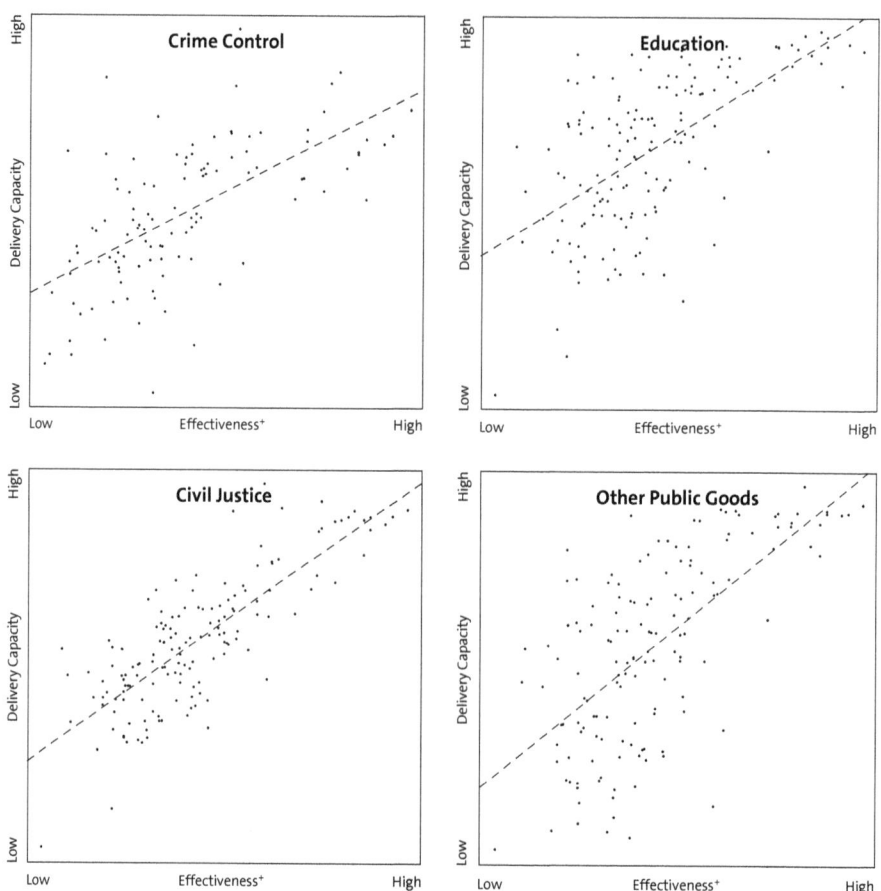

Figure 5.4 **Delivery capacity, disaggregated by policy field, and effectiveness+ ('Weberianness')**

somewhat above average. In detail, the data indicate that China is somewhat better than average on all the delivery outcomes sub-dimensions, with the important exception of civil justice delivery, where it scores a bit below average. At the same time China scores quite low both in the impartiality score and in the career advancement variables; in addition, its statistical capacity score (unlike India's) is just slightly above average.

The small plots in Figure 5.4 display the relationship between effectiveness (the effectiveness+ score) and the delivery outcomes scores for four of the policy areas we examined, namely public education, crime control, civil justice, and other public goods. The main message one can draw from the data is that there is a positive relationship between effectiveness+ and delivery outcomes even when looking at the indexes disaggregated by policy field. However, there is some variation in how tight the relationship is. This might imply that a Weberian bureaucracy might be more useful in some policy areas, such as education and civil justice, than others.

In addition, while one can conclude that having a Weberian structure might help improve delivery outcomes, a Weberian bureaucracy is–to some extent unsurprisingly–neither a sufficient nor a necessary condition for delivery capacity. Clearly, other factors are also involved.

Impartiality and autonomy of regulators, regulatory quality, and regulatory outcomes

It is generally accepted that in order to be effective, regulatory agents within the government have to enjoy autonomy from external interference and act based on criteria of impartiality. The data included in the regulatory capacity sub-dashboard allows us to examine various questions. The first set of questions has to do with which countries seem to display more impartiality and autonomy and higher regulatory quality. The second set of questions explores the relationship between institutional and 'throughput' characteristics and outcomes.

The plot in Figure 5.5 displays the aggregated sub-index of regulatory quality, i.e. measures of effective enforcement and of the absence of delays and excessive burdens on the regulated agents, on the vertical axis and that of impartiality on the horizontal axis. At first glance, impartiality and quality seem to go together: the quadrants with high impartiality and low quality and with low impartiality and high quality are essentially empty. Needless to say, this information cannot be used to infer that one factor has a causal effect on the other. Among the countries that perform best on these indicators are the 'usual suspects', countries that also usually score towards the top in other governance indicators: New Zealand, the Scandinavian countries, the two Asian city-states, and the United Kingdom. Similarly, towards the bottom are Somalia, Liberia, and Cambodia.

One interesting outlier is Ireland, whose regulatory quality is much higher than one would expect based on its level of impartiality. Ireland's score of impartiality and autonomy is quite low due to the absence of mechanisms to prevent 'revolving door' phenomena involving judges and civil servants and lack of provisions to exclude from office public servants convicted of corruption. India and Argentina, among others, score much lower on regulatory quality than one would expect given their impartiality and autonomy scores. India scores low especially because of the relatively poor quality of environmental regulation and because of the general assessment regarding effective enforcement and unreasonable delay; Argentina because of a low score on the corporate director liability index and because of the relatively high amount of time spent by firms to deal with regulation. Malaysia, with an impartiality and autonomy score similar to that of India and Argentina, scores well above average in terms of regulatory quality, in particular because of its very high scores on investor protection and on some of the environmental protection variables.

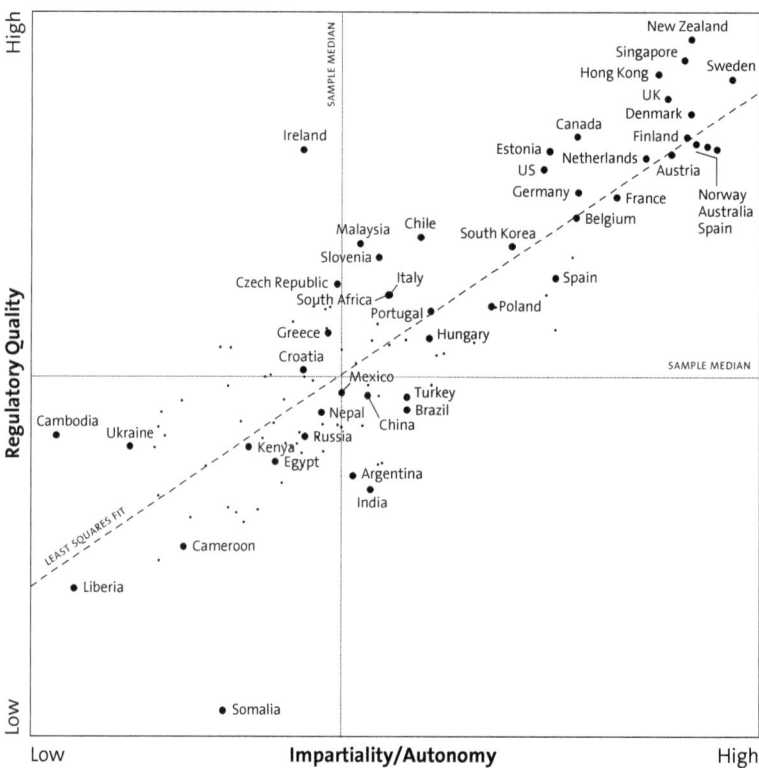

Figure 5.5 **Regulatory quality and impartiality/autonomy**

Figure 5.6 displays the relationship between regulatory outcomes on the vertical axis and impartiality and autonomy on the horizontal axis. Countries located in the top right quadrant have high impartiality and good outcomes, while countries located in the bottom left quadrant have low impartiality and relatively poor outcomes. As shown here, the relationship between impartiality and the outcomes-based measure of regulatory capacity is positive, and the relationship is relatively tight, but there are some exceptions. In particular, Botswana (usually considered an example of best practice in sub-Saharan Africa), Uruguay, and Georgia[9] have lower regulatory capacity, as estimated from outcome data, than one would expect based on measures of impartiality. On the other hand, two emerging economies, China and Indonesia, along with some advanced countries like Ireland, the Czech Republic, and to a lesser extent Italy, display a better performance in terms of regulatory outcomes than one would expect based on the impartiality and independence of their regulators.

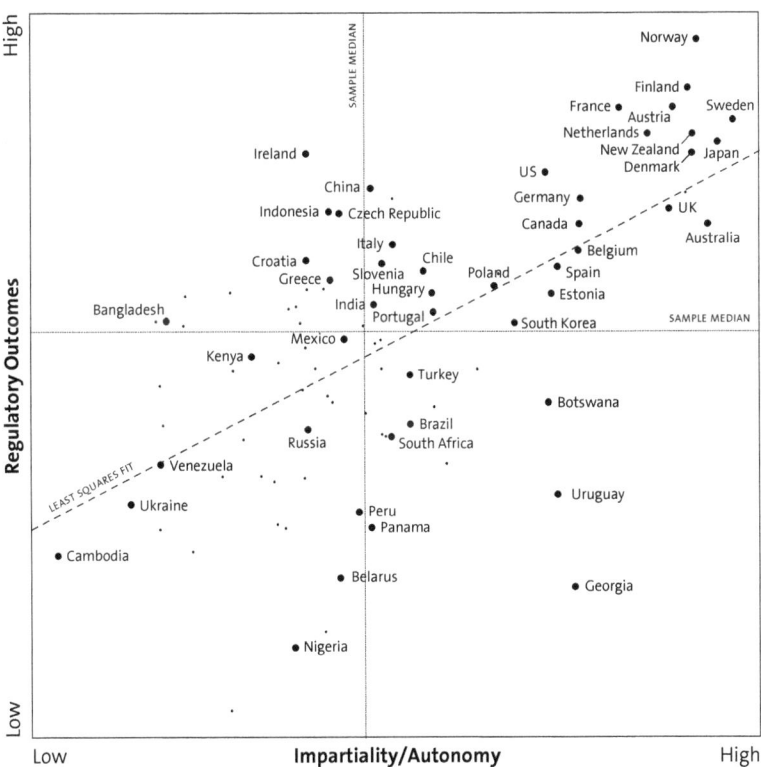

Figure 5.6 **Regulatory outcomes and impartiality/autonomy**

As shown in Figure 5.7, the same tight positive association holds in the case of regulatory quality and regulatory outcomes. One of the countries with greatest discrepancy between outcomes and regulatory quality is Switzerland. In fact, Switzerland has the highest score in regulatory outcomes, but its regulatory quality index is just above the median. The reason for this is that Switzerland scores quite low on the measures relating to investor protection: disclosure requirements are extremely low, shareholder lawsuits are not easy to initiate and carry out, and overall investor protection is very weak. Otherwise, Switzerland scores well on environmental regulation and on overall regulatory quality. That Switzerland does not consider financial transparency a priority does not come as a surprise.[10]

It is interesting to notice how China's regulatory outcomes are, like in the case of delivery, better than one would expect based on evaluation of its (formal) regulation quality. In fact, China scores quite low on all the regulatory quality variables, with the exception of financial disclosure. On the other hand, its regulatory outcomes rival those of several advanced Western

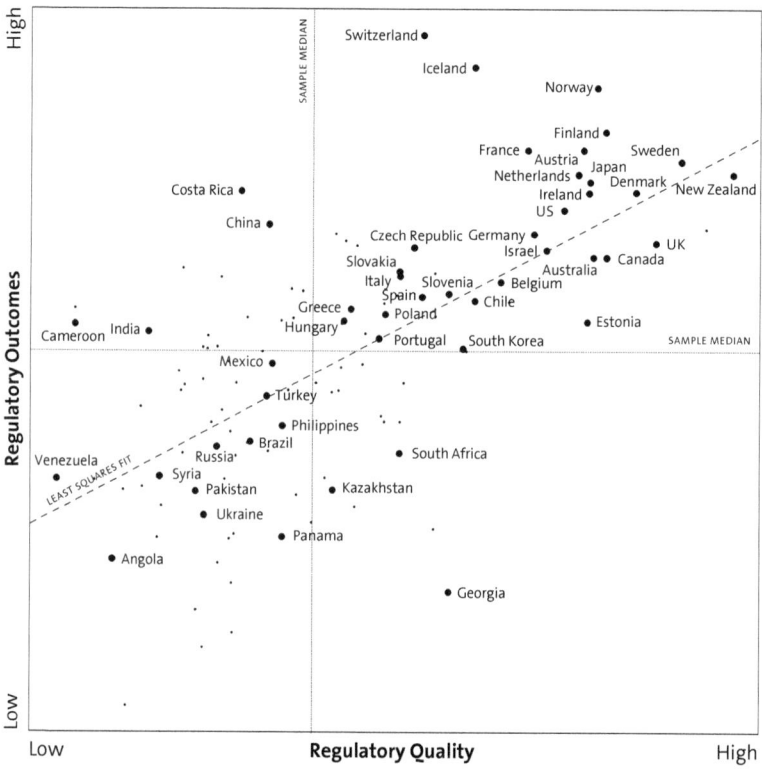

Figure 5.7 **Regulatory outcomes and regulatory quality**

countries that tend to score high on regulatory quality, including Germany, the UK, and the US. In particular, China seems to be good at preventing economic activity from escaping its reach: the size of the shadow economy is estimated to be quite small. In addition, China displays good performance when controlling utility prices. Its environmental performance, on the other hand, is below average. While not as dismal as earlier work has found it to be, it lags behind the performance in other policy areas (Wu 2009).

Another country whose outcomes are better than one would expect based on its regulatory quality score is Costa Rica, a country that performs somewhat above average on all the measured phenomena, and does particularly well in utilities price control. Yet, its regulatory quality is scored low for two reasons: for one, its investor protection scores are very low, and entrepreneurs find regulation to be a serious obstacle.

Coordination capacity: institutions and outcomes

As explained above, the dashboards contain relatively limited data on coordination capacity. First of all, the expert observations regarding, among others, the degree of coordination or division within an administration and the coherence of public policies (CEPII 2012) give a credible, yet rough, assessment of the coordination capacity of a country, but, coming from a single source, might yield a relatively imprecise index when aggregated. In addition, coordination capacity is inferred from coordination outcomes in one specific policy area, that is, the ability of governments to coordinate their administrative procedures for businesses. In any case, it is interesting to look at the relationship between the more formal aspects of coordination, as perceived by experts, and the extent to which procedures related to the operation of a business are easy to navigate. This then provides some indication of how coordination might play out. Figure 5.8 displays the data about the complexity of procedures to start a business, i.e. coordination outcomes, on the vertical axis and coordination quality as estimated from the expert survey data on the horizontal axis.

As with the other capacities, Figure 5.8 shows a strong positive correlation between the perceived quality of the institutional framework and the outcomes of that capacity. Yet, in this case, the observations are more scattered than in the case of delivery and regulatory capacity. Only around 15% of the variation in outcomes is explained by variation in the expert ratings of quality. This stems from the fact that a smaller set of variables is involved and that the outcomes included in the sub-index, unlike in the case of the two previous capacities, are limited to one specific policy area. Future research should expand the number and breadth of the indicators of coordination capacity.

Looking at some specific cases of countries whose performance in terms of outcomes is not in line with expectations based on quality proves to be informative. In particular, some countries have much higher outcome-based scores than one would expect based on their somewhat disappointing expert ratings. Among these, Saudi Arabia, Mexico, and Romania, are among the strongest outliers.

Take Saudi Arabia. According to the expert survey, this country has very poor coordination both between and within ministries and weaker-than-average overall coherence of public policies. Yet, Saudi Arabia does better than average on all the outcome-related dimensions, with the exception of the number of procedures to start a business, where it performs below average. Overall, its performance is above average. Similarly, Mexico is evaluated by experts as performing quite poorly in terms of quality of coordination, and the level of overall coherence of policies is lower than that of Saudi Arabia. Yet, on a majority of the coordination outcomes measures, Mexico does better than the global average (and particularly so when it comes to import-related documents). By contrast, Kuwait, a country that scores somewhat higher than Saudi Arabia, Mexico and Romania on the expert assessment

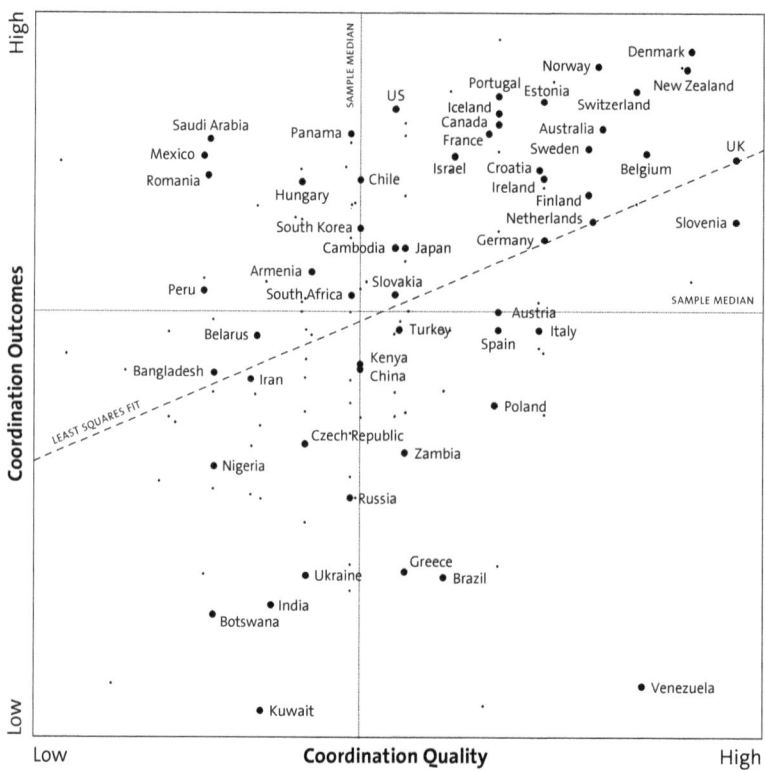

Figure 5.8 **Coordination outcomes and coordination quality**

of coordination quality, is at the same time one of the worst-performing countries when it comes to easy navigation of business-related procedures. Indeed, Kuwait has not improved its procedures over many years (The World Bank, Doing Business).

There are also some countries that perform poorly in terms of outcomes in spite of receiving very high quality of coordination scores from experts. Among these, Venezuela is the starkest case. It is ranked as one of the most well-coordinated countries, but it has one of the worst performances in providing a coherent set of procedures for entrepreneurs. One could very well think that, in such a case, simplification of procedures to start a business was not a policy priority, and therefore, in spite of a potential ability to coordinate, the outcomes look as if no coordination capacity were available. In reality, however, Venezuela introduced more stringent requirements to start a business in the past few years (The World Bank, Doing Business). This is an important reminder of a general consideration, namely that capacities and policy priorities are not always in line with each other: a government might have the capacity to achieve a given outcome, but if the outcome is not a policy priority, the capacity can be left unused. Venezuela's government has a general anti-business stance, therefore it does not mobilize its highly-coordinated administration to make the life of entrepreneurs easier.

Coordination: self-monitoring capacity and other types of capacity

Part of our indicator set on coordination deals with what we called 'self-monitoring' capacity: the ability of the government (as a complex set of apparatuses) to monitor how its various parts operate, and to oversee whether self-interested behaviour diverts administrative action related to other capacities (like delivery and regulation). Figures 5.9 and 5.10 display on the vertical axis, respectively, delivery and regulatory outcomes and on the horizontal axis the aggregated sub-index on self-monitoring capacity. While there is a positive relationship between self-monitoring capacity and the two main outcomes-based sub-indexes (for delivery and regulatory capacity), the relationship is far from tight. In fact, while the relationship between self-monitoring and delivery outcomes is statistically detectable, only 3% of the variation in delivery outcomes is explained by such mechanisms. Furthermore, there is no statistically discernible relation between self-monitoring capacity and regulatory outcomes.

One tentative conclusion is that some of the most popular policies to reduce corruption and 'shirking', like independent anti-corruption agencies, disclosure rules, and whistle-blower protection, might be linked only very loosely, and somewhat indirectly, to actual bureaucratic performance in terms of policy implementation. Note, for example, the outlier case of

Austria, which received a remarkably low score in self-monitoring capacity. This is not due to a data error. In fact, Austria is reported to not have many of the provisions identified within self-monitoring capacity, including whistle-blower protection, financial disclosure systems, and other conflict of interest legislation. For instance, Djankov et al. (2010) show that Austria does not have strict requirements for its parliamentarians to disclose the amount or sources of their assets.

Analytical capacity

The concept of analytical capacity introduced in Chapter 2 is, to an extent, very close in nature, definition, and intuition to what was called 'efficacy' in *The Governance Report 2013*. As Anheier, Stanig, and Kayser (2013) claimed, problem-solving and good governance might be the consequence of the availability of resources, within as well as outside of the government, to

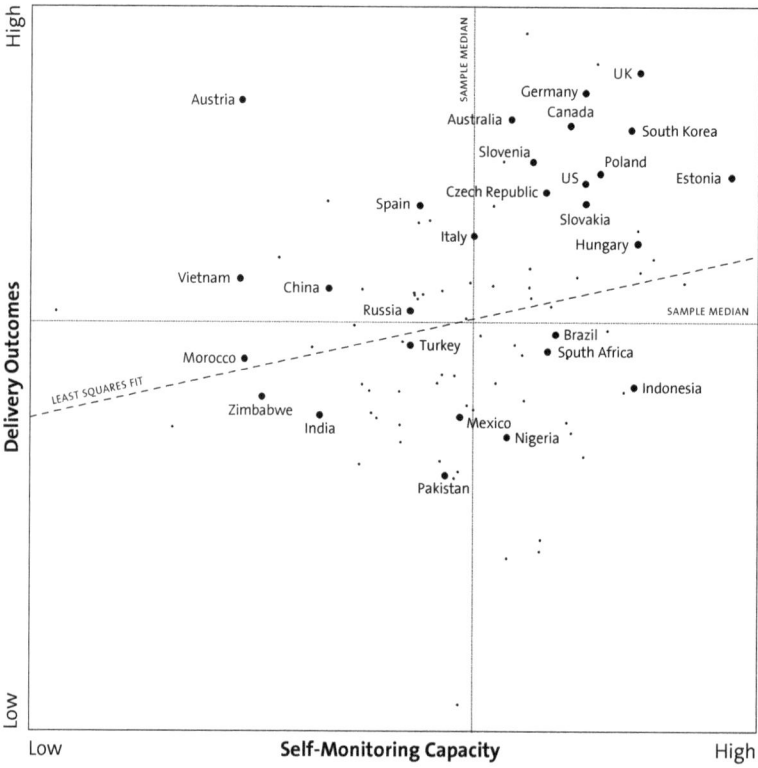

Figure 5.9 **Delivery outcomes and self-monitoring capacity**

sustain an active marketplace of ideas and propose innovative policy solutions. In the analytical capacity sub-dashboard, the efficacy+ score reflects the existence and quality of such a vibrant marketplace of ideas that can feed into the policy-making process. Figure 5.11 then shows the relationship between a country's administration's analytical capacity as rated by experts (on the vertical axis) and its efficacy+ score (on the horizontal axis).

It is interesting to note that the countries that have high efficacy (that is, nongovernmental resources for policy design) also tend to be assessed by experts as having high analytical capacity within the government. The United Kingdom, as well as Germany, Australia, and Japan, among others, have high efficacy and also rank very high on the experts-based analytical capacity score. Interestingly, the country that scores highest in the nongovernmental resources index of efficacy, the United States, is not ranked particularly high (it is actually right at the median) when it comes to analytical capacity as scored in the expert-survey dataset.

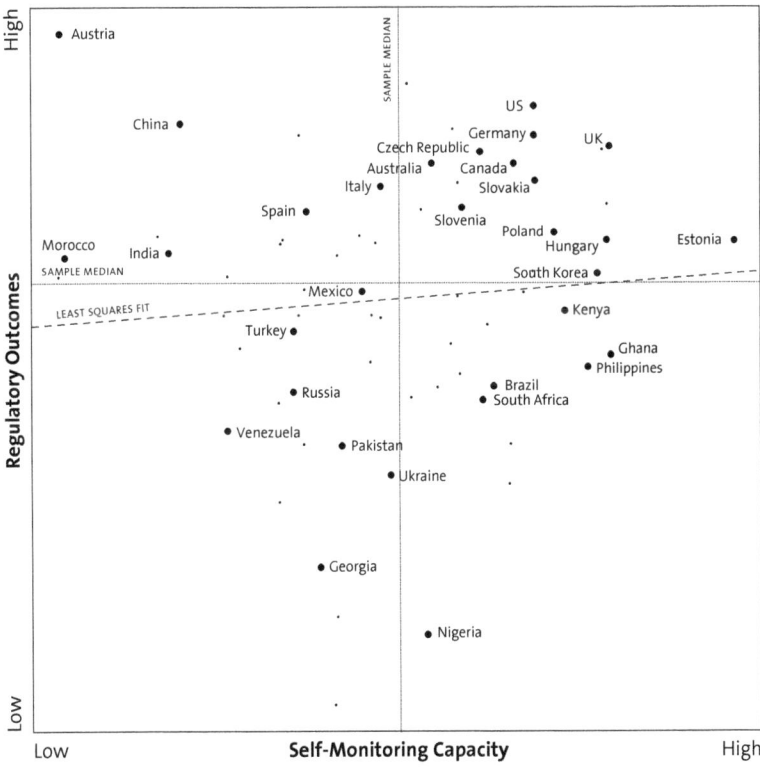

Figure 5.10 **Regulatory outcomes and self-monitoring capacity**

General patterns in the relationship between capacities

As noted at the beginning of this part of the chapter, it is far from surprising that most of the countries that show the highest capacity tend to be among the most developed countries in the world (see Figures 5.2a-d). Countries scoring high on delivery capacity also score high on regulatory capacity, and so on, just because rich countries have an easier time achieving high delivery capacity and also achieving high regulatory capacity. Thus, any correlation tells us little about possible causal relations between the two and about the potential role other 'third variables' (but not economic development itself) play in determining different aspects of bureaucratic capacity.

To detect relationships independent of a country's wealth, we adjust the four main capacity indexes to remove the effect of development.[11] While no longer directly informative of the absolute level of capacity in a given country, these adjusted indexes help us look at two (related) issues.

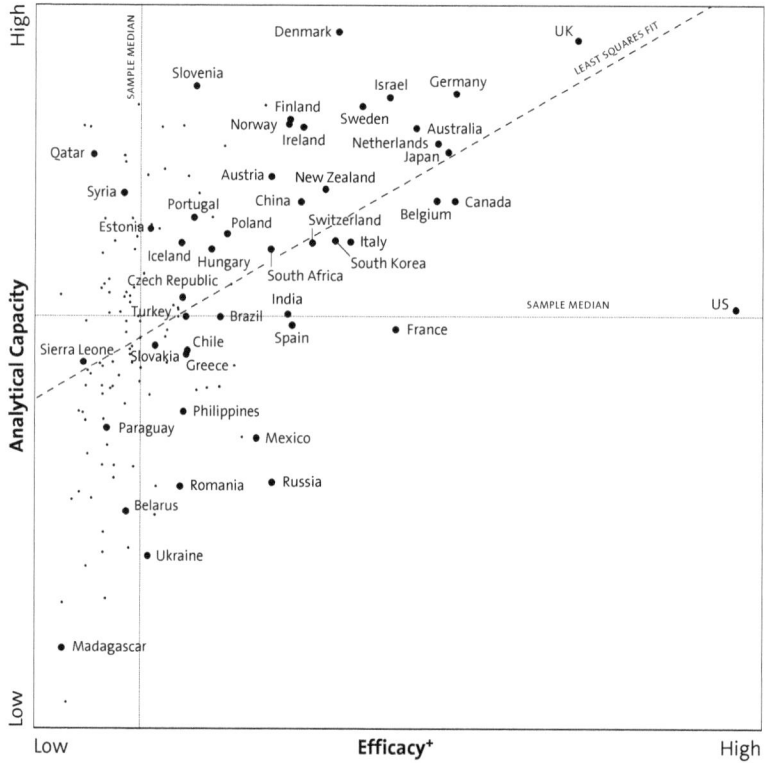

Figure 5.11 **Expert evaluations of analytical capacity, and efficacy+**

First, the adjusted score can be interpreted as the level of capacity that each country would be expected to display if all countries had the same GDP per capita (i.e. were at the same level of development). From a slightly different perspective, the adjusted scores are informative of how much a country over- or under-performs relative to the level of capacity it is expected to display given its level of development. Figure 5.12 plots the adjusted score of regulatory capacity and the adjusted score of delivery capacity to highlight countries that perform better or worse, in comparative terms, than their level of development leads one to expect. Among these, Ghana and, to a lesser extent, Senegal stand out as over-performers in terms of both regulatory and delivery capacities; Vietnam performs well in adjusted terms in delivery capacity; and Indonesia, the Philippines, and Nepal in regulatory capacity. On the other hand, the performance of some advanced and emerging economies turns out to be disappointing once their level of development and, indirectly, the resources on which they could draw to build capacity are accounted for. Among OECD members, Mexico, Turkey, Greece, and Italy per-

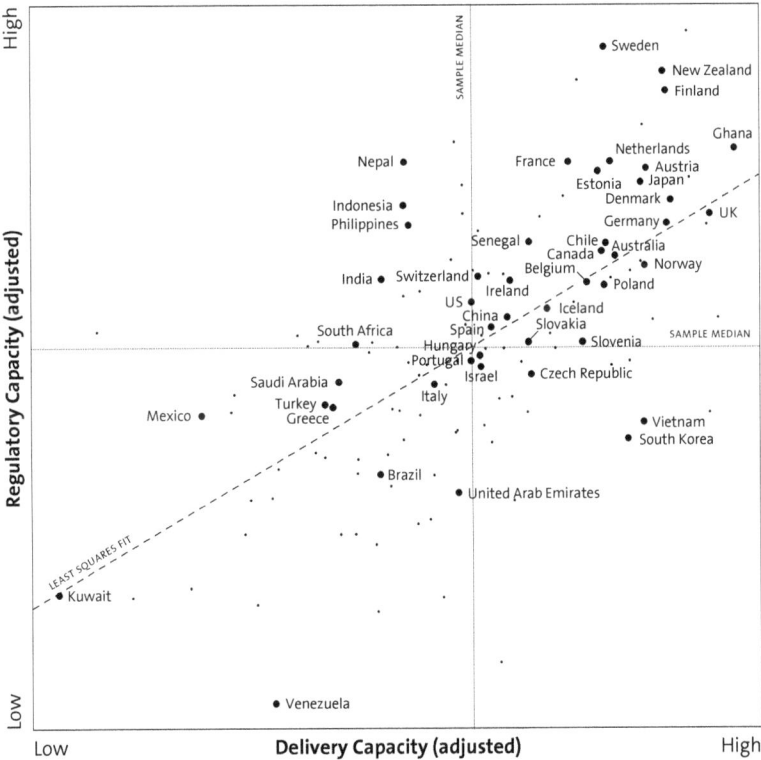

Figure 5.12 **Regulatory capacity and delivery capacity, adjusted for level of development**

form below the median in both capacities once their level of development is accounted for; similarly, the performance of Brazil, and that of wealthy Arab oil counties (Kuwait in particular, but also Saudi Arabia and the Emirates) is quite disappointing given the resources they could mobilize to build capacity.

The second issue, which is more important in our view, has to do with what correlations exist between different capacities. After the adjustment, any correlation between different capacities is, by construction, not related to level of development and reflects either direct causal relations between capacities, or the existence of third variables (a general latent 'governance capacity'?) that positively affect different capacities.

The four plots in Figure 5.13 display only the relationship between pairs of the adjusted measures of administrative capacity. The important fact one can

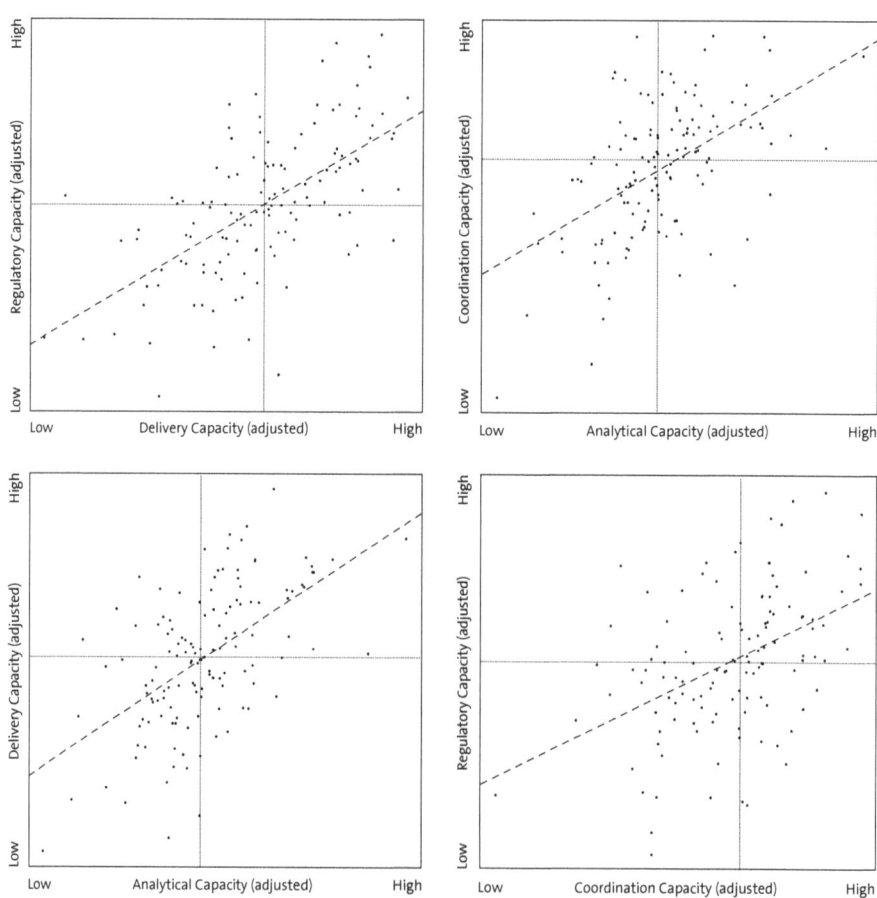

Figure 5.13 **The interrelation between administrative capacities, after adjustment for level of development**

observe is that, even after the adjustment, there is a strong positive correlation among the capacities. This means that, to some extent, some underlying connection (driven, potentially, by an overall 'institutional quality' factor, or due to causal connections between the capacities) exists that makes it easier for countries to perform better whether they deliver, regulate, coordinate, or analyse.

Legitimacy and bureaucratic capacities

As stressed in Anheier, Stanig, and Kayser (2013), one important dimension of the broader governance phenomenon has to do with legitimacy, and specifically with the public perception that government deserves confidence for its ability to deliver services to the population. Along the same lines, legitimacy and trust in government are considered in Chapter 2 to be key components of an administration's delivery capacity. As noted earlier, data about the level of confidence that citizens declare to have in public services (police, education system, and public servants in general) were aggregated within the sub-dashboard on delivery capacity into a legitimacy index. To examine the relationship between legitimacy and each of the four administrative capacities more closely, both the capacity and legitimacy scores were adjusted for GDP per capita so that any remaining correlation is not due to the fact that, for instance, wealthier countries might at the same time have higher capacity and a more confident public in general.

As shown in Figures 5.14a-d, many Asian countries stand out as those with highest (adjusted) legitimacy. Perhaps more remarkable, however, is that the only positive (and statistically detectable) association is between regulatory capacity and legitimacy, though it is not that strong (see Figure 5.14b). There is no strong (or statistically detectable) association between any of the other three capacities and legitimacy. Thus, a significant part of the variation in legitimacy might be explained by cultural differences. Still, it is interesting to note how one of the countries that has the highest adjusted delivery capacity, Rwanda, also enjoys significantly high (adjusted) legitimacy (Figure 5.14a).

The dashboards allow an even more detailed search for possible relationships between legitimacy and aspects of administrative capacity, for example, some of the outcomes-based sub-indexes of capacity. In the case of delivery outcomes in four different policy fields, for example, the relationship between capacity and legitimacy is always positive, but it is statistically discernible (at conventional confidence levels) only in the case of crime control (Figure 5.15a) and education (Figure 5.15b). The relationship is tightest in the case of crime control[12], something that is not surprising given the importance of the basic law and order functions in how citizens perceive the state. What is somewhat more surprising, and to an extent troublesome, is that good delivery capacity in the field of education seems to not be rewarded by citizens as steeply as crime control.

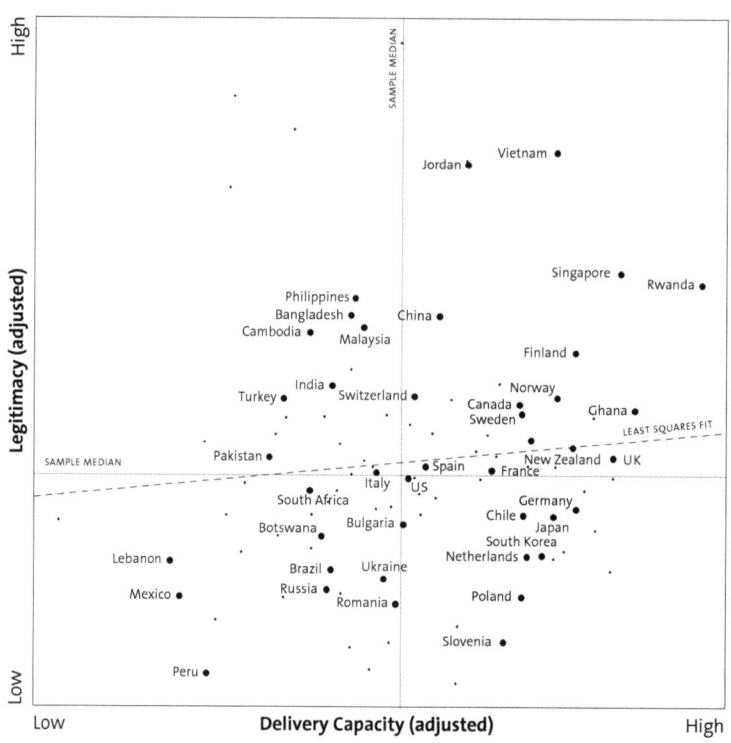

Figure 5.14a–d Legitimacy and administrative capacities, both adjusted for level of development

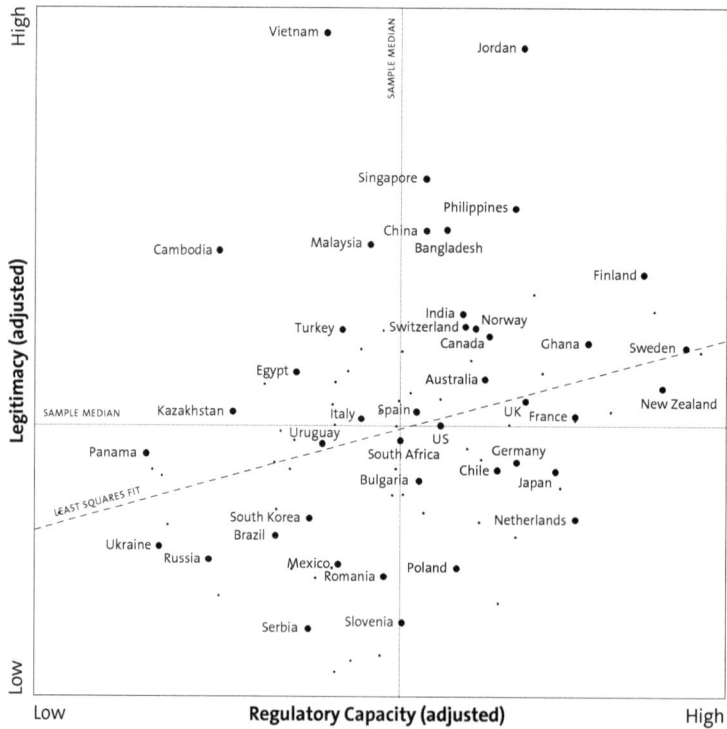

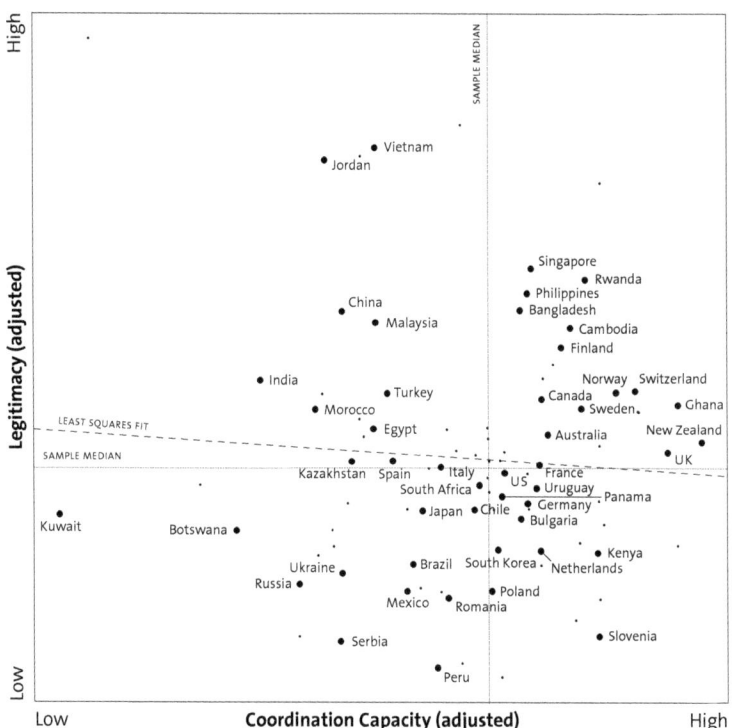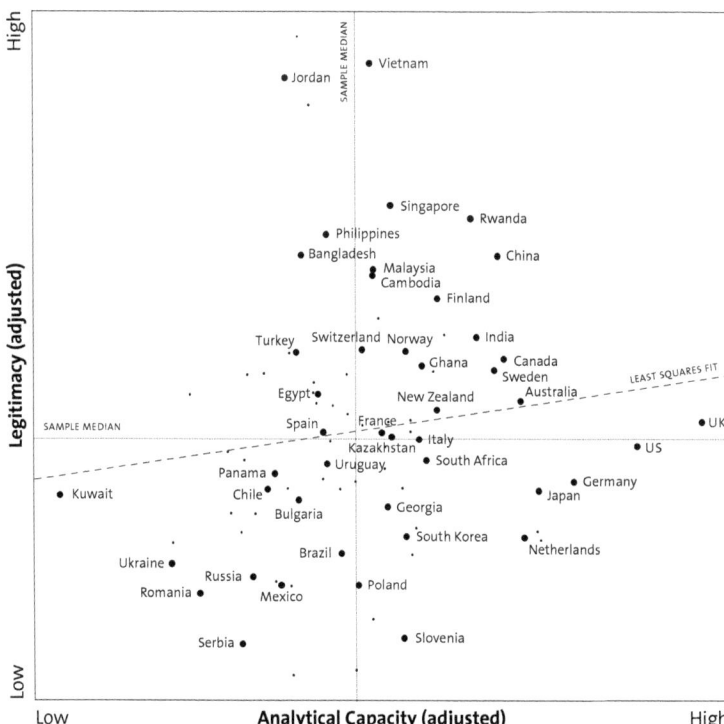

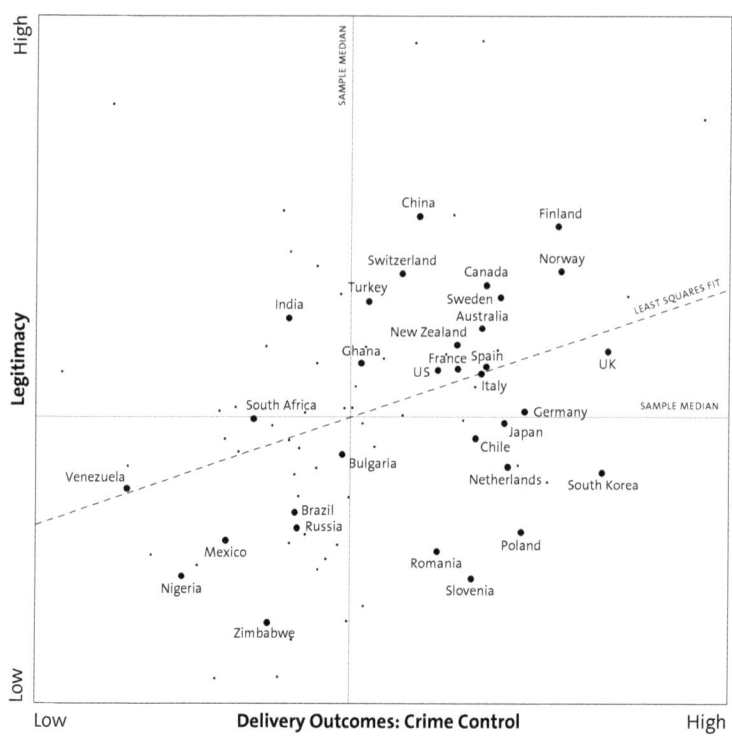

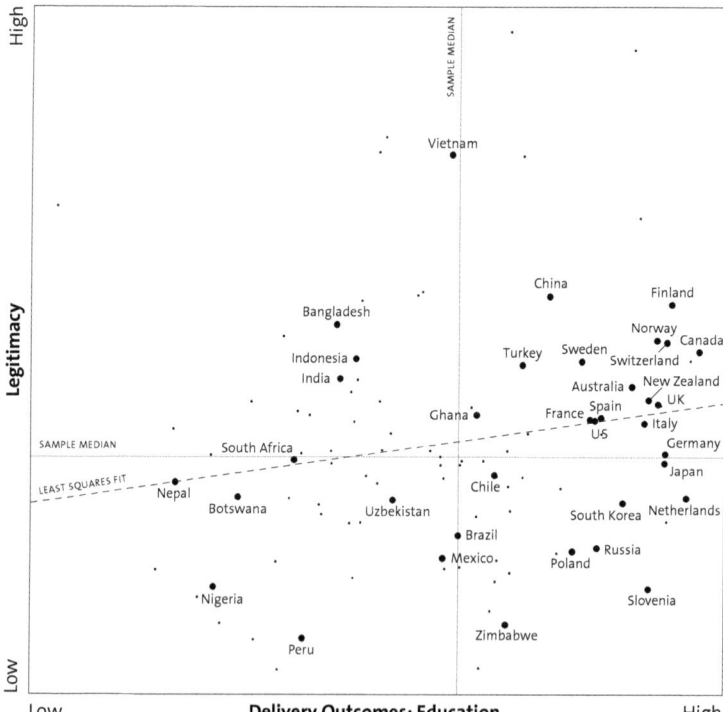

Figure 5.15a–b **Legitimacy and delivery outcomes for selected policy areas**

As for the relationship between regulatory outcomes and legitimacy, only control of the shadow economy has a statistically discernible relationship with legitimacy (Figure 5.16a). More disappointing is the fact that environmental regulation outcomes have basically no association with legitimacy (Figure 5.16b). It seems, then, the capacities that are more strongly associated with legitimacy are those of a 'command' type like law and order and accounting of economic activity, while more progressive, 'post-materialist' policy fields like education and the environment are not associated with legitimacy. In plain words (and stretching the association a bit, to interpret it causally) a government might be better able to increase the confidence that citizens have in it by deploying more police officers and more tax auditors, than by hiring more teachers or by reducing particulates in the air and preventing deforestation.

Conclusion

Several important messages can be drawn from the preliminary analyses of the Administrative Capacity Dashboard presented above. First of all, the fact that there is a positive correlation among capacities after adjusting for level of development implies that the four capacities, estimated by our indicators, are linked to each other either directly, in the sense that there are positive feedback effects across different capacities, or that variation in the various capacities is explained by some underlying 'prime mover'. In substantive terms, two (not necessarily mutually exclusive) phenomena might be operating. On the one hand, capacities feed each other, so that, for instance, increased analytical capacity improves delivery capacity; the capacity to coordinate improves regulatory capacity; and so on. On the other hand, one single, not directly observable (hence 'latent'), factor might determine the ability of governments to build capacity. This latent factor, which one could call the 'capacity to build administrative capacity', explains patterns in all four administrative capacities, and is what one might call 'governance capacity'.

In addition, the indicators provide other interesting insights. One important empirical finding is that administrative capacity is not necessarily reserved for advanced economies. While OECD countries and high-income Asian city-states tend to perform at the top levels on most indicators, several emerging economies and some developing countries display high capacity, at least in some fields. One could also conjecture that emerging economies owe their 'emerging' status at least in part to their capacity, especially in delivery and regulation. China's performance on many of the sub-indicators is the obvious example of this phenomenon.

The data also point to the potential existence of functional substitutes for an impartial, Weberian bureaucracy. Some countries in fact are able to

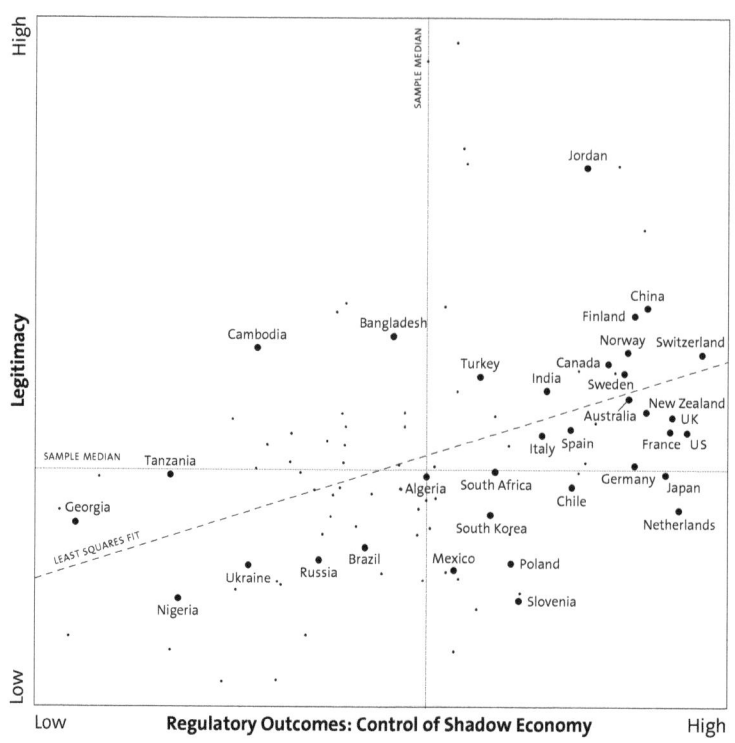

Figure 5.16a–b **Legitimacy and regulatory outcomes for selected policy areas**

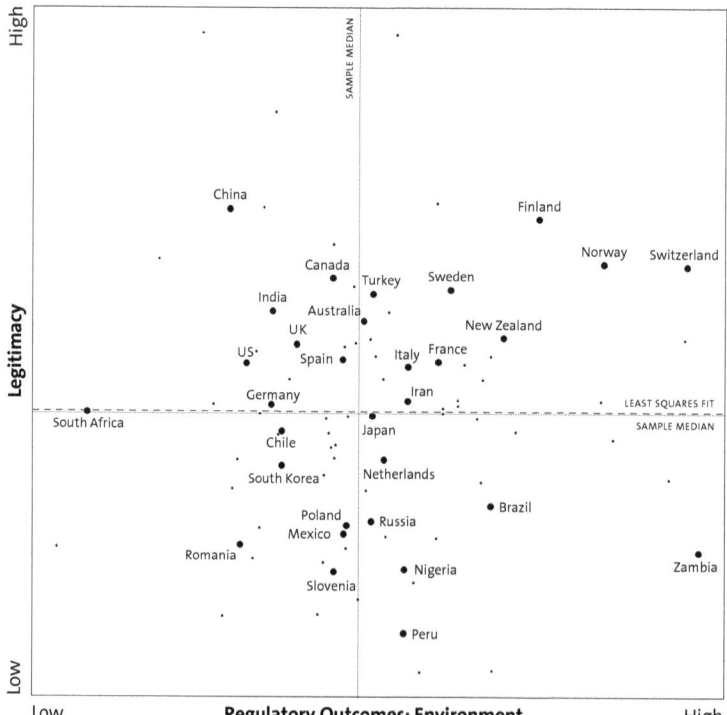

achieve outcomes that are quite better than one would expect based on the formal institutional framework within which they operate. China provides again the starkest example, but other Asian countries, like Vietnam and Indonesia, also display an analogous pattern of seemingly mediocre institutional design paired with good outcomes in specific policy areas, for instance, control of the shadow economy. Furthermore, a formally Weberian state apparatus is not a guarantee of good governance: some countries have close approximations to what are traditionally considered 'good' institutions, but their outcomes are disappointing. For instance, India's administrative capacities, as estimated from policy outcomes, are rather lower than one could expect based on measures that capture the main features of its institutional design.

Finally, a lot of attention has been given, in the literature and in the policy world, to what we call 'self-monitoring' provisions. While these institutional provisions might have some effect in terms of preventing or repressing illegal behaviour and outright corruption, they might not be that effective if the aim is building capacity in terms of delivery and regulatory outcomes. The value of these self-monitoring provisions, if any, might be then limited to the initial stages of administrative reform, but doubts have been cast about their overall effectiveness (Meagher 2005; see also Rothstein 2011). In fact, their existence does not seem to be associated, in our data, with measures of administrative capacity.

The full Administrative Capacity Dashboard prepared for the Governance Report, and the aggregate medium-range indexes, make it possible to empirically address many pressing questions related to governance and bureaucratic capacity. The findings presented in this chapter are just some examples of the type of analysis that can be carried out with this indicators dashboard. The data, and additional estimates, are available at www.governancereport.org.

Endnotes

1 More complicated methods to aggregate indicators exist: see Stanig and Kayser (2013) for some discussion and our website (www.governancereport.org) for an alternative aggregation of the data into indexes, using a Bayesian factor analysis approach that estimates the weights assigned to each variable from the data themselves. The results of the more complicated method do not differ in a major way from those reported here; yet, the approach is more conservative (in the statistical meaning of the term) in that it discounts, to some extent, individual indicators that tend to disagree with the picture painted by the majority of indicators for a given capacity. In addition, it makes it possible to estimate, in a rigourous way, the margins of error of the thematic indexes for each country. On the importance of margins of error for governance indexes, see Kaufmann, Kraay, and Mastruzzi (2010).

2   From the econometric point of view, the errors (i.e. the stochastic components of the measures) from the same source might be correlated across indicators (see Stanig and Kayser (2013) for a discussion of this issue and its relation with the conditional independence assumptions required to use factor-analytical models to estimate aggregate indexes). In plain words, if one source (say, the expert survey in the Institutional Profiles Data) over-reports the amount of capacity on one indicator in one country, it might over-report capacity in that country on another indicator, and so on. These over- and under-ratings would cancel each other out (on average) if one were to aggregate variables from different sources, but they compound each other when one aggregates variables from the same source.

3   New data were available for this edition on statistical capacity and the presence of expertise in the administrative apparatus and have thus been updated. However, the values for professionalism and impartiality are based on the scores used in the 2013 edition since the Quality of Government survey had not been updated.

4   In this indicator set, revenue collection is considered part of the delivery capacity. While it is not a service to citizens in direct terms, revenue collection shares with delivery some central features. In particular, it operates 'at the frontline' and, like delivery, it requires what can be called 'infrastructural power' (Mann 1984). In addition, revenue collection is a prerequisite to finance the provision of those services that naturally fall into the delivery rubric. Some features of revenue collection (in particular, the fact that by its own nature, it distorts private decisions) might induce one to classify it under the regulatory capacity rubric. Yet, even if the tax system can be used to implement regulatory policies (for instance, to set incentives so that certain activities become unattractive or more appealing to private agents), this is not always the purpose for which taxation and revenue collection are carried out.

5   In order to account for differences across countries at different levels of development, and for the potential effects of country size, all the price measures are adjusted for level of development (measured with GDP per capita) and for country size (measured with population of the country). In practice, we use the residuals from a regression of each price indicator on log population and log GDP per capita.

6   Negative values of inflation are turned into zeros. Values for countries experiencing hyperinflation (and therefore have values of inflation that are, from the point of view of textbook statistics, severe statistical outliers) are top-coded.

7   Some might wonder why we include these variables. We recognise that the rankings of academic departments can be found lacking from the point of view of completeness, given that they are based on self-selected authors in the most popular article repository. At a minimum, yet, they measure the presence of academic economics departments whose members participate in the international scientific community. Academically successful economists are more likely to stay on top of the developments in the field and produce innovative ideas. In fact, any of several disciplines in the social sciences could be used for this indicator, but the compulsion of economists for self-ranking greatly simplifies data collection. See Stanig and Kayser (2013).

8   The low score for Austria might seem not very plausible: What drives the poor recorded performance of Austria on this capacity is explored in some detail below.

9   The outlier status of Georgia can be explained by reform timing. While many of its recent reforms put it towards the top in terms of regulatory quality and impartial-

ity, its outcomes—some of which are measured pre-reforms—are still quite lower than might be expected. To an extent, this could be driven by outdated measures as much as a time lag between reform and improvement in performance.

10. Another outlier, Iceland, also has a mediocre performance on the investor protection indicators.

11. In practice, in this subsection we work with the residuals from regressions of the capacity indexes on log GDP per capita.

12. It is also worth noting that this relationship is not explained simply by the fact that more advanced countries have better crime control. In fact, the relationship survives after conditioning on level of development (measured with log GDP per capita).

VI. Enhancing Administrative Capacities for Better Governance
Seven Recommendations

MARTIN LODGE and KAI WEGRICH

Seemingly mundane topics such as 'bureaucracy' might seem of only marginal importance at first. However, as this Report has shown, the presence of administrative capacities is fundamental to ensuring that governance outputs and outcomes can be achieved. In other words, questions about administrative capacities are at the heart of debates regarding legitimacy. The interplay between regime legitimacy and governance performance mediated by efficacious and effective administrative systems is at the core of governance readiness, as already argued in *The Governance Report 2013*. In this concluding chapter of the 2014 Report, we develop seven recommendations on how to enhance the capacity and contributions of public administrations for improved governance.

> *Taking administrative capacities seriously will challenge some of the established ways of discussing public sector and governance reform.*

Saying that policy-makers and observers should have a well-considered discussion about delivery, regulatory, coordination, and analytical capacities might be seen as unhelpful academic advice. Nobody is likely to disagree that administrative capacities are important–but how important they are, and what should be done about them, is more contentious and goes beyond the widespread search for a 'fit for purpose' bureaucracy. Taking administrative capacities seriously will challenge some of the established ways of discussing public sector and governance reform.

The starting point of our approach to administrative capacities as developed in this Report is the governance challenges contemporary states face. These are likely to entail a considerable resource transfer between generations and to have significant consequences for the way in which states can be governed. More generally, any recommendation to develop governance readiness through strengthening administrative capacities needs to consider the context of what we called the depleted state (Lodge and Wegrich 2012a; Lodge 2013), where many governments have to face crises with resources incommensurate to the challenges at hand, be it climate change, social security and health, or infrastructure.

Our recommendations may be criticised for their lack of concreteness. However, governance readiness is not about prescription; it is about asking the appropriate questions that then should encourage an open search for answers within specific and very different governance systems. The more debates vanish in broad declarations and vague answers, the less the traction of these debates in actual organisational and system-wide behaviours. At the same time, the more concrete and precise reform proposals are, the more likely it is that they will be dismissed as 'irrelevant' or 'old-fashioned'. Such rejection is likely as governance systems vary in terms of actor constellations, dominant guiding policy principles, and institutional trajectories.

The following seven recommendations therefore emphasise the importance of asking questions so that an enlightened debate about administrative capacity can be had. They do not, however, seek to prescribe what the outcome of such discussions should be or how such discussions should be conducted. After all, such a naïve institutionalism (Roberts 2010: 15) has done more harm than good in debates about public sector reform and (good) governance.

Recommendations

Recommendation 1: Ask the central question: What capacities do bureaucracies need to ensure governance readiness?

This Governance Report has approached the issue of governance readiness from the vantage point of public administration. Governance readiness is about the creation of conditions in which state and non-state actors engage in active problem-solving rather than lowest common denominator decision-making, jealous turf-protection, or other blame-avoiding strategies. What, then, is the role of bureaucracy in the context of dispersed governance where power is fragmented and interdependently exercised by a variety of public, para-public, and private actors at different levels of governance, from the transnational to the local?

Asking what is expected and demanded of bureaucracy may seem a trivial question. However, contemporary discussions are usually pre-occupied by output or outcome measures, or by bland statements about bureaucratic challenges. For example, suggesting that coordination is a challenge is at best an understatement, given the variety of configurations in which coordination is required. So too, chanting that 'leadership' is essential ignores the lack of agreement on what 'leadership' might involve (and what 'following' in the context of bureaucracy might entail).

Too little attention has been paid to the activities that bureaucracies actually perform or are expected to perform. Any discussion about government modernisation should therefore start with the simple question: What skills and capabilities are required to perform particular tasks? In particular, the search for answers to this question will aid understanding of the kind of administrative capacities that are likely to be in high demand. Once there is a discussion about what capacities are required, then there can be an informed debate about how such capacities might be exercised, and by whom.

Starting with the simple focus on problems and moving on to a focus on 'what bureaucracies actually do and are expected to do' contrasts with the wider public sector modernisation discourse over the past thirty years. Animated by criticisms that bureaucracies were too 'monolithic', 'non-entrepreneurial', 'dysfunctional', or 'non-collaborative', much effort has been expended to make the public sector in general, and bureaucracies in particular, 'leaner and meaner' and more 'collaborative'. What has been missing in this cacophony of reform mantras has been an interest in the actual demands on bureaucracy, especially from a comparative perspective. We can only speculate as to why there has been such a limited interest in exploring the actual demands on bureaucracy. On the one hand, it is unlikely that reform-announcement-hungry politicians are keen to ask questions that may point to key problems in the interface between them and an army of bureaucrats. On the other hand, concentrating reform discussions on actual tasks rather than on bland statements leaves bureaucracies less wriggle room to adapt to demands for change in their own self-interested ways: it reduces the scope for them to draw on highly selective examples and ill-justified analogies from other countries and experiences.

However, it is important to acknowledge that demands regarding the type of skills and competencies have changed over the past three decades. While the discourse of management-oriented reform is still dominant (despite repeated announcements that we have entered the post-New Public Management age), this Report highlights that administrative capacities are not just about expertise (the classical idea of the bureaucrat who possesses both substantive and procedural expertise) or about delivery (the managerial idea that bureaucrats are supposed to make things happen). Rather, current debates need to acknowledge that contemporary bureaucracy is about operating across organisational, territorial, and sectoral boundaries and about aligning various actors. Such boundary-spanning skills have not been a prominent part of the Human Resource Management canon, but they should be. At the same time, the increasing demand on understanding complex debates requires a stronger emphasis on analytical skills which cannot simply be procured from consultancies (that are often staffed by former civil servants). Thus, we need more experts in government (which should not be confused with simplistic calls for more 'specialists' both because the idea of what a 'specialist' is is contested and because there are widely diagnosed problems with over-specialisation in government as well, see Jann and Wegrich 2008). By experts we mean individuals who are able to span boundaries and who are able to apply analytical capacities to particular problems. However, attracting such analytical capacities and 'boundary spanners' as well as those with other skills and competencies is challenging as bureaucracies compete for talent with other parties. Such competition for talent is particularly problematic in an age of depleted resources and of political commitment towards reducing bureaucracy.

In short, any discussion about the future of bureaucracy needs to begin by asking what administrative capacities are required in light of the different diagnoses and solutions advocated to address today's governance challenges.

Recommendation 2: Policy-makers and affected parties need to acknowledge the challenges of dispersion and the limits of bureaucracy.

Asking what bureaucracies actually need to do represents one aspect of an agenda that takes administrative capacity seriously. To do so in an informed way, it is important to acknowledge that contemporary governance is taking place in a context of power dispersion. Therefore, public administration cannot be said to be in a privileged and all-powerful position.

A context of dispersion challenges the view that administrative capacity can be measured in terms of formal legal provisions, staff numbers, the extent to which particular industries have been privatised, or whether finance ministers have PhDs in economics or finance. It is similarly unhelpful to suggest that the presence of formal units that deal with a particular task (such as a 'delivery unit' or an 'evaluation unit') is a good indicator that such tasks are being exercised in any capable way (or in a more capable way than in administrations that do not have such a unit on their organisational chart). Simplistic benchmarking exercises that place too much emphasis on league positions in perception-based exercises (such as those involving corruption), announcements that celebrate the cutting of jobs or rules, or reform proclamations are unlikely to advance governance readiness. We do not deny that corruption is problematic or that a lack of resources will make implementation taxing. But we need other analytical tools and conceptual approaches to capture the role of bureaucracies in today's world of governance.

To address the limits of bureaucracy it is more helpful to start with those challenges that have been diagnosed to affect the performance of bureaucracy. The academic literature distinguishes among two problems that affect the performance of bureaucracies in general. One is the 'trust-honor game' problematic (see Miller 2000). According to this game, once bureaucrats are unsure whether their efforts will be rewarded, it is increasingly less likely that they will seek to perform to the best of their ability (this might also be called a 'commitment problem'). It is unlikely that anyone will speak 'truth to power' if they face the proverbial chop for doing so. To resolve this problem, devices that enhance the autonomy of the bureaucracy are advocated. In exchange, the loyalty of bureaucrats is ensured through guaranteeing certain benefits, such as pensions.

The other problem affecting the performance of bureaucracy emerges from the relation between principals, in this case political superiors, and agents, in this case bureaucrats. Bureaucrats can exploit information asymmetries to shape and implement their jobs in their preferred ways rather than those designated by their political superiors. The standard recipe to make bureaucrats more responsive to their superiors is to advocate procedural and other performative incentives.

Combining the two problems points to the inherent paradox that affects much of present-day reform talk about public administration, namely the trade-off between insulating bureaucrats from political interference ('Weberianisation') and making them more responsive to overall political objectives. Any conversation about governance readiness needs to accept that any choice will not be able to avoid this basic trade-off. Rather, it might be more important to be explicit about such tensions rather than to pretend that they do not exist.

Furthermore, useful as calls for 'Weberianism' or 'responsiveness' are, they do not take sufficient account of the context in which governing is taking place today. As noted, contemporary governance is characterised by dispersion. We have accounted for the demands triggered by the context of dispersion by considering four specific administrative capacities: delivery, regulation, coordination, and analysis. Dispersion raises particular challenges: delivery is more problematic as increasing reliance is being placed on private providers of public services; the exercise of regulation is more difficult as authorities are shared across levels of government and between state and non-state actors; coordination turns more demanding as the number of participants becomes more numerous and heterogeneous; and analysis is challenged by competing knowledge claims.

Governance readiness therefore involves different mixes of administrative capacities, i.e. requiring more coordination than regulatory capacities in some rather than other cases (such as in the area of immigration/integration compared to broadband internet provision). These differences also extend to the specific form that each individual capacity requirement takes (for example, the difference between 'underlap' and 'overlap' forms of coordination capacity in the fields of immigration/integration and sustainability/energy).

Another requirement is to acknowledge the inherent strengths and weaknesses of bureaucratic organisation. The 'secret' of (legal-rational) bureaucratic organisation is decomplexification. This means that adding more complexity is hardly a helpful recipe for advancing administrative capacity. Bureaucracy is about standardisation through decomplexification: in order to collect information, to make sense of this information, and to identify what needs to be done in order to achieve a certain desired state of the world, bureaucracy needs to standardise by categorising information, by specialising activities, and by encouraging procedural regularisation. In other words, as every incident or case is inherently *sui generis*, without processes that categorise or classify these observations or incidents, bureaucratic life (and any other life) would come to a standstill as the demands stemming from the need to process information in a bespoke way would be overwhelming. In the case of public administration, processes of standardisation are reinforced by demands for accountability. Without being able to trace decisions, accountability of a procedural kind would be unobtainable. Therefore, any reform that fails to acknowledge the importance of standardisation is unlikely to succeed: one cannot ask an organisation that is inherently about decomplexification to intentionally generate complexity and to be accountable for it.

It is, however, possible to address inherent tendencies within bureaucratic organisations that generate excessive decomplexification. For example, inertia in classification and categorisation can be balanced by introducing challenge functions (e.g. the need to justify decisions); over-specialisation can be addressed by creating linkages across different units; and routinisation (leading to embedded power structures and entrenched views of how to go about things) can be shaken up through rotation. However, none of these responses will ultimately overcome the inherent tendency towards decomplexification. Expecting bureaucracies of any kind to suddenly turn more agile and responsive in ways that deny their intrinsic nature will inevitably lead to disappointment.

In sum, any discussion of what kind of administrative capacities should be expected of bureaucracy today needs to bear in mind, first, the dispersed nature of contemporary governing and, second, the inherent logic of bureaucratic life. In developing policy and regulatory regimes, policy-makers and stakeholders therefore have to take into account the capacity requirements of a particular policy option or governance regime as well as the 'capacity stock' that a particular regime can offer. The assessment of policy options and governance approaches should therefore systematically take these capacity considerations into account.

Recommendation 3: To address major governance challenges, policy-makers need to focus on demand and supply mismatches and capacity bottlenecks.

Contemporary challenges are often portrayed as 'wicked problems' (Rittel and Webber 1973). Problems are said to be 'wicked' when they are characterised by complexity (interdependencies across sectors, regions, and time), high uncertainty about cause and effect relations, and contention over rival norms and values. We certainly agree with this diagnosis. It is also difficult to disagree with the recommendation that governance arrangements should mirror the complexity and 'wickedness' of policy challenges. At the same time, hiding behind the academically attractive term of 'wicked problems' is hardly going to address at least some of the problems affecting contemporary governing. This Report notes that many of today's governance challenges result from a mismatch between (excess) demand and (under-) supply. For example, health costs are likely to increase especially with the growing demands posed by ageing societies. Energy networks require decisions as to how to match demand and supply in the light of competing preferences about climate change, 'cheap' energy, and stable energy supplies.

This mismatch between (expected, but uncertain) demand and (a likely lack of) supply offers scope to advance the discussion about administrative capacity in at least two ways. First, administrative capacities are essential to address the mismatch between demand for and supply of goods and services. Second, the focus on administrative capacities raises questions about the inherent limitations and tensions of administrative capacities themselves.

Considering administrative capacities in the light of the mismatch between demand and supply is not without its own pitfalls: it could lead to the conclusion that administrative capacity bottlenecks are all about resource gaps. Recommendations stemming from this conclusion would then possibly be that administrative capacity could be improved by advancing material benefits, enhancing the status of public administration, or allowing for greater discretion and professionalisation. Any one (or a mixture of all) of these suggestions has been made in the context of administrative reform. For instance, the literature on 'high reliability' offers examples where complex organisations succeed in avoiding disaster (La Porte 1996). They do so by allowing for redundancy, by relying on extensive ex ante training that instils a strong sense of error intolerance and a 'system-wide' perspective in terms of performance, and by offering stability. None of these basic recipes can be assumed as given in contemporary governance scenarios where politics provides for instability, where career patterns are short-term, and where performance-related incentive regimes emphasise the measurement of an individual's contribution rather than the overall organisational or system-wide performance.

However, especially in an age of austerity, arguing for more money, more staff, and other resources is unlikely to be acceptable to political elites and electorates alike. It is also questionable whether the solution to administrative capacity bottlenecks can be found through extensive outsourcing to private parties, as risk transfer has been proven to be problematic and transferring ultimate responsibility for vulnerable people in care homes to private providers is unlikely to prove an acceptable solution. Similarly, simply abandoning administrative engagement in the kind of governance challenges outlined in this Report will not necessarily lead to desirable outcomes.

To enhance administrative capacities requires a careful discussion of the inherent functional problems that need to be tackled, an understanding of the capacities and motivations that are brought to the table by public and private actors, and what the role of bureaucracy might be to contribute to problem-solving capacity. In other words, it is not sufficient to say that 'coordination' is a problem. Instead, the discussion has to start with the actual problem that must be 'coordinated' and why coordinated action within a set actor constellation is perceived to be a problem. Similarly, announcing particular targets and then hoping for the best (such as 'reducing emissions by 40%') is not a particularly credible governance strategy. Headline-grabbing targets might be the stuff of the contemporary age of media-savvy politicians, spin-doctors, and think tankers. However, to advance governance readiness, any reform announcement needs to consider the administrative capacities that are required to 'make things happen'.

Furthermore, Chapter 3 identified bottlenecks that inhibit the exercise of administrative capacities. None of these bottlenecks can be resolved by simply throwing more resources into each of these capacities. For coordination capacity, for example, the key bottleneck is the trade-off between the overall desire to have organisations selflessly work with each other and the reality that the individual organisation's self-interest is all about turf-protection. Such a self-centred orientation is aggravated when organisations are subject to performance management regimes that rely on easily measurable activities. This will lead, for example, to a focus on complying with organisational-specific targets, whilst neglecting the wider system-wide consequences of target-hitting behaviours (such as the exclusion of particular sets of patients from particular forms of treatment).

In the case of regulatory capacity, the key bottlenecks are formal power and reputation. Formal power can be measured in terms of legal provisions, staff resources, and expertise. However, formal status is not a reliable indicator as to whether regulatory capacity can be exercised in meaningful ways. Rather, regulatory capacity needs to be associated with a shared reputation for competency. Reputation involves the capacity to shape perceptions about what is appropriate or not, and such reputation (which also means a higher degree of autonomy from political and other interference) can be generated through procedural and technical expertise that lead to effective and fair decisions. Reputation, therefore, is far more about relationships among actors than about formal legal provisions, budgetary provisions, or staffing numbers. Furthermore, reputation is not just about the action of bureaucratic actors alone; it also depends on those political and industry actors, other stakeholders as well as the wider public that represent the key audiences of regulators. In other words, administrative capacity is about understanding the inherent inter-connectiveness and relational character of governing.

Analytical capacity similarly encounters this 'more is not enough' problem: without some level of resources and staffing to either purchase expertise or to provide expertise in-house, there will be lack of analytical capacity. But just increasing spending on (academic) reports, consultancy, or some more or less high flying whiz kids in government will not necessarily result in better policies or governance (as anyone who studies the history of policy analysis will confirm). A key bottleneck is the trade-off and disconnect between generalist knowledge of the consultancy or academic type, on the one hand, and the specialist knowledge that is both produced and required by frontline policy actors, on the other. This disconnect is a product of different logics of action and knowledge bases. While analysis at the centre is usually of a generic and cross-cutting kind and produced by those whose careers depend on making an impression in order to quickly rise up the career ladder, frontline knowledge is the result of the continuous interaction with the messy real world of domain-specific practice, where resources are limited, incidents require interpretation to make sense in the light of official provisions, and sectoral experiences appear to be *sui generis* and also uniquely important. Advancing analytical capacity therefore requires the joining-up of different policy experiences, ranging from the front-lines of delivery (i.e. the giving and receiving ends of policy delivery) and experience with cross-sectoral and cross-national experiences, to the more analytical capability present within government. Such joining-up is, however, far from straightforward, if alone for the mutual distrust between the various parties, with people at the 'centre' often being disappointed with the lack of change evidence at the street-level and actors at the street-level considering people at the 'top' to be ill-informed.

Delivery capacity is confronted with the same problem. Alleviating resource constraints will not address all problems affecting delivery. Control over delivery is frustrated by the power of street-level bureaucrats to filter out the convenient from the inconvenient and to concentrate on the former, while target populations are likely to be highly adept at counter-learning and other forms of creative compliance. Such tensions cannot be wished away by prescribing particular remedies. However, strategies that require actors to have meaningful exposure to different parts of the policy process (and to different sides of the policy frontline) as part of their career trajectories would at least reduce the lack of understanding to some extent.

In short, advancing administrative capacities requires a view of the specific demand and supply mismatches. In responding to mismatches, policymakers need to consider not only the resources but also the administrative capacities required. This implies that a standard operating procedure that asks for 'more' resources to deal with any challenge, or to criticise the lack of resources to justify failure, is inherently problematic. Instead, it is important to carefully consider the ways in which capacities can be advanced by understanding the specific bottlenecks that inevitably occur. Especially under conditions of depleted budgets, a discussion of administrative capacity requirements needs to be included in policy analysis and policy planning exercises.

Recommendation 4: Move beyond checklist and scoreboard exercises towards adaptive learning.

The contemporary debate about 'good governance' has generated a number of contributions that engage with administrative capacity, broadly defined. For example, Fukuyama (2013) suggests that ranking exercises, as provided by the World Bank and other international organisations, offer very little insight into administrative capacity. In an age in which it is fashionable (at least among public administration scholars) to 'rediscover bureaucracy' (Olsen 2006), it is important to understand how capable bureaucracy actually is. However, this requires an agreement as to what administrative capabilities should achieve in the first place.

Rothstein (2013; Rothstein and Teorell 2008) suggests that the key indicator for 'quality of government' is impartiality: no favours should be granted or specific discrimination should be exercised in the application of particular laws. Such accounts say little about the quality of the laws themselves (although nobody is suggesting that normative concerns about the intent of a law should be ignored). They also favour meritocratic organisations. However, questions of whether bureaucracies are capable of addressing critical governance challenges feature neither in calls for balancing autonomy and control of bureaucracy (Fukuyama 2013) nor in the arguments in favour of impartiality as the key criterion for quality of government (Rothstein 2013). These approaches thus tell us little about the type of capacities required for 'governance'. They also tend to overlook the conditions under which active problem-solving is taking place (Longo 2008).

Our contribution to this debate is twofold. One is to argue that the condition of dispersed governance requires a view that sees bureaucracy as one actor among many. In other words, simply to find that merit-based bureaucracies are good for economic growth may be interesting, but to actually understand how such a correlation emerges requires insight into the underlying causal mechanism and the way in which power is actually distributed among actors. Our second contribution is to argue that administrative capacity needs to be understood by separating out four key dimensions, namely delivery, regulatory, coordination, and analytical capacities. Such a distinction moves beyond an emphasis on non-politicised appointment and promotion, which defines a 'Weberian' bureaucracy and suggests that such a 'Weberian' bureaucracy will be good for political, economic, and social development.

Indeed, the approach advocated here avoids the accusation that much of the contemporary 'good governance' literature represents a cocktail of well-intentioned individual reform recipes that, in combination, risk turning into self-defeating and contradictory reform packages. We therefore advise policy-makers not to adopt some kind of checklist derived from various (best, good or not so good) practices in a variety of contexts. Of course, it is always attractive to legitimise policy and administrative reforms by drawing on checklists and templates that have been endorsed by one international organisation or another, as is widely practiced in various fields, for example, in education or 'red tape' cutback attempts. Checklists might be vital in hospital operating theatres, but they are not helpful when it comes to addressing complex governance challenges.

Instead, what is helpful is to draw on international experiences captured in dashboards of indicators that allow for the exploration of specific relations between factors as a starting point for then examining the interaction of factors in individual cases, taking into account their historical development in a particular context. Such an approach that is based in 'adaptive learning' approaches will provide an advantageous starting point as it questions established practices. Policy-makers should systematically draw on indicators, comparisons, and benchmarks to challenge 'their' bureaucracy, but these should be consulted with consideration and in a reflecting way. Checklists should not become the sole occupation of organisational life. Furthermore, they should reflect actual challenges, rather than merely decontextualised reform templates downloaded from other governments' websites or endorsed by international organisations or consultancies.

Put more positively, to establish a capacity for adaptive learning and therefore to advance governance readiness requires two things. One is a perspective that avoids the narrowing of capacity-related debates to the pursuit of league-table positions or benchmark-hitting, but is willing to consider the capacity requirements. Furthermore, it requires a willingness to incorporate challenge functions into governance systems. Most systems have a tendency to protect their own practices by excluding dissent. While it is problematic to bring dissent into political organisations where ministerial careers might be even more short-lived in the presence of open deliberations about political priorities, it is nevertheless essential that challenge functions are incorporated into the policy-making process. While Bismarck may have compared law-making to sausage production and therefore advised against too close involvement in the production process, we argue that governance readiness is exactly about being interested in the production stage, even though this may not be as pretty as a focus on outputs and outcomes.

Recommendation 5: Make debates on innovation problem-focused and consider administrative capacity implications.

As noted at the outset of this chapter, bureaucracy has been the subject of much criticism. Similarly, 'public administration' is seen as somewhat of a backwater given the far sexier terms of governance, management, public affairs, or even public policy. These intellectual fashions have had the regrettable consequence that the 'administrative factor' has been underplayed in contemporary policy discussions. Instead, bureaucracy (and the public sector more generally) is usually seen as unwilling to reform, risk averse, and non-responsive. These criticisms are also evident in those accounts that do feature ways of improving administration. This is particularly regrettable since innovation is definitely required to overcome demand and supply mismatches and deal with capacity bottlenecks.

One standard innovation recipe is to emphasise the importance of 'collaborative' innovation. As noted in Chapter 4, innovative practices that span across organisational and sectoral boundaries are widely seen to promise a response to innovation deficits and the limited innovation capacity of the public sector. The challenge is to come to a better understanding as to what capacities are required to allow for collaboration to work. In particular, this raises issues in terms of access rules and mediating conflict. Furthermore, while collaboration elicits particular concerns about coordination capacity, it also raises the spectre of strategies that seek to avoid blame through the diffusion of responsibility (Hood 2011). Collaboration also precipitates questions about the ways in which institutional memory is maintained under conditions of diffused responsibility (Pollitt 2009). In sum, too little is known about the importance of administrative actors in facilitating innovative collaborative practices among state and non-state actors.

A second standard recipe is to stress the importance of 'technology' (Dunleavy et al. 2006). It is undoubtedly true that the growth in computing power has enhanced the capacities of data handling and storage, and information gathering more generally. It has also allowed for greater automatisation of administrative processes. However, again, technology is not the answer to the problem of administrative capacities. In contrast, technology as a means to facilitate governance innovation requires distinct administrative capacities. It is highly questionable, given the considerable number of studies about IT procurement, for example, whether contemporary administrative capacities are well-developed enough to deal with IT management. Delivery capacities therefore involve issues of contract design and project management.

Elsewhere, too, the application of information technology has not necessarily generated the intended results. For example, the UK Red Tape Challenge, an attempt to consult about and abolish existing legislation and regulation through online crowdsourcing, led to a result in which the quality of crowdsourced information was arguably below that generated through 'analogue' consultation processes. This raised administrative capacity concerns not just in terms of assessing crowdsourced comments, but also in terms of finding alternative means to challenge the existing stock of regulation, as intended by the political interests that had animated the initiative in the first place (Lodge and Wegrich 2012d). In other words, technology needs to be understood as a challenge for administrative capacity and not as a solution.

A third standard recipe for promoting innovation in public administration is to stress the importance of more incentives and competition. This is supposed to enhance performance, as economic rents are no longer allocated to politically important monopolies, public servants can be materially incentivised to work harder to achieve outcomes, and performance among organisations can be compared. However, a reliance on 'incentives' needs to take into consideration the particular demands that emerge in the context of the administrative capacities that are required to regulate, coordinate, and ensure the delivery of public services. None of these activities can be 'incentivised' in simple ways.

A fourth standard recipe is to rely on special offices or individuals ('czars') to bash heads together, to link up departmental silos, and to appear as an advocate of specific issues and interests. Again, however, it is important to understand the administrative prerequisites that make such an office viable (apart from the need to have high-level political support). This requires the presence of analytical capacity to combine different sources of knowledge, the coordination capacity to bring different interests and departments together, the delivery capacity of making 'joined-up' decision-making happen, and regulatory capacity to oversee whether actors in departments respond to demands from outside the line hierarchy. In particular the two latter capacities are usually a scarce commodity in a unit that depends on others to make and implement policies.

In sum, therefore, the four standard recipes presented to encourage innovation in public administration differ widely in the kind of public services they wish to see and in the ways in which they advocate how contemporary governance challenges might be resolved. However, they share the weakness of paying insufficient attention to the (different mixes of) administrative capacities that they require.

More generally, much of the recent work on governance innovation is about how particular problems were resolved creatively by often non-traditional actors. The key focus therefore is on innovations that happened without or with little involvement of the state. However, the implications of such innovations for administrative capacities are rarely considered. Governance innovations that rely, for example, on social investors to invest resources that governments are unable (or unwilling) to raise may have positive implications for the state (e.g. no need to seek funding), but it may also be harmful in that the more tasks are being undertaken outside the confines of public bureaucracy, the less capable these bureaucracies will become over time.

The preceding discussion illustrates that a recipe-driven approach towards addressing governance challenges is unlikely to offer much insight into the type of administrative capacities that are required in each particular case. A more informed approach would be problem-centred rather than recipe-driven. Indeed, the key to addressing governance challenges is to approach problems by focusing on the actual administrative situation and asking what constraints on actors and organisations prevent them from performing particular tasks (Simon 1947). Simplifying the kind of tasks or capacity requirements into four (delivery, regulatory, coordination, and analytical) concentrates the debate and allows for a focus on the type of bottlenecks that featured in Chapter 3 (and, more briefly, above). In short, asking what the problem is–why do people not comply, what is the actual communication flow within and among organisations, what kind of information is necessary for informed decision-making, who needs to be regulated to achieve policy objectives, etc.–is important to avoid that innovation processes are driven by the availability of solutions and patterns of 'provider capture'.

Recommendation 6: Consider administrative capacities when balancing the tension between reform paradigms (and their supporters) and specialists in policy domains.

The success or failure of particular administrative reform programmes has more to do with processes of social support and persuasion than the 'proof' of functional superiority (Hood 1998). The success of the various doctrines that have come to be known as the New Public Management (NPM) can be explained as a persuasive reaction to the perceived failures of public administration in the late 1970s and early 1980s. In short, reform is about argumentation and persuasiveness and less about 'hard facts'. The study of bureaucracy can hardly be said to have evolved in a cumulative fashion (Hood 1998), but to have involved recurring themes and doctrines (Hood and Jackson 1991).

Administrative reform programmes, especially those of a cross-cutting nature, require broad appeal to be successful. Support for particular programmatic ideas is often detached from the underlying technologies (or methodologies) that gave rise to the reform programme in the first place. For example, Michael Power (1997) has suggested that the spread of the 'audit' language in public sector reform resembles a diffusion process. Whereas the language and programmatic ideas of 'audit' are marching on and penetrate ever more social domains, the (ambiguous) technology of 'audit' is largely being left behind. At the same time, such cross-cutting reform programmes will always face resistance among sectoral actors who criticise such reforms as ill-informed and not reflecting their particular experience.

Similarly, domain-based reforms, i.e. those that emerge from within a particular sector, are also problematic. They will reflect the dominant thought-patterns and power structures of domain-interested actors in bureaucracies, parliamentary committees, and interest organisations (Jann and Wegrich 2008). Such 'iron triangles' will filter external reform demands, i.e. by adapting to demand for changes in ways that will sustain if not strengthen their power position. Domain-based innovation will therefore be largely about reinforcing dominant patterns rather than about improving particular governance arrangements and revenue flows.

Neither of these paradigm- or domain-based ways of administrative reform pays much attention to administrative capacities. The former is largely about drumming up support for a reform programme backed by visions of impending peril ('if we don't change we will all die') or the need to follow inevitable trends of modernisation ('these changes are all an inescapable part of becoming modern'). The latter, domain-based strategy is about selling reform by emphasising the importance of maintaining particular arrangements and merely updating them.

A focus on administrative capacities is unlikely to gain much social support: it neither promotes a particular recipe, nor does it claim to represent the insights of a particular policy domain or sector. However, this is as much an opportunity as it is problem. After all, administrative history is littered with examples of reform attempts that started with grandiose claims, but then quickly ended on the scrap heap of abandoned efforts, leaving behind disillusionment. Focusing on questions about what is expected of bureaucracies in the light of a context that is highly demanding (i.e. dispersion and the key governance challenges) is unlikely to witness rapid disillusionment. In other words, it is a kind of proposal that allows for incremental and 'small-win' progress that is likely to generate cumulative capacity increases rather than one-off headlines (Weick 1984).

Moreover, anchoring the debate to administrative capacities allows for a different type of engagement between the generalist reform champions and the domain specialists. While presented in generic form, the framework of administrative capacities can be used to balance the requirements and capacities of a particular sector or domain and the calls for engagement with particular reform paradigms. While attempts to assess administrative capacities as part of reform programmes, for example, the UK government's capability reviews of the mid 2000s, have used the managerial language of the NPM type (and hence have repeated the problem of miscommunication between domain specialists and reform generalists), we suggest that the framework provided in this Report provides a basis for an assessment exercise that provides for feedback in terms of what is needed by and demanded from domain specialists and their respective organisations.

Recommendation 7: Combine the use of indicators with peer reviews.

The final, and most problematic, question is how to assess whether, and to what extent, administrative capacities exist. In contrast to output and outcome measures, administrative capacities, as conceptualised in this Report, do not lend themselves easily to measuring and ranking exercises. Chapter 5 has offered an extensive discussion of this problem and also offers a dashboard of indicators of administrative capacities.

Benchmarking exercises have their place and so do arguments about taking national league positions in various public service rankings seriously. However, such practices tell us little about administrative capacity and the capacities of states more generally to tackle the key governance challenges of the financial crisis, of demographic change, and of climate change. Benchmarking exercises–be they cross-national, cross-sectoral or otherwise– can only be part of a conversation–one that is informed by an understanding of the purpose of the performance management system and by an interest in understanding the underlying processes that lead to the performance. Instead, most performance management attempts lead to immediate attempts to summarise performance in one single number that then can be used for 'benchmarking' and 'league-tabling' attempts. Again, such simplifications might be helpful to attract newspaper headlines and to generate enough panic to set the agenda for policy initiatives. However, they are less likely to enhance governance readiness in terms of administrative capacity. To enhance administrative capacities requires a perspective that sees performance management as driven by the motivation to solve problems, to accept contrasting perspectives, and to utilise measured outputs and outcomes as the starting point and not the end point of a conversation.

But how then can we assess and advance administrative capacity? Our recommendation is to combine indicator-based measurements with in-depth studies of how dispersed systems of governing go about problem-solving. A central question could, therefore, be how dispersed actors coordinate (or not) their activities, how different companies negotiate access agreements in the shadow of regulatory oversight, or how care homes are being inspected across different jurisdictions. The goal, therefore, is not only to develop measures as accurately as possible. Indicators not only require further methodological groundwork, but they also require interpretation and context-specific analysis of how a particular combination of factors plays out in a given country and sector. The goal is also to understand better how processes operate and how they overcome (or not) particular bottlenecks that are generally seen to affect bureaucratic life.

In academic terms, the interest is in extrapolation (Bardach 2004)–finding out why certain organisations or systems appear to be successful and exploring how such experiences could be incorporated within the context of one's own system. For example, it is not about the observation that independent regulators are good for lowering energy prices. Rather, the fascinating question is about how regulatory authorities interact with powerful political and economic interests in order to establish their autonomy and credibility. Similarly, an interest in budgetary processes would not resort to ticking boxes as to whether finance ministries have adopted accrual accounting or have access to particular budgetary techniques. In contrast, the interest turns to far more prosaic (but labour-intensive) questions about how finance ministries develop knowledge about expenditure patterns in other departments, how negotiations between departments are organised, and how spending patterns are being adjusted.

One proposal for such an extrapolation-oriented exercise would be to conduct 'peer reviews'. Such peer reviews would not be on the lines of the OECD reviews that follow common scripts and assess whether countries' approaches follow agreed guidelines that have been declared as 'best practice'. Instead, our understanding of 'peer review' focuses on the way in which different governance challenges are being addressed. In particular, such peer reviews would focus on key bottlenecks and on inherent tensions, such as the need for governance systems to mediate between the competing administrative values of fairness, efficiency, and redundancy (Hood 1991). By putting a particular spotlight on how bottlenecks are being negotiated and addressed, it is more likely that organisations will be able to learn from each other.

Of course, such a peer review variant that focuses on how to deal with particular problems or challenges is resource intensive. It requires an interest in studying the ways in which organisations go about their work and an interest in moving towards cross-sectoral and cross-national assessments. Nevertheless, it is likely that such a learning exercise will prove more effective than content-free ranking exercises.

In Conclusion

This Report argues that, to advance governance readiness, we need to have a radically different view of administrative capacities. First of all, it contends that the administrative factor matters, and that this administrative factor has to be considered in varied ways, namely in its delivery, regulatory, coordination, and analytical variants. Second, it maintains that any recipe as to how to address governance challenges needs to incorporate a discussion about the administrative capacities that are required. Third, it argues that a reliance on benchmarks and league-tabling is unlikely to advance governance readiness (apart from possibly generating interest so as to generate resources to advance a particular reform initiative). Rather than copying, extrapolation is likely to offer some promise in terms of advancing governance readiness. Fourth, we argue that a problem-focused approach that involves peer reviews is more likely to advance governance readiness than indices that seek to rank bureaucracies on some scale or another.

The seven recommendations that we advance in this chapter emphasise the importance of asking the kind of questions that will allow policy-makers, those who are charged with implementing policy, and other stakeholders to engage in an enlightened debate about the administrative capacities required to solve public problems. They will of course be criticised. Some will say that the recommendations are irrelevant as systems of governance have already embraced such an agenda and are 'getting there', although they are still 'learning' (the typical bureaucratic response). Others will say that the recommendations are not radical enough and that only root-and-branch type reforms will be able to deal with the problems of governing (the typical political response).

In conclusion, we want to 'pre-buttal' four types of objections to these recommendations and the overall tone of this Report and thereby clarify our argument further. It is only by openly discussing these criticisms that a more informed discussion is likely to ensue. In doing so, we realise that many other criticisms can and will be made.

The first set of criticisms suggests that we are 'too technocratic'. By classifying administrative competencies and by suggesting that bureaucracy has a role to play in addressing governance challenges, we seem to be offering a model of reform that hardly reflects contemporary societal and political demands, which should in any case be identified by politicians and citizens, and not academics. Furthermore, we might be accused of having a far too benevolent and upbeat view about the workings of bureaucracy. From this viewpoint, any active role for public administration in facilitating governance problem-solving is bound to end up with more red tape, dysfunctional processes, empowered producer groups, and unintended effects, and thus our recommendations may be seen as merely adding to the dysfunctional workings of bureaucracies without offering any support to advance governance capacity. Finally, we may also be criticised for being 'too technocratic' in ignoring the importance of politics.

In response, we are hardly technocratic in that we fully acknowledge the political context of administrative reform. It is one of the key insights of executive politics that there is no public administration without politics, as there is no politics without public administration (Lodge and Wegrich 2012c). We therefore are more than aware of the problem in focusing on the 'administrative factor' when concerns could be raised about the quality of the political system more broadly. However, we stress the importance of considering administrative capacities as an essential aspect for any programme of wider reform. If states seek to maintain their legitimacy through problem-solving (rather than through coercive repression), then considering how particular administrative demands are being resourced and organised is essential. Legitimacy-enhancing measures that rely on improved administrative capacities are important, but they cannot represent a substitute for those claims that stress the importance of legitimacy in terms of inputs and procedures.

The second potential criticism is that our recommendations are of an 'anything goes' kind that offer some nice-sounding words that are potentially universally agreeable, but that therefore also offer no real guidance as to how to enhance administrative capacity or how to innovate governance in order to improve problem-solving capacity. Governance readiness, as noted, is about being prepared to adapt to uncertain conditions. In our view, administrative capacities should not follow any blueprint; they also do not require any constitutional debates about whether particular tasks should be pursued in the public sector or not. Instead, in the light of dispersed governance, administrative capacities need to be seen through the prism not of an institutional argument that focuses on charts and units, but through the pursuit of functional requirements or problems. At the heart of such an endeavour are devices that allow for an exchange of experiences, as well as a degree of slack to allow for such exchanges to take place. By exchange we do not mean conversations about league tables that are obfuscated in international diplomatic language. Rather, we advocate an exchange of views about how particular problems are being addressed, such as those involving coordination in dispersed systems of governing or those regarding delivery in the context of highly heterogeneous target populations.

A third criticism could be that our recommendations fail to acknowledge the importance of individualised incentives. According to this view, bureaucratic organisation–given that it is all about standardisation and decomplexification–is simply no longer appropriate, and therefore greater emphasis should be placed on new organisational forms, such as networks, or market-type mechanisms. We do not believe that market-type arrangements or collaborative networks on their own will be able to address key governance challenges. As noted throughout the Report, bureaucracy plays a considerable part in facilitating and 'orchestrating' non-state actors so as to fulfil governance roles. It would be therefore somewhat naive to suggest that new forms of organisations and actors will overcome the diagnosed shortcomings of existing governance arrangements, and that, therefore, administrative capacities are not that important.

The final criticism might be that we do not sufficiently account for the inherent values of public service and bureaucracy. According to this criticism, we do not pay sufficient attention to the qualitative difference a professional public administration makes in providing particular public services. The key demand emerging from this viewpoint would be to emphasise the importance of a more autonomous and well-resourced public service. Such criticisms are clearly important. However, dispersion suggests that authority is not solely in the hands of the state, much less the public administration.

In reality, authority is shared across levels of government and between state and non-state actors. Furthermore, it is questionable whether analytical capacities, for example, can be provided in-house at all times. Therefore, it is open to debate whether 'best in world' knowledge should or even can be provided in ministerial departments or even within national policy 'communities'. In short, this Report is not about developing professionalism inside a public administration, but rather about raising greater awareness of what administrative systems should be considering in order to be able to co-govern in the future.

In an age in which the capacity of states to deal with today's problems has, once again, become a central concern in the study and practice of politics and public administration, the issue of administrative capacity deserves to play a central role. Emphasising the importance of administrative capacity places us at odds with those who argue that the contemporary (late capitalist) state has 'lost' its steering capacity, either because of its dependence on a low interest rate environment on international financial markets (Streeck and Schäfer 2013), or because of its hollow character that reduces its capacity to 'steer', regardless of the panic responses that various governments embarked on in the late 2000s (Matthews 2012). This argument also places us at odds with those who contend that contemporary states are at best hollowed out (via internationalisation and privatisation) and that therefore we need to primarily look at sources outside the traditional state to locate governance capacity. Instead, we need to take seriously the realities of depleted states, the fundamental complexities that arise from the key governance challenges that have been outlined in this Report, and the ways in which administrative capacities can contribute to problem-solving, within the constraints noted above.

> *National and local administrative systems are the backbone of any governance regime.*

National and local administrative systems matter as they are central to the design and operation of goods and services that 'real people' consume; they are the backbone of any governance regime. We cannot therefore afford to lose sight of administrative capacity, even if we live in an age of the depleted or hollowed-out state.

References

Agrast, M. D., Botero, J. C., Martinez, J., Ponce, A., and Pratt, C. (2012-2013). WJP Rule of Law Index 2012-2013. Washington, D.C.: The World Justice Project.

Andrews, M. (2010). 'Good Government Means Different Things in Different Countries', *Governance*, 23(1): 7–35.

Andrews, M. (2008). 'The Good Governance Agenda: Beyond Indicators without Theory', *Oxford Development Studies*, 36(4): 379–407.

Anheier, H. K. (2013). 'Governance: What are the Issues?', in Hertie School of Governance (ed), *The Governance Report 2013*. Oxford: Oxford University Press, 11–31.

Anheier, H. K., and Korreck, S. (2013). 'Governance Innovations', in Hertie School of Governance (ed), *The Governance Report 2013*. Oxford: Oxford University Press, 83–116.

Anheier, H. K., Stanig, P., and Kayser, M. (2013). 'Introducing a New Generation of Governance Indicators', in Hertie School of Governance (ed), *The Governance Report 2013*. Oxford: Oxford University Press, 117–48.

Anti-Corruption Authorities [website]. *Diagnostic Survey*. Retrieved from http://www.acauthorities.org/diagnostic-survey (accessed 21 November 2013).

Appleby, J. (2013). Spending on Health and Social Care over the next 50 Years: Why Think Long Term? London: The King's Fund.

Arndt, C. (2008). 'The Politics of Governance Ratings', *International Public Management Journal*, 11(3): 275–97.

Ayres, I., and Braithwaite, J. (1992). *Responsive Regulation: Transcending the Deregulation Debate*. New York: Oxford University Press.

Baldwin, R., Cave, M., and Lodge, M. (2012). *Understanding Regulation: Theory, Strategy, and Practice*. 2nd ed. New York: Oxford University Press.

Baldwin, R., Cave, M., and Lodge, M. (2010). 'Introduction: Regulation – The Field and the Developing Agenda', in R. Baldwin, M. Cave, and M. Lodge (eds), *The Oxford Handbook of Regulation*. Oxford: Oxford University Press, 3–16.

Banting, K., and Kymlicka, W. (2010). 'Canadian Multiculturalism: Global Anxieties and Local Debates', *British Journal of Canadian Studies*, 23(1): 43–72.

Barcelona City Council (2013). Barcelona Social Inclusion Plan for 2012-2015. Barcelona: Barcelona City Council.

Bardach, E. (2004). 'The Extrapolation Problem: How Can We Learn from the Experience of Others?', *Journal of Policy Analysis and Management*, 23(2): 205–20.

Baumert, K. A., Herzog, T., and Pershing, J. (2005). *Navigating the Numbers: Greenhouse Gas Data and International Climate Policy*. Washington, D.C.: World Resources Institute.

BBC News (2013) [website]. *UK Nuclear Power Plant gets Go-Ahead*. Retrieved from http://www.bbc.co.uk/news/business-24604218?print=true (accessed 4 December 2013).

BBSR (Bundesinstitut für Bau-, Stadt- und Raumforschung) (2012) [website]. *Schnelles Internet – Breitbandkluft in Deutschland*. Retrieved from http://www.bbsr.bund.de/nn_601066/BBSR/DE/Raumbeobachtung/AktuelleErgebnisse/Raumentwicklung/Breitband/breitband.html (accessed 19 November 2013).

Benington, J., and Moore, M. H. (2011). *Public Value: Theory and Practice*. Basingstoke: Palgrave Macmillan.

Bernstein, M. H. (1955). *Regulating Business by Independent Commission*. Princeton: Princeton University Press.

Black, J. (2010). 'Risk-Based Regulation: Choices, Practices and Lessons Being Learnt', in Organization for Economic Co-operation and Development (OECD) (ed), *Risk and Regulatory Policy: Improving the Governance of Risk*. Paris: OECD, 185–224.

Blom, M., Bergsman, G., and Korteland, M. (2008). *Economic Instruments for Biodiversity: Setting Up a Biodiversity Trading System in Europe*. Delft: CE Delft.

BMG (Bundesministerium für Gesundheit) (2013). Bericht des Expertenbeirats zur konkreten Ausgestaltung des neuen Pflegebedürftigkeitsbegriffs. Berlin: BMG.

BMG (Bundesministerium für Gesundheit) [website]. *Verbesserungen für pflegende Angehörige durch das Pflege-Neuausrichtungs-Gesetz (PNG)*. Retrieved from http://www.bmg.bund.de/pflege/das-pflege-neuausrichtungs-gesetz/pflegende-angehoerige.html (accessed 4 December 2013).

BMU (Bundesumweltministerium für Umwelt, Naturschutz und Reaktorsicherheit) (2013) [website]. *Treibhausgasausstoß im Jahr 2012 um 1,6 Prozent gestiegen*. Retrieved from http://www.bmu.de/bmu/presse-reden/pressemitteilungen/pm/artikel/treibhausgasausstoss-im-jahr-2012-um-16-prozent-gestiegen/?tx_ttnews[backPid]=82 (accessed 5 December 2013).

BMWi (Bundesministerium für Wirtschaft und Technologie) (2013). Dritter Monitoringbericht zur Breitbandstrategie des Bundes. Berlin: BMWi.

BMWi (Bundesministerium für Wirtschaft und Technologie) (2012a). Die Energiewende in Deutschland: Mit sicherer, bezahlbarer und umweltschonender Energie ins Jahr 2050. Berlin: BMWi.

BMWi (Bundesministerium für Wirtschaft und Technologie) (2012b). Möglichkeiten der Breitbandföderung: Ein Leitfaden. Berlin: BMWi.

Boucher, A. (2013). 'Bureaucratic Control and Policy Change: A Comparative Venue Shopping Approach to Skilled Immigration Policies in Australia and Canada', *Journal of Comparative Policy Analysis*, 15(4): 349–67.

Braithwaite, J. (2008). *Regulatory Capitalism: How it Works, Ideas for Making it Work Better*. Cheltenham, Northampton: Edward Elgar.

Breitbandnetz (2011). Breitband für Alle. Breklum: Breitbandnetz.

Breusch, T. (2005). Estimating the Underground Economy Using MIMIC Models. Canberra: The Australian National University.

Brodkin, E. Z. (2011). 'Policy Work: Street-Level Organizations under New Managerialism', *Journal of Public Administration Research and Theory*, 21(Supplement 2): i253-i277.

Brown, T. L., Potoski, M., and van Slyke, D. (2006). 'Managing Public Service Contracts', *Public Administration Review*, 66(3): 323–31.

Carpenter, D. P. (2001). *The Forging of Bureaucratic Autonomy: Reputations, Networks, and Policy Innovation in Executive Agencies, 1862-1928*. Princeton: Princeton University Press.

Carrera, S., and Hernández i Sagrera, R. (2011). 'Mobility Partnerships: "Insecurity Partnerships" for Policy Coherence and Migrant Workers' Human Rights in the EU', in R. Kunz, S. Lavenex, and M. Panizzon (eds), *Multilayered Migration Governance: The Promise of Partnership*. London, New York: Routledge, 97–117.

Carrera, S., and Hernández i Sagrera, R. (2009). The Externalisation of the EU's Labour Immigration Policy, CEPS Working Document No. 321. Brussels: Centre for European Policy Studies.

Cassarino, J.-P. (2009) [website]. *Mobility Partnerships: Expression of a New Compromise*. Retrieved from http://www.migrationinformation.org/Feature/display.cfm?ID=741 (accessed 5 May 2013).

Castles, S. (2006). Back to the Future? Can Europe Meet its Labour Needs through Temporary Migration? Oxford: International Migration Institute.

CEC (Commission of the European Communities) (2009). Mobility Partnerships as a Tool of the Global Approach to Migration: Commission Staff Working Document. Brussels: CEC.

CEC (Commission of the European Communities) (2006). The Global Approach to Migration One Year on: Towards a Comprehensive European Migration Policy. Brussels: CEC.

CEPII (Centre d'Etudes Prospectives et d'Informations Internationales) (2012) [website]. *Institutional Profiles Database (IPD)*. Retrieved from http://www.cepii.fr/institutions/EN/ipd.asp (accessed 28 November 2013).

Christensen, T., and Lægreid, P. (2006). *Autonomy and Regulation: Coping with Agencies in the Modern State*. Cheltenham: Edward Elgar.

Cohen, T. (2012). 'Canada Census 2011: Immigrants and Newcomers Drive Population Growth', *National Post*, 8 February 2012. Retrieved from http://news.nationalpost.com/2012/02/08/canada-census-2011-immigrants-and-newcomers-drive-population-growth/ (accessed 15 June 2013).

Colombo, F., Llena-Nozal, A., Mercier, J., and Tjadens, F. (2011). *Help Wanted? Providing and Paying for Long-Term Care*. Paris: OECD.

Crowe, C., and Meade, E. E. (2007). 'Evolution of Central Bank Governance Around the World', *Journal of Economic Perspectives*, 21(4): 69–90.

Daley, B. (2013). 'Massachusetts to Lower Cap on Emissions by Power Plants', *eBoston Globe*, 8 February 2013. Retrieved from http://www.bostonglobe.com/lifestyle/health-wellness/2013/02/08/massachusetts-and-other-states-cut-allowed-power-plant-emissions/IsSzXaN111BoZ4nvyY3WdJ/story.html (accessed 5 May 2013).

Darbi, M., Ohlenburg, H., Herberg, A., Wende, W., Skambracks, D., and Herbert, M. (2009). International Approaches to Compensation for Impacts on Biological Diversity. Dresden: Leibniz Institute of Ecological and Regional Development.

Dayson, C. (2011). 'The Personalisation Agenda: Implications for Organisational Development and Capacity Building in the Voluntary Sector', *Voluntary Sector Review*, 2(1): 97–106.

DEC (Department of Environment and Conservation New South Wales) (2006a). BioBanking: An Investigation of Market-Based Instruments to Secure Long-Term Biodiversity Objectives. Sydney: DEC.

DEC (Department of Environment and Conservation New South Wales) (2006b). Guide to the Threatened Species Conservation Amendment (Biodiversity Banking) Bill 2006. Sydney: DEC.

Dessai, S. (2001). The Climate Regime from The Hague to Marrakech: Saving or Sinking the Kyoto Protocol, Tyndall Centre Working Paper No. 12. Norwich: University of East Anglia.

Deutschlands Zukunft gestalten: Koalitionsvertrag zwischen CDU, CSU und SPD 18. Legislaturperiode (2013). Retrieved from https://www.cdu.de/sites/default/files/media/dokumente/koalitionsvertrag.pdf (accessed 6 December 2013).

Dilnot, A. (2011). Fairer Care Funding. London: Commission on Funding of Care and Support.

Djankov, S., La Porta, R., Lopez-de-Silanes, F., and Shleifer, A. (2010). 'Disclosure by Politicians', *American Economic Journal: Applied Economics*, 2(2): 179–209.

Djankov, S., La Porta, R., Lopez-de-Silanes, F., and Shleifer, A. (2002). 'The Regulation of Entry', *The Quarterly Journal of Economics*, 117(1): 1–37.

Döhler, M. (2012). 'Gesetzgebung auf Honorarbasis – Politik, Ministerialverwaltung und das Problem externer Beteiligung an Rechtsetzungsprozessen', *Politische Vierteljahresschrift*, 53(2): 181–210.

Domberger, S., and Jensen, P. H. (1997). 'Contracting Out by the Public Sector: Theory, Evidence, Prospects', *Oxford Review of Economic Policy*, 13(4): 67–78.

Dunleavy, P. (1995). 'Policy Disasters: Explaining the UK's Record', *Public Policy and Administration*, 10(2): 52–70.

Dunleavy, P. (1991). *Democracy, Bureaucracy and Public Choice: Economic Explanations in Political Science*. New York, London: Harvester.

Dunleavy, P., Margetts, H., Bastow, S., and Tinkler, J. (2006). 'New Public Management is Dead – Long live Digital-Era Governance', *Journal of Public Administration Research and Theory*, 16(3): 467–94.

EC (European Commission) (2012) [website]. *Quality of Broadband Services in the EU*. Retrieved from http://ec.europa.eu/digital-agenda/en/news/quality-broadband-services-eu-march-2012 (accessed 28 November 2013).

Ellis, B. (2013) [website]. *Nursing Home Costs Top $80,000 a Year*. Retrieved from http://money.cnn.com/2013/04/09/retirement/nursing-home-costs/index.html (accessed 31 October 2013).

Emerson, J. W., Esty, D. C., Hsu, A., Levy, M. A., Sherbinin, A. d., Mara, V., and Jaiteh, M. (2012). 2012 Environmental Performance Index and Pilot Trend Environmental Performance Index. New Haven: Yale Center for Environmental Law and Policy.

Eurocities (Eurocities Network of Local Authority Observations on Active Inclusion) (2011). The Quality of Social Services in Cities: Barcelona. Eurocities.

Eurostat [website]. *Statistics: Crime and Criminal Justice; Energy*. Retrieved from http://epp.eurostat.ec.europa.eu/portal/page/portal/statistics/themes (accessed 21 November 2013).

Evans, P. B. (1995). *Embedded Autonomy: States and Industrial Transformation*. Princeton: Princeton University Press.

Evans, P. B., and Rauch, J. E. (2000). 'Bureaucratic Structure and Bureaucratic Performance in Less Developed Countries', *Journal of Public Economics*, 75(1): 49–71.

Evans, P. B., and Rauch, J. E. (1999). 'Bureaucracy and Growth: A Cross-National Analysis of the Effects of "Weberian" State Structures on Economic Growth', *American Sociological Review*, 64(5): 748–65.

Fischer, F. (2009). *Democracy and Expertise: Reorienting Policy Inquiry*. Oxford: Oxford University Press.

Fletcher, S. R. (2005). Global Climate Change: The Kyoto Protocol. Washington, D.C.: Congressional Research Service.

Fox, A. (2012). Personalisation: Lessons from Social Care. London: Royal Society for the Encouragement of the Arts, Manufacturing and Commerce (RSA).

Fry, M. (2000). 'Key Issues in the Choice of Monetary Policy Framework: Introduction', in L. Mahadeva, and G. Sterne (eds), *Monetary Policy Frameworks in a Global Context*. London, New York: Routledge, 3–17.

Fukuyama, F. (2013). 'What Is Governance?', *Governance*, 26(3): 347–68.

Fung, A., Graham, M., and Weil, D. N. (2007). *Full Disclosure: The Perils and Promise of Transparency*. Cambridge: Cambridge University Press.

Gadsby, E. W. (2013). *Personal Budgets and Health: A Review of the Evidence*. Kent: Policy Research Unit in Commissioning and the Healthcare System.

Gertler, M. S. (2004). *Creative Cities: What are They for, how do They Work, and how do We Build Them?* Ottawa: Canadian Policy Research Networks Inc.

Global Integrity [website]. *Global Integrity Report 2011*. Retrieved from http://www.globalintegrity.org/report (accessed 21 November 2013).

Global Integrity [website]. *Global Integrity Report 2010*. Retrieved from http://www.globalintegrity.org/report (accessed 21 November 2013).

Goodhart, C. A. (2005). 'Regulation and the Role of Central Banks in an Increasingly Integrated Financial World', in P. Gijsel, and H. Schenk (eds), *Multidisciplinary Economics: The Birth of a New Economics Faculty in the Netherlands*. Boston: Springer, 267–78.

Goodhart, D. (2004). 'Too diverse?', *Prospect Magazine*, 20 February 2004. Retrieved from http://www.prospectmagazine.co.uk/magazine/too-diverse-david-goodhart-multiculturalism-britain-immigration-globalisation/#.UpdKk9JDv2E (accessed 28 November 2013).

Guiraudon, V. (2003). 'The Constitution of a European Immigration Policy Domain: A Political Sociology Approach', *Journal of European Public Policy*, 10(2): 263–82.

Hanley, N., Shogren, J. F., and White, B. (2001). *Introduction to Environmental Economics*. Oxford, New York: Oxford University Press.

Hibbard, P. J., Tierney, S. F., Okie, A. M., and Darling, P. G. (2011). *The Economic Impacts of the Regional Greenhouse Gas Initiative on Ten Northeast and Mid-Atlantic States: Review of the Use of RGGI Auction Proceeds from the First Three-Year Compliance Period*. Boston, Chicago, Dallas: Analysis Group.

HM Government Cabinet Office (2007). *Building on Progress: Public Services*. London: Prime Minister's Strategy Unit.

Hood, C. (2011). *The Blame Game: Spin, Bureaucracy, and Self-Preservation in Government*. Princeton: Princeton University Press.

Hood, C. (1998). *The Art of the State: Culture, Rhetoric, and Public Management*. Oxford, New York: Clarendon Press.

Hood, C. (1991). 'A Public Management for all Seasons?', *Public Administration*, 69(1): 3–19.

Hood, C. (1976). *The Limits of Administration*. London, New York: Wiley.

Hood, C., and Jackson, M. W. (1991). *Administrative Argument*. Aldershot, Brookfield: Dartmouth Publications.

Hood, C., and Lodge, M. (2006). *The Politics of Public Service Bargains: Reward, Competency, Loyalty – and Blame*. Oxford, New York: Oxford University Press.

Hood, C., and Margetts, H. (2007). *The Tools of Government in the Digital Age*. Basingstoke: Palgrave Macmillan.

Hood, C., Dixon, R., and Beeston, C. (2008). 'Rating the Rankings: Assessing International Rankings of Public Service Performance', *International Public Management Journal*, 11(3): 298–328.

Hood, C., James, O., Peters, B. G., and Scott, C. (eds) (2004). *Controlling Modern Government: Variety, Commonality, and Change*. Cheltenham: Edward Elgar.

Horenkamp, W., Hube, W., Jäger, J., Kleimaier, M., Kühn, W., Nestle, D., Pickhan, R., Pokojski, M., Raphael, T., Scheffler, J., Schulz, C., Schwaegerl, C., Wielsch, D., and Witzmann, R. (2007). *Dezentrale Energieversorgung 2020*. Frankfurt: VDE.

Hoßmann, I., and Karsch, M. (2011) [website]. *Deutschlands Integrationspolitik: Online-Handbuch Demografie*. Retrieved from http://www.berlin-institut.org/online-handbuchdemografie/bevoelkerungspolitik/deutschland/deutschlands-integrationspolitik.html (accessed 4 December 2013).

Huber, J., and McCarty, N. (2004). 'Bureaucratic Capacity, Delegation, and Political Reform', *American Political Science Review*, 98(3): 481–94.

Huber, J. D., and Shipan, C. R. (2002). *Deliberate Discretion? The Institutional Foundations of Bureaucratic Autonomy*. Cambridge: Cambridge University Press.

Hupe, P., and Hill, M. (forthcoming). 'Delivery Capacity', in M. Lodge, and K. Wegrich (eds), *The Problem-Solving Capacity of the Modern State: Governance Challenges and Administrative Capacities*. Oxford: Oxford University Press.

Jann, W., and Wegrich, K. (2008). 'Wie bürokratisch ist Deutschland? Und Warum? Generalisten und Spezialisten im Entbürokratisierungsspiel', *dms – der moderne staat*, 1(1): 49–72.

Johansson, M. V., Samakovlis, E., and Treich, N. (2011). On the Cost-Efficiency of an Investment Subsidy to Greenhouse Gas Reductions: Empirical Evidence from Sweden. Rome: The 18th Annual Conference of the European Association of Environmental and Resource Economists.

Joppke, C. (2007). 'Beyond National Models: Civic Integration Policies for Immigrants in Western Europe', *West European Politics*, 30(1): 1–22.

Jordana, J., and Levi-Faur, D. (2004). *The Politics of Regulation: Institutions and Regulatory Reform for the Age of Governance*. Cheltenham: Edward Elgar Publishing.

Kanter, R. M. (1983). *The Change Masters: Innovations for Productivity in the American Corporation*. New York: Simon and Schuster.

Kaufmann, D., Kraay, A., and Mastruzzi, M. (2010). The Worldwide Governance Indicators: Methodology and Analytical Issues, World Bank Policy Research Working Paper No. 5430. Washington, D.C.: The World Bank.

Kaul, I. (2013). 'Meeting Global Challenges: Assessing Governance Readiness', in Hertie School of Governance (ed), *The Governance Report 2013*. Oxford: Oxford University Press, 33–58.

Keskitalo, E. C. (ed) (2010). *Developing Adaptation Policy and Practice in Europe: Multi-Level Governance of Climate Change*. Dordrecht, New York: Springer.

Kettl, D. F. (2013). *System Under Stress: The Challenge to 21st Century Governance*. 3rd ed. Thousand Oaks: CQ Press.

Kim, Y., Kelly, T., and Raja, S. (2010). Building Broadband: Strategies and Policies for the Developing World. Washington, D.C.: Global Information and Communication Technologies Department, World Bank.

Köberle, R., Fiedeldey, M., Brennauer, B., Meyer, E.-P., Metzger, M., Szabo, A., Bamberger, J., Krengel, S., and Wippenbeck, T. (2012). Messungen und Analysen für aktive Verteilnetze mit hohem Anteil regenerativer Energien und Elektromobilität. Berlin: VDE.

Koopmans, R. (2010). 'Trade-Offs Between Equality and Difference: Immigrant Integration, Multiculturalism and the Welfare State in Cross-National Perspective', *Journal of Ethnic and Migration Studies*, 36(1): 1–26.

Krause, G. A. (2010). 'Legislative Delegation of Authority to Bureaucratic Agencies', in R. F. Durant (ed), *The Oxford Handbook of American Bureaucracy*. Oxford: Oxford University Press, 521–44.

La Porte, T. R. (1996). 'High Reliability Organizations: Unlikely, Demanding and At Risk', *Journal of Contingencies and Crisis Management*, 4(2): 60–71.

Leadbeater, C., Bartlett, J., and Gallagher, N. (2008). *Making it Personal*. London: Demos.

Levi-Faur, D. (2012). 'From "Big Government" to "Big Governance"?', in D. Levi-Faur (ed), *The Oxford Handbook of Governance*. Oxford: Oxford University Press, 3–18.

Levy, B., and Spiller, P. T. (1996). *Regulations, Institutions, and Commitment: Comparative Studies of Telecommunications*. Cambridge, New York: Cambridge University Press.

Levy, B., and Spiller, P. T. (1994). 'The Institutional Foundations of Regulatory Commitment: A Comparative Analysis of Telecommunications Regulation', *Journal of Law, Economics & Organization*, 10(2): 201–46.

Lipsky, M. (1980). *Street-Level Bureaucracy: Dilemmas of the Individual in Public Services*. New York: Russell Sage Foundation.

Lodge, M. (forthcoming). 'Regulatory Capacity', in M. Lodge, and K. Wegrich (eds), *The Problem-Solving Capacity of the Modern State: Governance Challenges and Administrative Capacities*. Oxford: Oxford University Press.

Lodge, M. (2013). 'Crisis, Resources and the State: Executive Politics in the Age of the Depleted State', *Political Studies Review*, 11(3): 378–90.

Lodge, M., and Gill, D. (2011). 'Toward a New Era of Administrative Reform? The Myth of Post-NPM in New Zealand', *Governance*, 24(1): 141–66.

Lodge, M., and Hood, C. (2012). 'Into an Age of Multiple Austerities: Public Management and Public Service Bargains across OECD Countries', *Governance*, 25(1): 79–101.

Lodge, M., and Wegrich, K. (2012a). 'Conclusion: Executive Politics in a Changing Climate', in M. Lodge, and K. Wegrich (eds), *Executive Politics in Times of Crisis*. Basingstoke: Palgrave Macmillan, 284–96.

Lodge, M., and Wegrich, K. (2012b). *Managing Regulation: Regulatory Analysis, Politics, and Policy*. Basingstoke: Palgrave Macmillan.

Lodge, M., and Wegrich, K. (2012c). 'Public Administration and Executive Politics: Perennial Questions in Changing Contexts', *Public Policy and Administration*, 27(3): 212–29.

Lodge, M., and Wegrich, K. (2012d). The "Californication" of Government?: Crowdsourcing and the Red Tape Challenge. London: Centre for Analysis of Risk and Regulation LSE.

Longo, F. (2008). 'Quality of Governance: Impartiality is Not Enough', *Governance*, 21(2): 191–6.

Madsen, B., Carroll, N., and Moore Brands, K. (2010). State of Biodiversity Markets Report: Offset and Compensation Programs Worldwide. Washington, D.C.: Ecosystem Marketplace.

Majone, G. (1997). 'From the Positive to the Regulatory State: Causes and Consequences of Changes in the Mode of Governance', *Journal of Public Policy*, 17(2): 139–68.

Makkai, T., and Braithwaite, J. (1992). 'In and Out of the Revolving Door: Making Sense of Regulatory Capture', *Journal of Public Policy*, 12(1): 61–78.

Mann, M. (1984). 'The Autonomous Power of the State: Its Origins, Mechanisms and Results', *European Journal of Sociology*, 25(2): 185–213.

March, J. G., Sproull, L. S., and Tamuz, M. (1991). 'Learning from Samples of One or Fewer', *Organization Sciences*, 2(1): 1–13.

Maroukis, T., and Triandafyllidou, A. (2013). Mobility Partnerships: A Convincing Tool for the EU's Global Approach to Migration?, Policy Paper 76. Paris: Notre Europe - Jacques Delors Institute.

Matthews, F. (2012). 'Governance, Governing, and the Capacity of Executive in Times of Crisis', in M. Lodge, and K. Wegrich (eds), *Executive Politics in Times of Crisis*. Basingstoke: Palgrave Macmillan, 217–38.

Mautz, R. (2012). 'Atomausstieg und was dann? Probleme staatlicher Steuerung der Energiewende', *dms – der moderne staat*, 5(1): 149–68.

McCubbins, M. D., and Schwartz, T. (1984). 'Congressional Oversight Overlooked: Police Patrols Versus Fire Alarms', *American Journal of Political Science*, 28(1): 165–79.

McGann, J. G. (2013). 2012 Global Go To Think Tanks Index Report. Philadelphia: University of Pennsylvania.

Meagher, P. (2005). 'Anti-Corruption Agencies: Rhetoric Versus Reality', *The Journal of Policy Reform*, 8(1): 69–103.

Mendonça, M., Jacobs, D., and Sovacool, B. K. (2009). *Powering the Green Economy: The Feed-In Tariff Handbook*. Sterling: Earthscan.

Metzger, M., Bamberger, J., Köberle, R., and Meyer, E.-P. (2012). Herausforderungen und Lösungskonzepte für Verteilnetze im ländlichen Raum. Berlin: VDE.

Meyer-Sahling, J.-H., Lowe, W., and van Stolk, C. (2012). 'Towards NPM-ization of the Post-Communist State? Attitudes of Public Officials towards Models of Bureaucracy in Central and Eastern Europe', in M. Lodge, and K. Wegrich (eds), *Executive Politics in Times of Crisis*. Basingstoke: Palgrave Macmillan, 99–117.

Michalowski, I. (2004). 'Integration Programs for Newcomers – A Dutch Model for Europe?', in A. Böcker, B. d. Hart, and I. Michalowski (eds), *Migration and the Regulation*. Osnabrück: IMIS, 163–75.

Miller, G. J. (2000). 'Above Politics: Credible Commitment and Efficiency in the Design of Public Agencies', *Journal of Public Administration Research and Theory*, 10(2): 289–328.

Miller, G. J. (1992). *Managerial Dilemmas: The Political Economy of Hierarchy*. Cambridge, New York: Cambridge University Press.

Montagut, T. (2013). Personal Communication with Author. University of Barcelona.

Moore, M. H. (1995). *Creating Public Value: Strategic Management in Government*. Cambridge, MA: Harvard University Press.

Moran, M. (2003). *The British Regulatory State: High Modernism and Hyper-Innovation*. Oxford, New York: Oxford University Press.

MTC (Metropolitan Transportation Commission) (2013a). Draft Bay Area Plan: Draft Transportation Air Quality Conformity Analysis. Oakland: MTC.

MTC (Metropolitan Transportation Commission) (2013b). Environmental Impact Report: Final. Oakland: MTC.

MTC (Metropolitan Transportation Commission) (2009). Change in Motion: Transportation 2035 Plan for the San Francisco Bay Area. Oakland: MTC.

MTC (Metropolitan Transportation Commission) (2008). Transportation 2035 Plan for the San Francisco Bay Area: Performance Assessment Report. Oakland: MTC.

MTC (Metropolitan Transportation Commission) (2007). Transportation 2035 Financial Assumptions and Cost Review: Risk Assessment. Oakland: MTC.

Müller, B. (2012). 'Das Dorf der Energiepioniere', *Pictures of the Future*, 1: 46–9.

NAO (National Audit Office) (2013). The Rural Broadband Programme: Report by the Comptroller and Auditor General, HC 535 Session 2013-14. London: NAO.

NAO (National Audit Office) (2010). Assessing the Impact of Proposed New Policies: Report by the Comptroller and Auditor General, HC 185 Session 2010–2011. London: NAO.

Net Index (2013) [website]. *Household Download Index: Graph Period: May 29, 2011 - Nov 27, 2013*. Retrieved from http://www.netindex.com/download/allcountries/ (accessed 28 November 2013).

Nielsen, J. S. (2009). 'The Blue Card: EU's Race for Talent', MA Thesis (The University of British Columbia, Vancouver).

Niskanen, W. A. (1971). *Buraucracy and Representative Government*. Chicago: Aldine-Atherton.

OECD (Organization for Economic Co-operation and Development) (2013a). 'Nuclear Energy', in Organization for Economic Co-operation and Development (OECD) (ed), *OECD Factbook 2013: Economic, Environmental and Social Statistics*. Paris: OECD Publishing.

OECD (Organization for Economic Co-operation and Development) (2013b). 'Renewable Energy', in Organization for Economic Co-operation and Development (OECD) (ed), *OECD Factbook 2013: Economic, Environmental and Social Statistics*. Paris: OECD Publishing.

OECD (Organization for Economic Co-operation and Development) (2013c). *International Migration Outlook 2013*. Paris: OECD.

OECD (Organization for Economic Co-operation and Development) (2013d) [website]. *OECD Broadband Portal*. Retrieved from http://www.oecd.org/internet/broadband/oecdbroadbandportal.htm (accessed 4 December 2013).

OECD (Organization for Economic Co-operation and Development) (2011). National Broadband Plans. Paris: OECD.

OECD (Organization for Economic Co-operation and Development) (2006). *From Immigration to Integration: Local Solutions to a Global Challenge*. Paris: OECD.

OECD (Organization for Economic Co-operation and Development) [website]. *Overview of PISA 2009 Profiles by Country/Economy*. Retrieved from http://stats.oecd.org/PISA2009Profiles/# (accessed 21 November 2013).

OECD (Organization for Economic Co-operation and Development), and EC (European Commission) (2013). *A Good Life in Old Age? Monitoring and Improving Quality in Long-term Care*. Paris: OECD Publishing.

Olsen, J. P. (2008). 'The Ups and Downs of Bureaucratic Organization', *Annual Review of Political Science*, 11(1): 13–37.

Olsen, J. P. (2006). 'Maybe it is Time to Rediscover Bureaucracy', *Journal of Public Administration Research and Theory*, 16(1): 1–24.

Page, E., and Jenkins, W. I. (2005). *Policy Bureaucracy: Government with a Cast of Thousands*. Oxford, New York: Oxford University Press.

Papworth, J. (2013). 'Social Care Costs: What will the New Proposals Mean?', *The Guardian*, 12 February 2013: 15.

Parker, C. (2013). 'Twenty Years of Responsive Regulation: An Appreciation and Appraisal', *Regulation & Governance*, 7(1): 2–13.

Parrado, S. (forthcoming). 'Analytical Capacity', in M. Lodge, and K. Wegrich (eds), *The Problem-Solving Capacity of the Modern State: Governance Challenges and Administrative Capacities*. Oxford: Oxford University Press.

Perry, J. L. (1996). 'Measuring Public Service Motivation: An Assessment of Construct Reliability and Validity', *Journal of Public Administration Research and Theory*, 6(1): 5–22.

Pickard, L. (2013). 'A Growing Care Gap? The Supply of Unpaid Care for Older People by their Adult Children in England to 2032', *Ageing and Society*: 1–28.

Pollitt, C. (2009). 'Buraucracies Remember, Post-Bureaucratic Organizations Forget?', *Public Administration*, 87(2): 198–218.

Power, M. (2007). *Organized Uncertainty: Designing a World of Risk Management.* Oxford, New York: Oxford University Press.

Power, M. (1997). *The Audit Society: Rituals of Verification.* Oxford, New York: Oxford University Press.

Ramseur, J. L. (2013). The Regional Greenhouse Gas Initiative: Lessons Learned and Issues for Policymakers. Washington, D.C.: Congressional Research Service.

Raudla, R. (2013). 'Pitfalls of Contracting for Policy Advice: Preparing Performance Budgeting Reform in Estonia', *Governance*, 26(4): 605–29.

Reslow, N. (2010). 'Migration and Development? An Assessment of Recent EU Policy Initiatives', *Journal of Contemporary European Research*, 6(1): 3–21.

Rhodes, R. A. W. (1997). *Understanding Governance: Policy Networks, Governance, Reflexivity, and Accountability.* Buckingham, Philadelphia: Open University Press.

Ridley, F. F. (1968). *Specialists and Generalists: A Comparative Study of the Professional Civil Servant at Home and Abroad.* London: Allen and Unwin.

Rittel, H. W., and Webber, M. M. (1973). 'Dilemmas in the General Theory of Planning', *Policy Science*, 4(2): 155–69.

Roberts, A. (2010). *The Logic of Discipline: Global Capitalism and the Architecture of Government.* Oxford: Oxford University Press.

Rothstein, B. (2013). The Three Worlds of Governance: Arguments for a Parsimonious Theory of Quality of Government. Paper for the Annual Meeting of the American Science Association, Chicago, August 29 - Sept. 1, 2013.

Rothstein, B. (2011). 'Anti-Corruption: The Indirect "Big Bang" Approach', *Review of International Political Economy*, 18(2): 228–50.

Rothstein, B., and Teorell, J. (2008). 'What is Quality of Government? A Theory of Impartial Government Institutions', *Governance*, 21(2): 165–90.

Scharpf, F. W. (1986). 'Policy Failure and Institutional Reform: Why Should Form Follow Function?', *International Social Science Journal*, 38(2): 179–89.

Scheppele, K. L. (2013). 'The Rule of Law and the Frankenstate: Why Governance Checklists Do Not Work', *Governance*, 26(4): 559–62.

Schittenhelm, K., and Schmidtke, O. (2010). 'Integrating Highly Skilled Migrants into the Economy: Transatlantic Perspectives', *International Journal*, 66: 127-43.

Schneider, F. (2013). The Shadow Economy in Europe 2013. Linz: Johannes Kepler Universität, A.T. Kearney, Visa Europe.

Schneider, F., Buehn, A., and Montenegro, C. E. (2010). Shadow Economies All Over the World: New Estimates for 162 Countries from 1999 to 2007, Policy Research Working Paper 5356. Washington, D.C.: The World Bank.

Schwab, K. (2012). The Global Competitiveness Report 2012–2013. Geneva: World Economic Forum.

Shachar, A. (2006). 'The Race for Talent: Highly Skilled Migrants and Competitive Immigration Regimes', *New York University Law Review*, 81: 148–206.

Simon, H. A. (1947). *Administrative Behavior: A Study of Decision-Making Processes in Administrative Organization.* New York: Macmillan.

Slasberg, C., Beresford, P., and Schonfield, P. (2012). 'How Self Directed Support is Failing to Deliver Personal Budgets and Pesonalisation', *Research, Policy and Planning*, 29(3): 161–77.

Sørensen, E., and Torfing, J. (forthcoming). 'Collaborative Innovation and Governance Capacity', in M. Lodge, and K. Wegrich (eds), *The Problem-Solving Capacity of the Modern State: Governance Challenges and Administrative Capacities*. Oxford: Oxford University Press.

Stanig, P. (forthcoming). Methodological Notes on the 2014 Administrative Capacity Dashboard: Technical Report. Berlin: Hertie School of Governance.

Stanig, P., and Kayser, M. (2013). 'Governance Indicators: Some Proposals', in H. K. Anheier (ed), *Governance Challenges and Innovations: Financial and Fiscal Governance*. Oxford: Oxford University Press, 189–220.

Stigler, G. J. (1971). 'The Theory of Economic Regulation', *The Bell Journal of Economics and Managment Science*, 2(1): 3–21.

Stoker, G. (2006). 'Public Value Management: A New Narrative for Networked Governance?', *The American Review of Public Administration*, 36(1): 41–57.

Stoker, G. (1998). 'Governance as Theory: Five Propositions', *International Social Science Journal*, 50(155): 17–28.

Streeck, W., and Schäfer, A. (2013). *Politics in the Age of Austerity*. Cambridge: Polity.

Swedish Environmental Protection Agency (2009). Climate Investment Programmes: An Important Step Towards Achieving Sweden's Climate Targets. Stockholm: Swedish Environmental Protection Agency.

Tarr, A. (2011). Making the Work Programme Work for People with Health Conditions: Follow-On Report to "Pathways to What?". London: Centre for Economic and Social Inclusion.

Teelucksingh, C., and Galabuzi, G.-E. (2005). Working Precariously: The Impact of Race and Immigrants Status on Employment Opportunities and Outcomes in Canada. Toronto, Ontario: Canadian Race Relations Foundation.

ten Kate, K., Bishop, J., and Bayon, R. (2004). Biodiversity Offsets: Views, Experience, and the Business Case. Gland, Switzerland: IUCN-The World Conservation Union.

Teorell, J., Dahlström, C., and Dahlberg, S. (2011). The QoG Expert Survey Dataset. University of Gothenburg, Sweden: The Quality of Government Institute.

The World Bank (2013) [website]. *Bulletin Board on Statistical Capacity: 1999-2012 Overall Score*. Retrieved from http://data.worldbank.org/data-catalog/bulletin-board-on-statistical-capacity (accessed 21 November 2013).

The World Bank [website]. *Doing Business: Historical Data Sets and Trends Data*. Retrieved from http://www.doingbusiness.org/custom-query (accessed 21 November 2013).

The World Bank [website]. Enterprise Surveys. Retrieved from http://www.enterprisesurveys.org/ (accessed 21 November 2013).

The World Bank [website]. *World Development Indicators: 5.11 Power and Communications*. Retrieved from http://wdi.worldbank.org/table/5.11 (accessed 6 December 2013).

Torfing, J., Peters, B. G., Pierre, J., and Sørensen, E. (2012). *Interactive Governance: Advancing the Paradigm*. Oxford, New York: Oxford University Press.

Triadafilopoulos, T. (2012). *Becoming Multicultural: Immigration and the Politics of Membership in Canada and Germany*. Vancouver: UBC Press.

Tummers, L. G., Jilke, S. R., and Van de Walle, S. (2013). 'Citizens in Charge? Reviewing the Background and Value of Introducing Choice and Competition in Public Services', in Y. K. Dwivedi, M. A. Shareef, S. K. Pandey, and V. Kumar (eds), *Public Administration Reformation: Market Demand from Public Organizations*. London: Routledge.

'Turf Wars in Telecoms' (2006), *The Financial Times*, 29 June 2006: 16.

TÜV (TÜV Rheinland Consulting) (2012). Breitbandatlas 2012: Teil I des Berichts zum Breitbandatlas 2012 des Bundesministeriums für Wirtschaft und Technologie. Berlin: TÜV.

UN (United Nations, Department of Economic and Social Affairs, Population Division) (2013). World Population Prospects: The 2012 Revision, Highlights and Advance Tables. New York: United Nations.

UNEP (United Nations Environment Program Secretariat of the Convention on Biological Diversity) (2000). Sustaining Life on Earth: How the Convention on Biological Diversity Promotes Nature and Human Wellbeing. Montreal: UNEP.

UNESCO (UNESCO Institute for Statistics) [website]. Retrieved from http://stats.uis.unesco.org/unesco/ReportFolders/ReportFolders.aspx (accessed 21 November 2013).

Verweij, M. (forthcoming). 'Wicked Problems, Clumsy Solutions, and Messy Institutions in Transnational Governance', in M. Lodge, and K. Wegrich (eds), *The Problem-Solving Capacity of the Modern State: Governance Challenges and Administrative Capacities*. Oxford: Oxford University Press.

Voorberg, W., Bekkers, V., and Tummers, L. G. (2013). Embarking on the Social Innovation Journey: A Systematic Review Regarding of Co-Creation with Citizens. Paper for the IRSPM Conference, Prague, 10-12 April 2013. Prague: IRSPM.

Wegrich, K., and Stimac, V. (forthcoming). 'Coordination Capacity', in M. Lodge, and K. Wegrich (eds), *The Problem-Solving Capacity of the Modern State: Governance Challenges and Administrative Capacities*. Oxford: Oxford University Press.

Weick, K. E. (1984). 'Small Wins: Redefining the Scale of Social Problems', *American Psychologist*, 39(1): 40–9.

Whitten, S. M., Coggan, A., Reeson, A., and Gorddard, R. (2007). Putting Theory into Practice: Market Failure and Market Based Instruments (MBIs), Socio-Economics and the Environment in Discussion (SEED) Working Paper Series 2007-02. Canberra: Commonwealth Scientific and Industrial Research Organisation.

WHO (World Health Organization) [website]. *Global Health Observatory Data Repository*. Retrieved from http://apps.who.int/gho/data/node.main.1094?lang=en (accessed 21 November 2013).

Wildavsky, A. B. (1988). *Searching for Safety*. New Brunswick: Transaction Books.

Wilson, J. Q. (1989). *Bureaucracy: What Government Agencies Do and Why They Do it*. New York: Basic Books.

Wilson, J. Q. (1980). *The Politics of Regulation*. New York: Basic Books.

Winter, S. C. (2012). 'Implementation Perspectives: Status and Reconsideration', in J. Pierre, and B. G. Peters (eds), *The SAGE Handbook of Public Administration*. 2nd ed. London: Sage, 265–78.

Wohlgeannt, M. (2012). 'Feldtest für intelligente Stromnetze', *Netzpolitik*, 51(11): 42–5.

Wu, F. (2009). 'Environmental Politics in China: An Issue Area in Review', *Journal of Chinese Political Science*, 14: 383–406.

About the Contributors

Helmut K. Anheier (PhD, Yale) is Dean and Professor of Sociology of the Hertie School of Governance (Berlin, Germany). He also holds a chair of Sociology at Heidelberg University and serves as Academic Director of the Centre for Social Investment there. Previously, he was Professor of Public Policy and Social Welfare at UCLA's School of Public Affairs and Centennial Professor at the London School of Economics (LSE).

Regina A. List (MA, American University) is Managing Editor of the Governance Report project at the Hertie School of Governance. She is also Managing Editor of the *Journal of Civil Society* and has researched and written on various aspects of civil society and nonprofit organisations

Martin Lodge (PhD, London School of Economics) is Professor of Political Science and Public Policy in the Department of Government and the Centre for Analysis of Risk and Regulation at the London School of Economics and Political Science (LSE).

Piero Stanig (PhD, Columbia University) is Senior Research Scientist in Governance and Methodology at the Hertie School of Governance and a member of the Advisory Council of the Ibrahim Index of African Governance. His research interests span comparative voting behaviour and public opinion, the political economy of governance and corruption, and statistical methodology for political science.

Kai Wegrich (Dr. rer. pol., Potsdam University) is Professor of Public Administration and Public Policy at the Hertie School of Governance. Prior to this position, he was a Fellow at the London School of Economics and a Senior Researcher at RAND Corporation in Berlin and Cambridge. He is European Editor of *Public Administration* and co-editor of the book series on 'Executive Politics and Governance' (Palgrave). His main research interests are regulation, executive politics, and public sector reform.

Ramsey Wise (MPP, Hertie School of Governance) was Research Associate at the Hertie School of Governance at the time of writing, where she also studied social policy and comparative welfare states. Currently a PhD candidate at the Bremen International Graduate School of Social Sciences, her research interests include skill formation, comparative political economy, and labour market segmentation.

The manufacturer's authorised representative in the EU for product safety is Oxford University Press España S.A. of el Parque Empresarial San Fernando de Henares, Avenida de Castilla, 2 – 28830 Madrid (www.oup.es/en or product. safety@oup.com). OUP España S.A. also acts as importer into Spain of products made by the manufacturer.

www.ingramcontent.com/pod-product-compliance
Ingram Content Group UK Ltd.
Pitfield, Milton Keynes, MK11 3LW, UK
UKHW021320180426
11947UKWH00015B/1338